INJURY-FREE RUNNING

HOW TO BUILD STRENGTH, IMPROVE FORM, AND TREAT/PREVENT INJURIES

Written and Illustrated by
Dr. Tom Michaud

INJURY-FREE RUNNING

HOW TO BUILD STRENGTH, IMPROVE FORM, AND TREAT/PREVENT INJURIES

Tom Michaud, DC

Michaud Chiropractic
517 Washington Street
Newton, Massachusetts, 02458
USA
www.newtonbiomechanics.com

NEWTON
BIOMECHANICS

Published by Newton Biomechanics
517 Washington Street
Newton, Massachusetts 02458
USA
www.newtonbiomechanics.com

Discounts on bulk quantities are available to schools, professional associations, and other qualified organizations. For details and specific discount information, go to www.newtonbiomechanics.com, or call (617) 969-2225.

Every effort has been made to credit the authors responsible for specific illustrations. If an oversight has been made, please contact the author at www.newtonbiomechanics.com and it will be corrected.

Printed in the United States of America

Michaud, Thomas C.
Injury-Free Running: How to Build Strength, Improve Form, and Treat/Prevent Injuries / Thomas C. Michaud
p; cm.
Includes index.
ISBN 978-1-4675-8931-4
1. Running-training 2. Running-injury prevention. 3. Sports injuries
4. Stretches

Preface

We all know running has significant health benefits. Recreational running has been shown to lower blood pressure and reduce the risk of developing diabetes, depression, and Alzheimer's. Running as few as 10 miles per week can increase your lifespan by six years (1). Also, contrary to popular belief, running does not cause degenerative changes in our joints. The long-held belief that running would accelerate the development of arthritis was disproved in a 25-year study from Stanford University in which researchers confirmed that running altered neither the severity nor prevalence of knee arthritis (2). In fact, a recent review of the literature found that compared to nonexercisers, lifelong recreational runners were much less likely to become disabled as they got older (3).

While research confirms that recreational running does not cause long-term damage to our joints, runners are much more likely than the general population to suffer short-term injuries, such as sprains, strains, and stress fractures. Among the nearly 12 million recreational runners in the United States, the annual injury rate is close to 50% (4). This translates into nearly 2 million stress fractures and countless muscle and tendon injuries each year. To make matters worse, nearly 70% of injured runners will be reinjured within 12 months. The medical costs for treating these injuries are so high that despite the proven health benefits associated with exercise, many insurance companies are denying coverage to injured runners (5).

The injury and reinjury rates in runners do not have to be so high. While a few unlucky runners may be injury prone, the vast majority of running injuries can be avoided with simple modifications in running form and cadence, along with the addition of specific stretches/exercises. The problem is, it's difficult for runners to decide which preventive measures are right for them because experts have conflicting opinions on the best ways to treat and prevent injuries. The most obvious example of this is stretching. Some experts claim that in order to avoid injury you have to stretch regularly. Others say runners should never stretch because it increases the risk of injury and weakens muscles. Another glaring example is the selection of a running shoe. Many running authorities claim that all runners should wear minimalist shoes and strike the ground with their midfoot (like our ancient ancestors). Others suggest you should wear motion control running shoes and strike the ground with your heel. The conflicting information forces the typical runner to experiment with different exercise protocols, running shoes, and/or running styles that may or may not alter the potential for developing a running injury.

Another obstacle for injury-free running is that most doctors continue to treat runners with medications proven to be ineffective. The classic example of this is the overprescription of anti-inflammatory medications, such as aspirin, ibuprofen, and naproxen (better known by their trade names of Advil, Motrin, and Aleve). Given their widespread use in the management of running injuries, you would think there would be an abundance of scientific evidence suggesting these drugs accelerate the repair of muscle and bone injuries. This is not the case. Over a decade ago, common nonsteroidal anti-inflammatory drugs (NSAIDs) were shown to interfere with bone remodeling by suppressing activity of osteoblasts, specialized cells found inside bone that are responsible for repairing cracks. Subsequent papers have confirmed this finding (6,7). Nonetheless, the average physician continues to prescribe NSAIDs when treating runners with stress fractures. More recently, an award-winning paper published in the *American Journal of Sports Medicine* confirmed that many frequently prescribed NSAIDs may actually inhibit tendon repair following an injury (8). In spite of this, these popular drugs are still the first-line intervention for the management of the vast majority of running injuries.

Putting aside their ineffectiveness, NSAIDs are also deadly. In a study of nearly 8 million people presenting to 197 hospitals in Spain, NSAIDs were found to be responsible for 1.5 deaths per 10,000 NSAID users (9). Even low-dose aspirin was found to be dangerous and accounted for nearly a third of all deaths. Runners should be especially careful when taking NSAIDs because regular use of these drugs can accelerate the development of arthritis. In a 6-year study of nearly 1,700 people with hip and knee arthritis, researchers from the Netherlands determined that individuals who routinely took NSAIDs for pain management had a 240% increase in the development of hip arthritis and a 320% increase in the development of knee arthritis compared to individuals who rarely used these drugs (10). The authors state, "Whether this occurs because of a true deleterious effect on cartilage or because of excessive mechanical loading following pain relief remains to be investigated."

The goal of this book is to keep you running injury-free by showing you how to develop a running form based on your alignment, prior injuries, and desired running speed. You will learn how to choose a running shoe and design a personalized rehab program by evaluating your arch height, flexibility, strength, and coordination. Specific tests are described that can determine if you're injury prone. More importantly, the corrective stretches and exercises needed to prevent injury are illustrated.

Because parts of this book are slightly technical, the first chapter reviews human anatomy and movement as specifically related to running. A chapter on the evolution of bipedality has been included, in part to explain why the ability to get around on two legs has made us so successful as a species, but also to point out that we were not "born to run." Regularly running long distances is stressful on the body and, to avoid injury, you have to be strong, coordinated, and well informed. Chapters 3 and 4 discuss exactly what is happening while we walk and run and chapter 5 explains how to identify and correct possible problems that may lead to injury. The controversy regarding running shoe selection is addressed in chapter 6. The final chapter lists 25 of the most common running-related injuries and outlines the most up-to-date, scientifically justified treatment protocols necessary to get you running again. After spending thirty years reviewing the scientific literature on running injuries and evaluating the efficacy of these treatments on thousands of elite and recreational runners, I've seen firsthand how the information presented in this book can keep you running for decades without being sidelined with unnecessary injuries.

Tom Michaud, DC
Newton, Massachusetts

References

1. Schonhr P. Assessing prognosis: a glimpse of the future. Jogging healthy or hazard? In: Cardiology ESo, ed. EuroPrevent 2012. Dublin, Ireland: *European Heart Journal,* 2012.

2. Chakravarty E, Hubert H, Lingala V, et al. Long distance running and knee osteoarthritis: a prospective study. *Am J Prev Med.* 2008;35:133-138.

3. Bosomworth N. Exercise and knee osteoarthritis: benefit or hazard? *Canadian Family Physician.* 2009; 55:871-878.

4. van Mechelen W. Running injuries: a review of the epidemiological literature. *Sports Med.* 1992;4:320.

5. Erin Beresini. Distance Runners Are a Paradox for Insurers. *The New York Times.* October 24, 2010.

6. Simon AM, Manigrasso MB, O'Connor JP, COX-2 function is essential for bone fracture healing. *J Bone Miner Res.* 2002;17:963–976.

7. Zhang X, Xing L, Boyce BF, Puzas JE, Rosier RN, Schwarz EM, O'Keefe RJ. Cox-2 is critical for mesenchymal cell differentiation during skeletal repair. *J Bone Miner Res.* 2001;16:S1;S145.

8. Cohen D, Kawamura S, Ehteshami J, Rodeo S. Indomethacin and Celecoxib impair rotator cuff tendon-to-bone healing. *Am J Sports Med.* 2006;34:362-369.

9. Lanas A, Perez-Aisa M, Feu F, et al. A nationwide study of mortality associated with hospital admission due to severe gastrointestinal events and those associated with nonsteroidal anti-inflammatory drug use. *Am J Gastroenterol.* 2005 Aug;100(8):1685-93.

10. Reijman M, Bierma - Zeinstra S, Pols H, et al. Anti-Inflammatory drugs and radiological progression of osteoarthritis? The Rotterdam study. *Arthritis and Rheumatism.* 2005; 52(10);3137-42.

Table of Contents

Chapter Three   **The Biomechanics of Walking and Running**   **27**

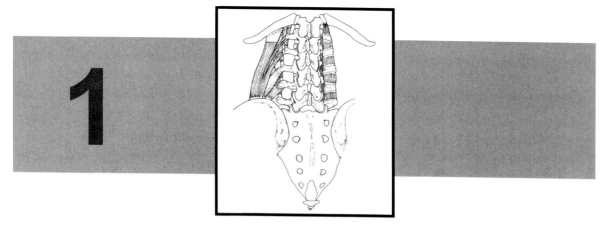

Chapter One

ANATOMY AND THREE-DIMENSIONAL MOTION

Leonardo da Vinci once said that in addition to being a work of art, the human body is also a marvel of engineering. Leonardo's statement is particularly true when it comes to the anatomical structures that allow us to run, since running on two legs presents an engineering conundrum: When the foot first hits the ground, the entire limb must be supple in order to absorb shock and accommodate discrepancies in terrain, while shortly thereafter, these same structures become rigid so they can tolerate the accelerational forces associated with propelling the body forward. This is in contrast to quadrupeds, which have the luxury of being able to absorb shock with their forelimbs while their hindlimbs are serving to support and accelerate (picture a cat jumping on and off a ledge).

Shock absorption is particularly important in marathon running, since the feet of long distance runners contact the ground an average of 10,000 times per hour, absorbing between 2 and 7 times body weight with each strike. In the course of a

marathon, this translates into a force of nearly 8,000 tons that must be dissipated by the body. Obviously, even a minor glitch in our shock absorption system will result in injury. To make matters worse, the forces associated with accelerating the body forward are even greater than the forces associated with initially contacting the ground.

To understand the complex structural interactions responsible for shock absorption and acceleration, it is important to understand how the different joints and muscles of the human body interact. Because most runners are not familiar with anatomy and clinical biomechanics, the following section provides an illustrated review of all the major muscles and bones associated with running. The Greek/Latin origins of the names are listed to emphasize that anatomy was never meant to be complicated. Early anatomists named muscles and bones mostly by their shape: the piriformis muscle was named because it is shaped like a pear, while the navicular bone is so named because it resembles a ship. If you understand the Greek and Latin origins of the various anatomical terms, learning this information is significantly less challenging. The final section of this chapter provides an illustrated review of the words used to describe motion. At first, terms like dorsiflexion and eversion seem complicated, but after hearing them a few times, they quickly become part of your vocabulary.

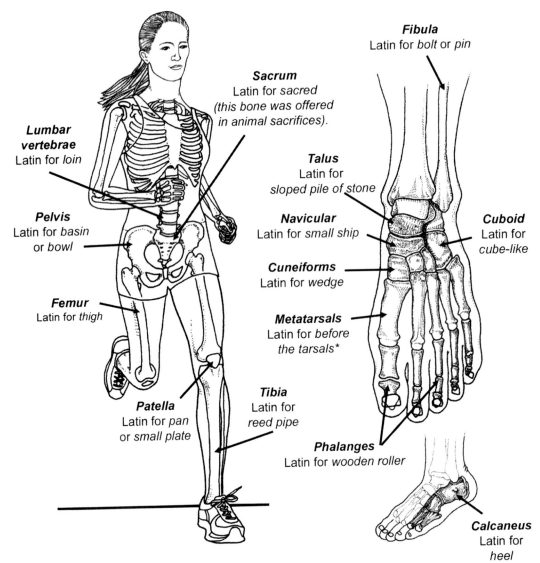

Fibula
Latin for *bolt* or *pin*

Sacrum
Latin for *sacred*
(this bone was offered
in animal sacrifices).

**Lumbar
vertebrae**
Latin for *loin*

Talus
Latin for
sloped pile of stone

Pelvis
Latin for *basin*
or *bowl*

Navicular
Latin for *small ship*

Cuboid
Latin for
cube-like

Cuneiforms
Latin for *wedge*

Femur
Latin for *thigh*

Metatarsals
Latin for *before
the tarsals**

Tibia
Latin for
reed pipe

Patella
Latin for *pan*
or *small plate*

Phalanges
Latin for *wooden roller*

Calcaneus
Latin for
heel

*The tarsals are all of the foot bones located
behind the metatarsals: the calcaneus, talus, cuboid, navicular, and the cuneiforms.
The word tarsal is Latin for *flat surface*

1.1. Skeletal anatomy.

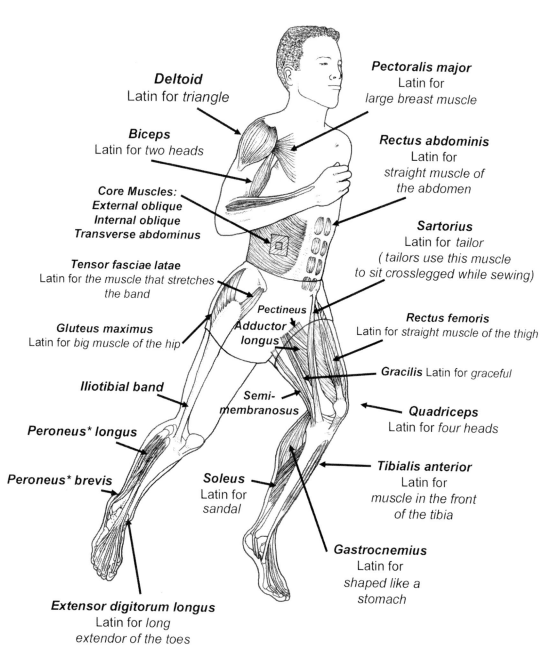

Deltoid
Latin for *triangle*

Biceps
Latin for *two heads*

Core Muscles:
External oblique
Internal oblique
Transverse abdominus

Tensor fasciae latae
Latin for *the muscle that stretches the band*

Gluteus maximus
Latin for *big muscle of the hip*

Iliotibial band

Peroneus* longus

Peroneus* brevis

Extensor digitorum longus
Latin for *long extendor of the toes*

Pectoralis major
Latin for
large breast muscle

Rectus abdominis
Latin for
straight muscle of the abdomen

Sartorius
Latin for *tailor*
(*tailors use this muscle to sit crosslegged while sewing*)

Rectus femoris
Latin for *straight muscle of the thigh*

Gracilis Latin for *graceful*

Quadriceps
Latin for *four heads*

Tibialis anterior
Latin for
muscle in the front of the tibia

Pectineus

Adductor longus

Semi-membranosus

Soleus
Latin for *sandal*

Gastrocnemius
Latin for
shaped like a stomach

*Peroneus is Latin for *pin of a brooch or buckle*

1.2. Muscle anatomy (front view).

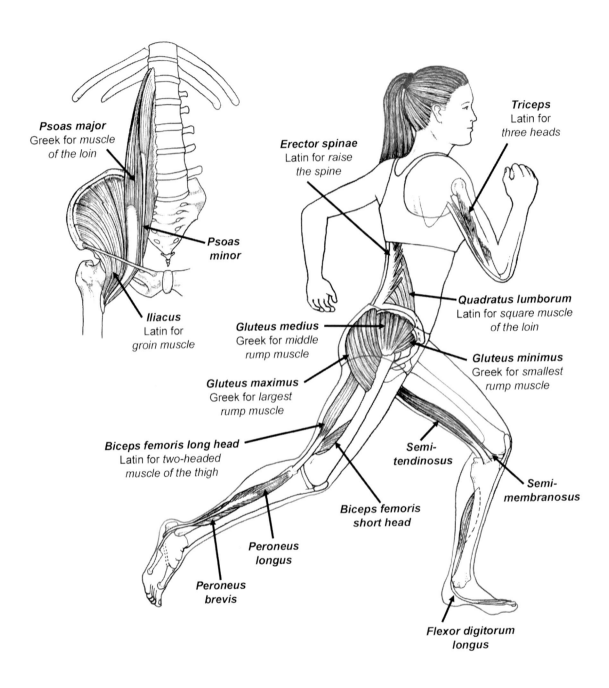

Psoas major
Greek for *muscle of the loin*

Psoas minor

Iliacus
Latin for *groin muscle*

Erector spinae
Latin for *raise the spine*

Triceps
Latin for *three heads*

Quadratus lumborum
Latin for *square muscle of the loin*

Gluteus medius
Greek for *middle rump muscle*

Gluteus minimus
Greek for *smallest rump muscle*

Gluteus maximus
Greek for *largest rump muscle*

Biceps femoris long head
Latin for *two-headed muscle of the thigh*

Semi-tendinosus

Semi-membranosus

Biceps femoris short head

Peroneus longus

Peroneus brevis

Flexor digitorum longus

1.3. Muscle anatomy (side view).

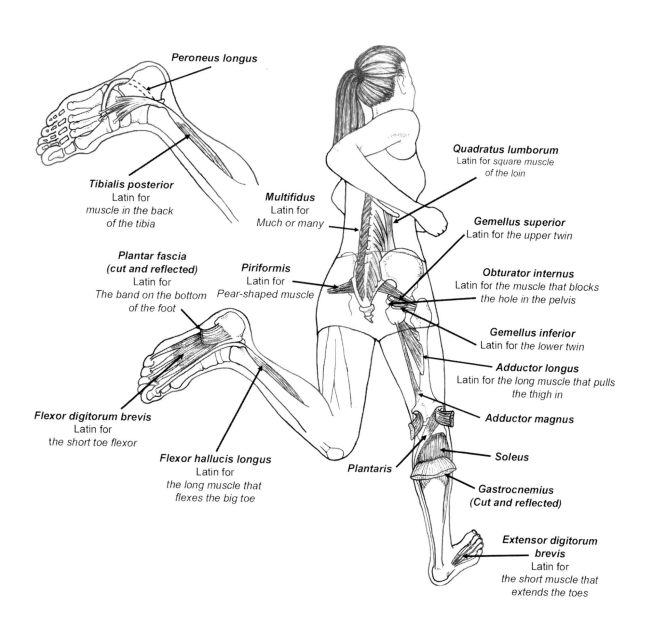

Peroneus longus

Tibialis posterior
Latin for
*muscle in the back
of the tibia*

Multifidus
Latin for
Much or many

Quadratus lumborum
Latin for *square muscle
of the loin*

Gemellus superior
Latin for *the upper twin*

**Plantar fascia
(cut and reflected)**
Latin for
*The band on the bottom
of the foot*

Piriformis
Latin for
Pear-shaped muscle

Obturator internus
Latin for *the muscle that blocks
the hole in the pelvis*

Gemellus inferior
Latin for *the lower twin*

Adductor longus
Latin for *the long muscle that pulls
the thigh in*

Flexor digitorum brevis
Latin for
the short toe flexor

Adductor magnus

Flexor hallucis longus
Latin for
*the long muscle that
flexes the big toe*

Plantaris

Soleus

**Gastrocnemius
(Cut and reflected)**

**Extensor digitorum
brevis**
Latin for
*the short muscle that
extends the toes*

1.4. Muscle anatomy (back view).

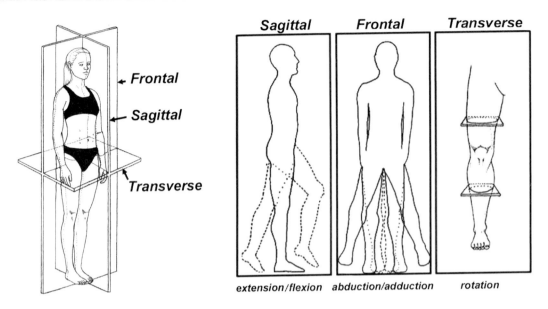

1.5. To describe motion, the body is divided into three reference planes: sagittal, frontal, and transverse.

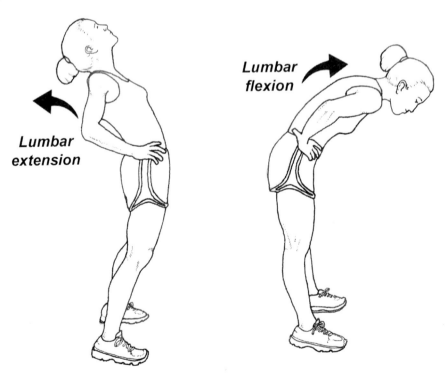

1.6. Sagittal plane motion of the spine.

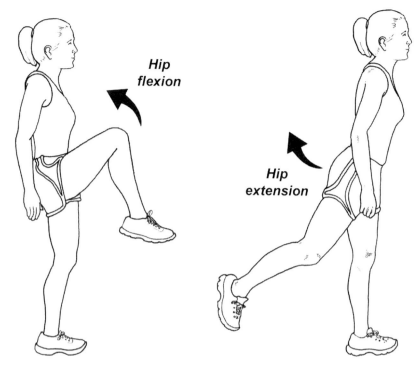

1.7. Sagittal plane motion of the hip.

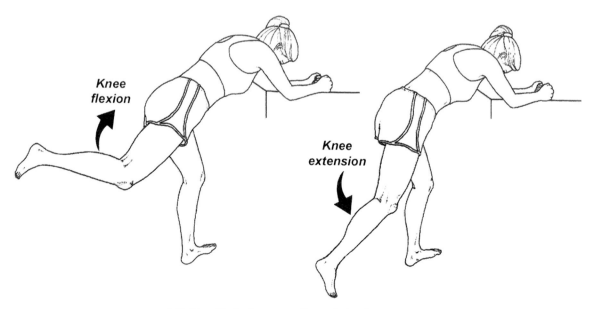

1.8. Sagittal plane motion of the knee.

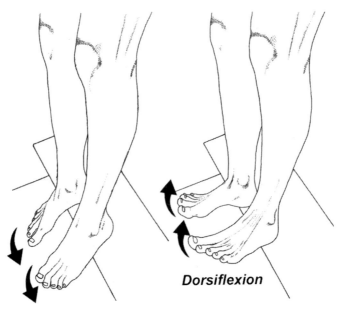

Dorsiflexion

Plantarflexion

1.9. Sagittal plane motion of the toes and ankles.

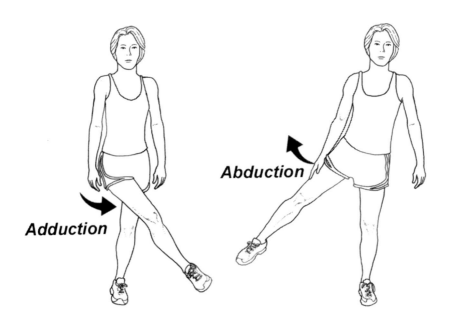

Abduction

Adduction

1.10. Frontal plane motion of the hip.

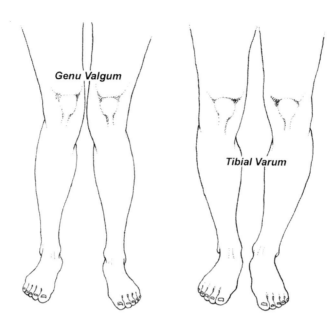

Genu Valgum

Tibial Varum

1.11. Fixed frontal plane positions of the knees.

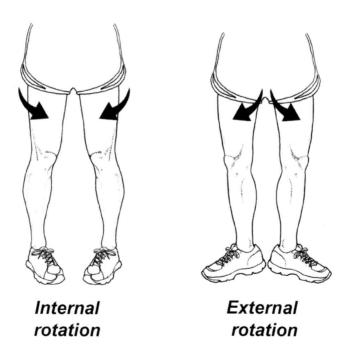

Internal rotation

External rotation

1.12. Transverse plane motions of the hips.

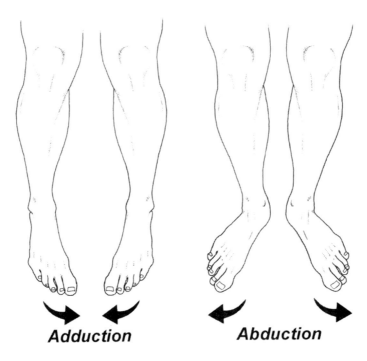

Adduction   **Abduction**

1.13. Transverse plane motion of the forefeet.

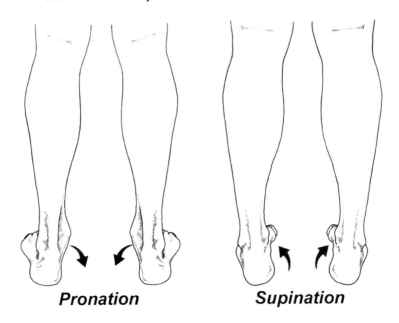

Pronation   **Supination**

1.14. **Pronation** and **supination** occur in all planes and represent lowering and elevation of the arch, respectively.

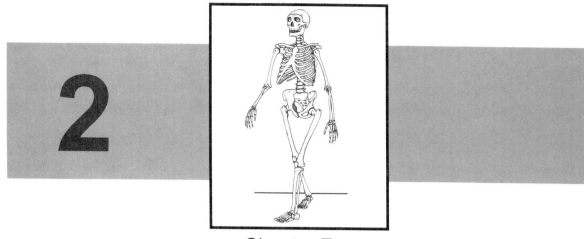

Chapter Two

THE EVOLUTION OF RUNNING

Even though running is good for your mental and physical health, contrary to popular belief, there is no proof that we were actually born to run. If we were, injury rates among marathoners would not average more than 90% per year (1). Longevity research also suggests we were not born to run. In a long-term study of 20,000 Danes followed since 1976, people who ran 10 to 15 miles per week lived almost six years longer than the runners averaging more than 25 miles per week (2). If we were really born to run, there wouldn't be a negative consequence associated with the higher weekly mileage.

Although some paleoanthropologists suggest we were designed to run because our hominid ancestors ran long distances in order to exhaust and then kill their prey (a type of hunting known as persistence hunting), proof of this theory is lacking. After studying the hunting and gathering habits of the sub-Saharan Hadza tribe (whose lifestyle and environment closely match that

of our hominid ancestors), Pickering and Bunn (3) made the important observation that Hadza hunters rarely run, and when they do it is usually in an attempt to "avoid approaching rain showers, stinging bees, and marauding elephants."

Pickering and Bunn emphasize that prior studies purporting the effectiveness of persistence hunting are flawed in that many of the persistence hunts referred to were prompted by researchers attempting to film the hunts for television documentaries. In many situations, the persistence hunts "were commenced from a vehicle and hunters refilled their water bottles during hunting." Even with the aid of the television crew, only 3 out of the 8 prompted persistence hunts were successful.

Ironically, in one of the few unsolicited persistence hunts witnessed by Bunn and a colleague, a tribal hunter identified the fresh footprints of a small deer and relentlessly *walked* after the animal for about 3 hours. The hunter kept forcing the deer away from the few shady areas available until the animal was exhausted and readily killed with a small club. Pickering and Bunn suggest that because running is metabolically expensive and greatly increases the risks of dehydration and heat exhaustion, it is unlikely that our ancient ancestors would have chosen such a risky and inefficient method of hunting.

The authors propose that our early ancestors obtained calories simply by being fortunate enough to have been foraging during a time period in which there was little competition from other carnivores (2.5 to 1.5 million years ago). Detailed evaluation of their food sources suggests that *Homo erectus* survived by "exploiting conditions of low competition while carcass foraging," not by endurance running in a highly competitive environment. The authors propose that rather than running prey to exhaustion, they might have functioned as "ambush predators," stealing prey killed by other animals.

In order to determine the role running might have played in the development of our species, researchers from Harvard University compared muscle forces associated with walking and running and determined that the transition to running resulted in a 520% increase in quadriceps muscle activity (4). This massive increase in quadriceps activity would have presented a significant problem to our hominid ancestors, as they would have had difficulty gathering the calories necessary to fuel such an inefficient form of transportation. Fast running on a hunter-gatherer diet is comparable to having a V8 engine in your car when you have a very limited gas budget: you'd only floor the engine in emergencies because it would be too expensive to go fast on a regular

basis. The Harvard researchers state that because of the inflated metabolic expense associated with conventional running, running efficiency was "unlikely a key selective factor favoring the evolution of erect bipedalism in humans."

The fact that we weren't running down unsuspecting prey in the hot savanna sun is consistent with the recent discovery that modern hunter-gatherers consume so few calories in the course of a typical day that they survive by expending almost no calories while hunting and foraging. By tracking the movements and energy expended by members of the Hadza tribe, Hunter College anthropologist Herman Pontzer concluded that the Hadza burn about the same number of calories per day while foraging as American office workers burn while sitting in their chairs. The main difference between the office workers and the Hadza foragers is that the Hadza eat much less than Westerners and their sparse diet contains none of the processed sugars and fats present in the typical modern diet. Pontzer emphasizes that Westerners are getting fat because we eat too much, not because we don't run long distances.

Becoming Bipeds

Since running long distances was most likely not a key factor in the evolution of bipedality, why exactly did we stand upright and take those first few steps? According to the classic theory of bipedal evolution, approximately 2.5 million years ago a seismic shifting of tectonic plates caused a rapid global cooling that quickly converted the once dense forests of eastern Africa into the open grasslands of the savanna. Because food sources

became more spread out, our early quadruped ancestors were forced to stand up and walk. This new
form of transportation theoretically allowed the
early hominids to see over the tall savanna grass-
es in order to more effectively forage for food.

The problem with the savanna hypothesis is
that recent discoveries show that the timing is
all wrong. In 2001, a team of French and Kenyan paleontologists announced the discovery
of multiple specimens of a 6-million-year-old
hominid they named *Orrorin tugenensis*. Discovered in the Tugin hills of Kenya, the femur
of this early hominid was remarkably humanlike
in that it possessed a groove on the back of its
hip for the obturator muscle. This groove is
present only in bipeds and confirmed that *Orrorin* most definitely walked upright (Fig. 2.1).

In 2002, a team of paleontologists led by Mi-
chael Brunet unveiled a newly discovered skull
from a 7-million-year-old hominid they called
Sahelanthropus tchadensis. Although no other remains have been found, the skull of this hominid
possessed an opening for the brainstem directly
in the center of the skull, strongly suggesting
Sahelanthropus was a dedicated biped; i.e., be-

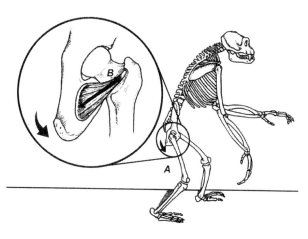

**2.1. Standing upright forces the pelvis to tilt
downward (arrow A), causing the obturator
externus tendon to press against the femoral
neck (B).**

cause bipeds walk with their heads balanced over
the center of their necks, their spinal cords enter
their skulls in a midline position. This contrasts
with almost all quadrupeds, which walk with
their heads down causing the brainstem to enter
the skull from the back (Fig. 2.2). The discovery
of *Sahelanthropus tchadensis* in Africa pushes
back the origins of bipedality from 4 million
years ago to a minimum of 7 million years ago,

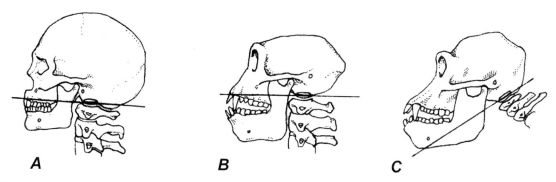

A   *B*   *C*

**2.2. In modern humans (A) and *Sahelanthropus tchadensis* (B), the spinal cord enters the skull
in a midline position.** Because they spend so much time looking down, the spinal cord in chimpanzees enters the skull from the back (**C**).

long before the shifting of the tectonic plates.

The controversy regarding the origins of bipedality continued until 2012, when researchers from the United States, England, Japan and Portugal published research suggesting that upright walking had nothing to do with the shifting of the tectonic plates and more than likely developed as a method for carrying scarce, high-quality food resources (5). This international team of researchers evaluated the behavior of wild chimpanzees while providing them access to two different types of nuts: the oil palm nut, which is widely available in their habitat, and the coula nut, which is relatively rare and highly prized by the chimpanzees. The researchers created three different feeding situations in which the prevalence of the rare versus the common nuts was varied.

When forced to compete for limited access to the rare coula nut, the frequency with which the chimpanzees started moving on two legs increased 400%. Bipedality allowed the chimpanzees to use their hands in order to carry greater quantities of the precious nuts. In a separate 14-month study performed by the same researchers (6), competition while the chimpanzees were raiding crops for rare and unpredictable resources again resulted in significant increases in the prevalence of bipedal movement, which the authors link to a clear attempt to carry as many resources as possible.

While our earliest ancestors were more than likely very unstable while standing upright and attempting to walk, the last 7 million years have provided enough time for natural selection to mold us into the extremely successful bipeds we are today. Compared to the well-known hominid Lucy, who could walk a mile in about 26 minutes, modern humans have developed specific anatomical traits designed to improve our ability to get around. Three million years after Lucy roamed the earth, modern humans can now run 26.2 miles in a little over 2 hours, a mile in 3 minutes 43 seconds, and achieve sprint speeds of almost 30 mph. Sometimes the anatomical changes were subtle (e.g., tendons thickened and rotated in order to store and return energy in a spring-like manner) and other times the changes were more dramatic (such as the complete rebuilding of our pelvis in order to allow the hip abductors and hamstrings to function efficiently). The precise anatomical changes responsible for producing these amazing running accomplishments are summarized in the following sections.

The First Walker

Although unable to run, the first hominid to get around routinely on two legs was *Ardipithecus ramidus*, better known as *Ardi*. A recently published 15-year analysis of this 4.4-million-year-old hominid confirmed that Ardi could easily stand upright and was in fact a dedicated biped (6) (Fig. 2.3). This finding was unexpected since scientists had assumed that 4.4 million years ago, while upright walking might have occasionally occurred in our hominid ancestors, it would not have been the primary form of transportation. The fact that *Ardi* walked upright as a habitual biped forced scientists to change the way they viewed our last common ancestor. Prior to *Ardi*, experts had assumed that the farther back they traced the evolutionary tree, the more chimpanzee-like

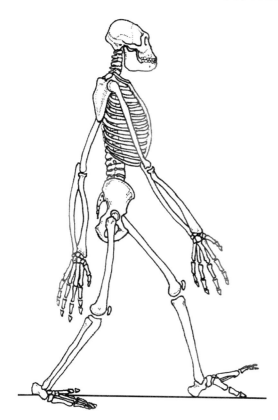

2.3. *Ardipithecus ramidus.* Modified and redrawn from an illustration by J. H. Matternes in Science. 2009;326:101.

our ancestors became. The discovery of *Ardi* changed that, because her skeleton possessed an unanticipated number of modern human traits.

The most surprising skeletal discovery related to bipedality was that *Ardi's* lumbar spine was so mobile that she could arch her back into an upright position, effectively allowing her to balance the weight of her upper body over her pelvis (Fig. 2.4). Because chimpanzees have such rigid lumbar spines (providing invaluable protection against spinal shear forces associated with twisting between branches) they are unable

to balance effectively in an upright position and can walk as bipeds only by excessively flexing their knees, hips, and spine (Fig. 2.5).

The shape of *Ardi's* upper pelvis was also unexpected because her upper pelvis angled forward allowing the hip abductors to support weight more effectively during single-limb support. This is in contrast to the chimpanzee pelvis that rests flat against the back and projects up towards the ribs (Fig. 2.5. A). Because the chimpanzee pelvis is so flat, the hip abductor muscles are unable to

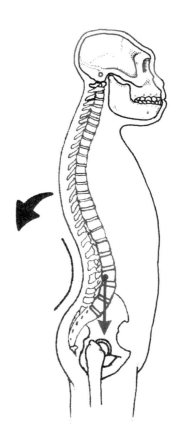

2.4. By arching its low back (arrow), *Ardipithecus* could balance the upper body over the pelvis, thereby reducing stress on the hip and back muscles.

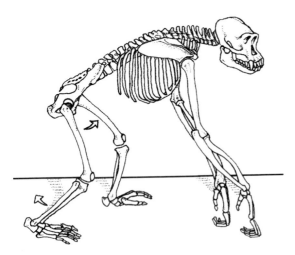

2.5. Unlike humans, a chimpanzee's longer pelvis and fused lumbar spine forces it to walk with its hips and knees flexed (white arrows).

stabilize the pelvis during single-limb stance (i.e., a chimpanzee cannot stand upright on one leg).

All of these findings confirm that our last common ancestor was not similar in shape to a modern chimp but more closely resembled a blend between chimpanzees and humans. *Ardi* confirmed what in hindsight seems obvious: while modern humans have spent the last 7 million years evolving into our present form, chimpanzees and apes have also evolved considerably, perhaps even more so, developing features that made them more efficient at hanging from branches and moving about in high trees.

Because our last common ancestor possessed a mobile lumbar spine and a pelvis that angled slightly forward, the transition to bipedality would have been much easier than previously believed when using the chimpanzee-centric model. This transition would have provided our ancient ancestors with a slight increase in effi-

ciency during upright postures, while also allowing them to use their hands, possibly supplying food to pregnant females. By supplying females with food, an environment was created in which natural selection heavily favored the most efficient bipeds. After meticulously analyzing every detail of *Ardi's* skeleton and comparing it to past and present hominids, a team of world-famous researchers concluded that our last common ancestor was not skilled at prolonged suspension or climbing high branches (6). These researchers go on to make the interesting statement that if the early hominids could have adapted to climbing as well as apes and chimps, "neither bipedality nor its social correlates would likely have evolved." In other words, if we weren't so bad at evolving, we'd have left the ground in search of the better food sources higher up in the trees and the world would have been a very different place.

The next significant change in our anatomy that set the stage for the development of our current running skills occurred in *Australopithecus anamensis*. The biggest change occurring in *anamensis* was that the upper portion of its leg flared outward, allowing for greater pressure distribution (Fig. 2.6). Oddly, while the legs of *Australopithecus anamensis* revealed significant changes that improved efficiency while upright, the skull and facial features of *anamensis* remained primitive and these hominids resembled walking orangutans.

After the development of a lumbar spine that could arch backward (first noted in *Ardi*) the second most important change allowing for efficient bipedality occurred in our 3-million-year-old ancestor, *Australopithecus afarensis*. More easily

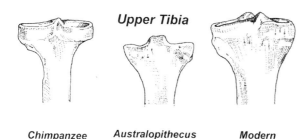

Upper Tibia

Chimpanzee   Australopithecus   Modern
                    anamensis   Human

2.6. Chimpanzees spend so little time upright that their upper legs (tibia) are very narrow. In contrast, *anamensis* is spending so much time upright that the upper tibia begins to widen.

recognized by her nickname Lucy (after the Beatle's song that frequently played at the archaeological site), this important ancestor developed a dish-shaped pelvis that dramatically improved efficiency while walking because it allowed her to use her hip abductors to stabilize her vertical upper body during single-limb support (Fig. 2.7).

Footprints of the *Afarenses*

The famous Laetoli footprints confirm that Lucy was an efficient biped. Discovered in Tanzania by Mary Leakey and her team of archaeologists (7), these 3.2-million-year-old footprints were formed as three *Australopithecus afarensis* walked along a steep slope of volcanic ash. Despite a significant incline, there was no evidence of hand contact with the ground confirming that these *afarensis* were indeed bipedal. While the Laetoli footprints lacked the detail necessary to evaluate the shape of the medial arch, recent research suggests that *Australopithecus afarensis*, like modern humans, exhibited variation in arch structure: some *afarenses* possessed well-developed arches; others were flat-footed (8).

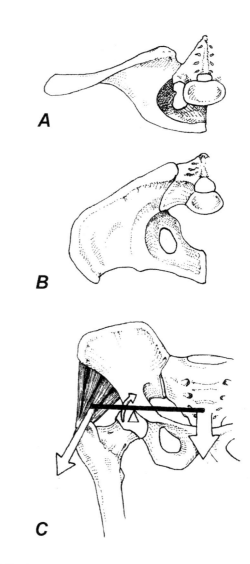

2.7. Compared to the chimpanzee pelvis (A), Lucy's pelvis flares forward (B), allowing the hip abductors to maintain a level pelvis while standing upright (C). Modified from Lovejoy O. Evolution of human walking. Scientific American. November 1988:118-125.

The most significant anatomical clue suggesting that Lucy was a biped is the distinctive groove for tibialis anterior tendon located on the inner side of her foot (Fig. 2.8). The location of this groove is an important prerequisite for getting around on two legs because it allows this tendon to prevent shifting of the bones of the inner forefoot. The authors note that in less efficient bipeds such as chimps and apes, the groove for tibialis anterior is positioned farther back, making the inner forefoot unstable.

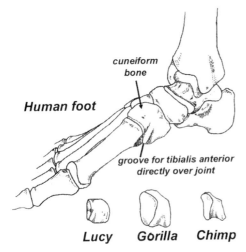

2.8. In humans and Lucy, a bony groove for the tibialis anterior tendon is located across a very mobile joint, while in gorillas and chimpanzees, the groove is positioned over the bone.

Another important change in the inner forefoot occurred at the base of the first metatarsal (Fig. 2.9). Unlike the chimpanzee, Lucy developed a ridge in the base of her first metatarsal. This is an extremely important change since it stabilizes the inner forefoot and creates a bony block that lessens muscular strain during the pushoff phase while walking. The changes present in Lucy's feet suggest that she gave up her opposable great toe in exchange for improved efficiency while walking.

Because Lucy's hip could not extend as far back as modern humans, she could not create significant force during push-off. The thick bones present in her forearms confirm that despite the lack of handprints present in the Laetoli footprints, Lucy frequently used her hands for support. Because she could walk on all fours or upright on two feet, Lucy serves as an excellent example of "mosaic evolution," in that she exchanged the grasping skills of the foot (which *Ardipithecus* found so invaluable) in favor of the improved stability necessary for bipedality (Fig. 2.10).

An additional hominid who played a significant role in our ability to walk and run efficiently is *Homo rudolfensis*. Named after Lake Rudolf in Western Kenya, where this hominid was first discovered, *Homo rudolfensis* possessed such a large braincase that it was the first of our ances-

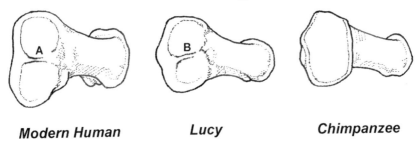

2.9. Back view of the first metatarsal. Compared to the chimpanzee first metatarsal, both Lucy and modern humans possess a bony ridge (**A** and **B**) that lessens rotation of the metatarsal.

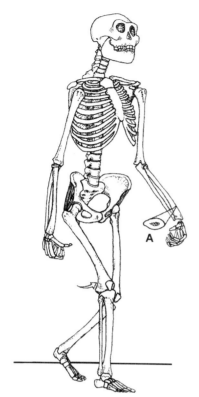

2.10. Lucy walking. The thick bones of her forearms (**A**) confirm that she frequently used her hands for support while her elongated and curved fingers prove that she spent a significant amount of time grasping branches and climbing. Compared to modern humans, her limited range of hip extension would have shortened her stride length and she most likely would have walked with exaggerated knee flexion.

tors to be classified as *Homo* (Greek for "same"). Skeletal remains of the pelvis and legs suggest that *Homo rudolfensis* spent almost all of its time walking on two legs. The joints of the low back and hips have increased surface areas capable of supporting body weight for long periods without assistance from the arms. The kneecaps face forward and there is a humanlike ankle that is aligned so that the foot moves forward in the same plane as the leg. Unlike Lucy, who walked with her feet pointing out, *Homo rudolfensis* walked with its knees and feet moving straight forward.

Bipedality and the Development of Language

An important by-product of *Homo rudolfensis*'s habitual bipedality is that it uncoupled breathing and locomotion. As noted by Carrier (9), animals that run on all fours time their respiration with their strides. When their legs extend forward they inhale, and when they hit the ground and their muscles contract to absorb shock, they exhale. This coupled pattern locks the breathing cycle to the stride rate during four-legged locomotion. In a full-time biped, breathing is no longer coupled with locomotion. This is essential for the development of speech since it allows for an adjustable rate of airflow. Whether our hominid ancestors began talking 50,000 years ago or 5 million years ago is a subject of debate, but it is clear that the process of walking on two legs was crucial for the development of language.

Until this point in evolution and despite changes in the forefoot, hips, and pelvis, the foot was still relatively unstable during the pushoff phase, and would buckle while walking at faster speeds. All this changed about 1.9 million years ago with the development of the calcaneocuboid joint locking mechanism (Fig. 2.11). First appearing in *Homo habilis*, (nicknamed *"The Handyman"* because it was the first hominid to routinely use tools) the development of this bony locking mechanism was critical for improved efficiency while walking because it prevents the arch from collapsing during propulsion. This simple change allowed for the increased stride lengths necessary

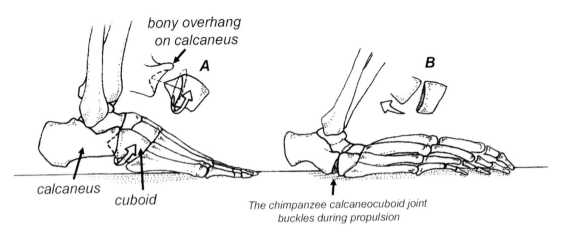

bony overhang
on calcaneus

A

B

calcaneus
cuboid

*The chimpanzee calcaneocuboid joint
buckles during propulsion*

2.11. In humans (A), heel lift occurs with the cuboid bone pivoting against a bony overhang on the calcaneus. This action locks the midfoot during pushoff, which stabilizes the entire foot. In a chimpanzee (**B**), the calcaneocuboid joint fails to lock and the midfoot buckles under the forces of propulsion.

for the gradual transition to running because the foot could now be placed behind the extended hip.

Homo Erectus: The First Runner

The first hominid believed to be capable of running is *Homo erectus*. Named *erectus* because of its upright stature and narrow frame, this hominid had a remarkably long species lifespan with fossil remnants dating from 1.9 million years ago to as recently as 27,000 years ago. Because no primates other than humans are capable of jogging even short distances, the ability to run could have provided significant advantages while searching for food, all the while freeing the hands for the efficient transportation of precious calories.

As explained by Bramble and Lieberman (10), one of the most important clues that *Homo erectus* was capable of occasional running is the enlarged size of the semicircular canals present in its inner ears. Confirmed on a CAT scan of a *Homo erectus* skull, the large semicircular canals (which are not

present in Lucy's skull) allowed this hominid to balance during the periods of single-limb support present while running. (Unlike walking in which both feet are on the ground for extended periods, running requires that the individual spend more time balancing on one leg.) The improved balance facilitated by the large semicircular canals would allow for the complex cutting and pivoting movements that occur while running.

Although there are no skeletal remains of *Homo erectus* feet, the discovery of 1.5-million-year-old *Homo erectus* footprints in Kenya revealed well-defined arches and a modern humanlike angle of the big toe. In contrast, Lucy's big toe tilted in more, comparable to a modern human with a large bunion. The tilted big toe would have made Lucy's forefoot significantly less stable during propulsion. A detailed analysis of the *Homo erectus* footprints revealed a greater depth of print beneath the inner forefoot, suggesting an efficient weight transfer towards the big toe during the push-off phase of walking (11). These findings are consistent with a long, modern, humanlike stride with push-off occurring with the hip extended and pressure centered over a stable inner forefoot.

In a great paper that went on to create the *Born to Run* movement, Bramble and Lieberman (10) claim that *Homo erectus* was so efficient at running they could chase prey for hours, eventually killing them by hand. According to the authors, the consumption of meat obtained by endurance running is the only way to explain the mystery of how *Homo erectus* was able to double its brain size in a relatively short time period about 2 million years ago. Bramble and Lieberman propose that because the brain consumes 16 times the calories of an equivalent mass of muscle, and meat provides four times the calories of an equal sized serving of fruit, the only way *Homo erectus* could have fueled such rapid brain expansion was if they were able to obtain calorie-dense meat by running prey to exhaustion. Because *Homo erectus* lacked the ability to use even the simplest of weapons, it seemed logical that chasing prey for hours was their only option for obtaining the amount of meat necessary to fuel their rapidly expanding brains.

The Real Reason for Brain Expansion

While there was an increase in the number of animal bones found in early *Homo erectus* archaeological sites confirming that meat consumption did correlate with brain expansion, a paper recently published in *Proceedings of the National Academy of Sciences* suggests that it wasn't long distance running that allowed for brain expansion: it was the ability to cook (12).

The authors of this paper prove that fire was discovered much earlier than previously believed and the ability to heat food was instrumental in brain expansion because heat softens tough fibers, speeding up the process of chewing and digestion. Cooking food also allows for a greater percentage of food to be metabolized by the body: 100% of cooked food is metabolized while only 30 to 40% of the nutrients present in raw foods can be digested. These researchers claim that by incorporating fire to cook their food, *Homo erectus* could easily obtain the calories necessary to fuel their expanding brains.

Fire may also have indirectly allowed for brain expansion by keeping predators at bay throughout the night. The improved sleep provided by a primitive campfire may have allowed for the rapid eye movement sleep proven to accelerate brain development. Apparently, our big brains developed not because we were able to run, but because we were able to control fire.

The Hobbit Hominid

Homo floresiensis is the next hominid in our evolutionary tree. Discovered in 2003 on the remote Indonesian island of Flores, this enigmatic hominid stood only 3 feet 6 inches tall, possessed an extremely tiny head, and was terrible at getting around on two legs. This hobbit-like hominid represented a step backwards in our transition towards efficient walking and running because *floresiensis* possessed a primitive foot with long, curled toes that would have been useless while upright but invaluable while climbing trees and grabbing branches. By far, the most unusual characteristic of the *Homo floresiensis* foot was its length: while modern humans typically have a foot measuring 55% the length of their thigh, the *Homo floresiensis* foot measured 70% the length of its thigh. Such an extremely long foot would have forced *Homo floresiensis* to walk with a steppage gait in which its hips flexed excessively in order to allow its big foot to clear the ground during swing phase, comparable to walking while wearing swim fins. Although *Homo floresiensis* may have been able to run, it would have been for extremely short distances and only in emergencies.

Short Legs: The Downfall of the Neanderthals

While *Homo floresiensis* remained isolated on a remote island and was inconsequential in making us efficient runners, Neanderthals played a more important role in the development of bipedality as they competed for food and coexisted with modern humans for most of the last 200,000 years. The prototypical caveman, almost all skeletal remains of *Homo neanderthalensis,* have been recovered from cave and rock shelters found throughout Europe and Asia. Although originally considered a primitive brute (skeletal remains revealed routine cannibalism), it is now known that Neanderthals buried their dead with rituals that included specific positioning, the use of markers and perhaps even the incorporation of flowers with the deceased.

The species lifespan for *Homo neanderthalensis* was from 175,000 to 27,000 years ago. Expanding glaciers throughout Europe and Asia during that time suggest that *neanderthalensis* was exposed to snow almost year-round. The consistent exposure to cold for tens of thousands of years allowed natural selection to favor a skeletal shape that lessened heat loss: the extremities (particularly the fingers, forearms and legs) were significantly shorter than modern humans while the torso was long, wide, and barrel-chested. These combined features make *Homo neanderthalensis* a little shorter than modern humans but about the same weight.

Because of their short legs and stocky thighs, it was originally assumed that Neanderthals walked with a stooped, bent-knee gait. However, the recent discovery of arthritis in the weight-bearing joints of a particularly old Neanderthal confirms that they most likely walked upright in a manner similar to modern humans, although their shorter legs resulted in reduced stride lengths making for a fairly inefficient gait (Fig. 2.12).

Since Neanderthals and modern humans inhabited the same geographic location for thousands of years, it has long been suspected that occasional interbreeding between humans and Neanderthals might have occurred. Although early DNA research suggested otherwise, a team of researchers from the Max Planck Institute for Evolutionary Anthropology in Leipzig, Germany evaluated 4 billion nucleotides from Neanderthal bone fragments and conclusively demonstrated that interbreeding did occur (13). In fact, between one and four percent of modern human DNA comes directly from Neanderthals, including genes coding for cognitive function and skeletal development. By comparing the Neanderthal genetic code to that of modern humans throughout the world, the authors concluded that interbreeding most likely took place between 50,000 and 80,000 years ago, somewhere in the Middle East. The offspring of Neanderthals and humans

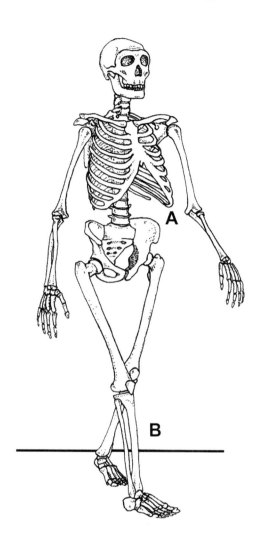

2.12. *Homo neanderthalensis* **walked with an upright posture similar to modern humans.** The primary difference in skeletal structure relates to the widened rib cage (**A**) and the shorter legs (**B**). The short legs and excessive muscle mass made Neanderthals very inefficient at getting around on two legs.

quickly spread: people from Papua New Guinea (where Neanderthals never lived) have just as much Neanderthal DNA as people from France. The only modern humans devoid of Neanderthal DNA are from Africa, since interbreeding occurred after our ancestors crossed into Eurasia.

Despite occasional interbreeding, the Neanderthal population slowly dwindled, becoming extinct approximately 30,000 years ago. While it was originally assumed that *Homo sapiens* unwittingly caused the extinction of *Homo neanderthalensis* through competition for food and/or by the spread of disease, more recent research suggests that metabolic inefficiency may have played an important role in their demise. In a detailed study of the energetic cost of locomotion as related to lower limb length, researchers from the University of Wisconsin prove that the Neanderthal's shorter legs would have increased the metabolic cost of locomotion by at least 30% (14).

Another group of paleoanthropologists went on to calculate the daily energy expenditure of Neanderthals versus that of modern humans and determined that because of their stockier frames and increased muscularity, *Homo neanderthalensis* had to spend anywhere from 100 to 350 calories per day more than their *Homo sapien* relatives (15). Because rapid climate change present at the time reduced the number of large prey available, and because Neanderthals continued to obtain more than 70% of their calories from meat, experts believe Neanderthals gradually starved themselves into extinction because they were spending more calories searching for food than they were able to obtain from the food itself.

Homo Sapiens and the Exodus from Africa

With Neanderthals, *Homo erectus,* and *Homo floresiensis* extinct, the last hominid left standing is us, the remarkably successful species known as *Homo sapiens* (from the Latin "The Knowing Man"). DNA evidence coupled with carbon dating of skeletal remains suggests that the first *Homo sapiens* appeared in Africa about 200,000 years ago. These early humans were quick to cover the planet. With a small band of modern humans leaving Africa about 100,000 years ago (estimated to be between 50 and 100 individuals), skeletal remains have been dated in the Middle East at 90,000 years ago, China 67,000, Australia 30,000, and the Americas starting at 11,000 years ago. Within a thousand years, our early ancestors spread from Alaska to the lower tip of South America (16).

The skeletal factors that allowed for such efficient long distance travel included the formation of a rigid arch and a thickening of our leg bones. Compared with our ancestors, our toes became shorter and the surface area of our weight-bearing joints increased. Our spinal columns developed three curves to improve mobility and distribute force more effectively. Our tails reduced in size forming the coccyx. Specific changes also occurred in our tendons that allowed them to store and return energy with little contribution from our muscles. This important change allowed us to travel farther on fewer calories, which is the ultimate goal of efficient walking and running.

Why Kenyans and Ethiopians Win Marathons

Given the fact that less than two percent of the world's population comes from sub-Saharan Africa, it's surprising that the lead pack in almost every major marathon consists primarily of Kenyans and Ethiopians. According to Sawyer, et al. (16), the world's best long distance runners are from sub-Saharan Africa because people from these countries have had more time to develop specific anatomical changes that allow them to tolerate extreme heat, and these same changes allow them to run long distances more efficiently. Just as Neanderthals and early humans living in cold environments became inefficient as bipeds because they developed massive torsos with short limbs that favored heat retention, the earliest *Homo sapiens* from Kenya and Ethiopia have had 200,000 years to develop the smaller torsos and longer extremities necessary for heat dissipation. Because it takes significantly less energy to carry a small torso 26.2 miles, and thin legs are easier to accelerate and decelerate, the structural changes that improved heat dissipation also allowed the sub-Saharan Africans to become some of the greatest marathon runners on earth.

References

1. van Gent RN, Siem D, van Middelkoop M, van Os AG, Bierma-Zeinstra SM, Koes BW. Incidence and determinants of lower extremity running injuries in long distance runners: a systematic review. *Br J Sports Med.* 2007;41:469–80.
2. Schonhr P. Assessing prognosis: a glimpse of the future. Jogging healthy or hazard? In: Cardiology ESo, ed. EuroPrevent 2012. Dublin, Ireland: *European Heart Journal.* 2012.
3. Pickering T, Bunn H. The endurance running hypothesis and hunting and scavenging in savanna woodlands. *J Human Evolution.* 2007;53:434-438.
4. Biewener A, Farley C, Roberts T, Temaner M. Muscle mechanical advantage of human walking and running: implications for energy cost. *J Appl Physiol.* 2004;97:2266-2274.
5. Carvalho S, Biro D, Cunha E, et al. Chimpanzee carrying behaviour and the origins of human bipedality. *Current Biology.* 2012; 22(6): R180.
6. White T, Asfaw B, Beyene Y, et al. Ardipithecus ramidus and the paleobiology of early hominids (summary). *Science.* 2009;326:64.
7. Leakey M, Harris J. Laetoli: A Pliocene Site in Northern Tanzania. New York:Clarendon, 1987.
8. Desilva J, Throckmorton Z. Lucy's flat feet: the relationship between the ankle and rearfoot arching in early hominins. *PLoS One.* 2010;5:14432.
9. Carrier D. The energetic paradox of human running and hominid evolution. *Current Anthropol.* 1984;25:483-495.
10. Bramble D, Lieberman D. Endurance running and the evolution of Homo. *Nature.* 2004;432:345-352.
11. Bennett M, Harris J, Richmond B, et al. Early hominin foot morphology based on 1.5-million- year-old footprints from Ilieret, Kenya. *Science.* 2009;323:1197-1201.
12. Berna F, Goldberg P, Horwitz L, et al. Microstratigraphic evidence of *in situ* fire in the Acheulean strata of Wonderwerk Cave, Northern Cape province, South Africa. Proceedings of the National Academy of Sciences. April 2, 2012.
13. Green R, Krause J, et al. A draft sequence of the Neandertal genome. *Science.* 2010; 328: 710-722.
14. Steudel-Numbers K, Tilkens M. The effect of lower limb length on the energetic cost of locomotion: implications for fossil hominins. *J Human Evolution.* 2004;47:95-109.
15. Froehle A, Churchill S. Energetic competition between Neandertals and anatomically modern humans. *Paleoanthropology.* 2009;96-116.
16. Sawyer G, Deak V, Sarmiento E, et al. The Last Human; A Guide to 22 Species of Extinct Humans. New York: Nevraumont Publishing, 2007.

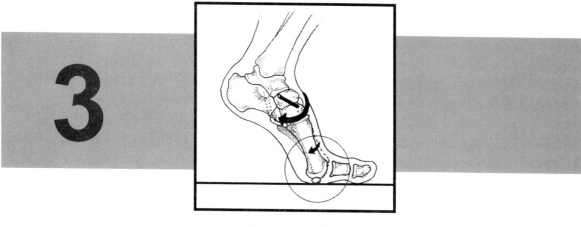

Chapter Three

THE BIOMECHANICS OF WALKING AND RUNNING

In order to understand what it takes to be a great runner (and remain injury-free), it's important to understand exactly what's going on while we're upright and moving around. To accurately describe the various anatomical interactions occurring while we walk and run, researchers have come up with the term gait cycle. Traced back to the 13th century Scandinavian word "*gata*" for "road or path," one complete gait cycle consists of the anatomical interactions occurring from the moment the foot first contacts the ground until that same foot again makes ground contact with the next step. The gait cycle consists of two distinct phases: stance phase, in which the foot is contacting the ground; and swing phase, in which the lower limb is swinging through the air preparing for the next impact (Fig. 3.1). Because of the complexity of stance phase motions, this portion of the gait cycle has been subdivided into contact, midstance, and propulsive periods. Although running is also divided

into the same three periods, the increased speed and the need for a more forceful propulsive period changes the timing of the events: the contact and midstance periods are slightly shorter and the propulsive period is longer (Fig. 3.2).

The neurological mechanisms necessary to complete the gait cycle are unusual in that swing phase motions are reflexive and present at birth (e.g., an unbalanced toddler will immediately swing the lower extremity into a protected position), while movements associated with stance phase represent a learned process. This statement is supported with the clinical observation that children born without sight make no spontaneous attempts to stand up and walk on their own and will only do so when physically guided.

As soon as we become toddlers, we begin experimenting with a wide range of walking and running patterns, subconsciously analyzing the metabolic expense associated with each variation in gait. This is a time-consuming process and

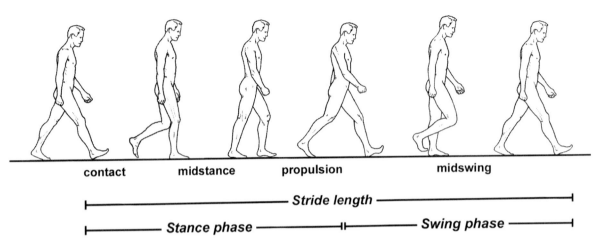

contact   midstance   propulsion   midswing

|————————————————— *Stride length* ————————————————|

|——————— *Stance phase* ———————|+|——————— *Swing phase* ———————|

3.1. Gait cycle of the right leg. Stance phase begins when the heel hits the ground and ends when the big toe leaves the ground. Swing phase continues until the heel again strikes the ground. Stance phase is subdivided into contact, midstance, and propulsive periods. Important components of the gait cycle are step length, stride length, and cadence. Step length refers to the distance covered between the right and left foot in a single step, while stride length refers to the distance covered by a single foot during the entire gait cycle; i.e., the distance covered during two steps. Cadence, or step frequency, is the number of times your feet make ground contact per minute. While walking, the typical person takes 115 steps per minute with an average stride length equal to 0.8 times body height.

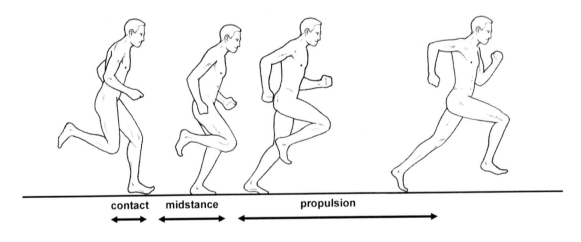

contact   midstance   propulsion

3.2. Stance phase while running. Although running is divided into the same phases, there is tremendous variation in stride length and cadence depending upon running speed. While recreational runners often possess stride lengths of about 4 feet and a cadence of around 175 steps per minute, Usain Bolt set the world record in the 100-meter sprint by running with a stride length of 16 feet and a cadence of more than 265 steps per minute.

perfecting the musculoskeletal interactions necessary to become metabolically efficient can take up to a decade to master. Even when adjusting for size differences, the average three year old consumes 33% more oxygen when traveling at a fixed speed than an adult. By the age of six, children continue to burn more calories while walking and running. Fortunately, by age ten, mechanical efficiency is equal to that of an adult and after almost a decade of practice, children are finally efficient at getting around on two legs.

What is Perfect Running Form?

Despite the controversy among coaches as to what constitutes perfect running form (they'll tell you to modify everything from the position of your wrist to the angle of your torso), the actual answer is pretty simple and can be traced back to a 1953 article published in the *Journal of Bone and Joint Surgery* (1). In this article, a team of orthopedic specialists conclude that in order to be efficient, we must learn to "move our center of mass through space along a path requiring the least expenditure of energy." (Located in the middle of the pelvis, the center of mass represents the point about which our bodies would rotate if we were to flip in the air.) We minimize energy expenditure by modifying the positions of our joints in such a way that the pathway of the center of mass through space is flattened (Fig. 3.3). For example, if we were to walk with our knees locked and our pelvis stiff (e.g., with a Frankenstein-like gait), the body's center of mass would move up and down through a series of abruptly intersecting arcs, which would significantly increase the metabolic cost of locomotion

because specific muscles would tense to accommodate the exaggerated up-and-down motions.

Try taking a few paces mimicking Frankenstein's gait and you'll quickly feel yourself accelerate downward before reversing direction and suddenly accelerating upward. The rapid acceleration/deceleration is made more apparent by trying to walk while holding a glass of water: the water in the glass splashes forward the moment the heel strike occurs and moves backward as you accelerate up. The extreme version of this gait occurs when trying to walk while wearing stilts, when the abrupt transitions be-

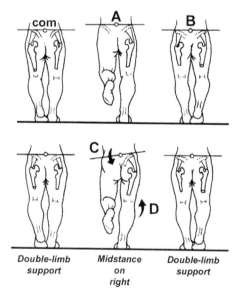

Double-limb   Midstance   Double-limb
support   on   support
                right

3.3. Movement of the center of mass (COM). If we walk with our hips and knees stiff, the center of mass moves up and down through a large range of motion (compare the height of **A** and **B**). The excessive up-and-down movement of the center of mass is metabolically expensive because muscles have to work hard to move the center of mass up-and-down. By dropping the opposite hip (**C**), flexing the knee (**D**), and moving the ankle, we can keep our center of mass moving along a straight line.

tween low and high points become more obvious.

Considering the inefficiency associated with excessive up-and-down motions, you would think that the ideal gait would be one in which the pathway of the center of mass was flattened into a straight line: this is often suggested by many running experts who claim the most efficient gait is the one with the least vertical oscillation. The problem is that flattening the progression of the center of mass too much can be just as costly as not flattening it at all. For example, try walking in a manner similar to the comedian Groucho Marx (you can find videos of him walking on *YouTube*). Although excessive flexion of the knees and hips associated with this style of gait will flatten the pathway of the center of mass, it is metabolically expensive because the caloric cost associated with exaggerated knee flexion is high. In fact, research has shown that walking with a "Groucho gait" results in a 50% increase in oxygen consumption (2). Excessive flattening of the pathway of the center of mass accomplished by flexing our limbs explains why small mammals are so inefficient compared to large mammals; e.g., on a gram per gram basis, a mouse consumes 20 times more energy than a pony (3).

It turns out that moderately flattening our center of mass allows us to maximize efficiency while walking and running. The catch is that the precise movement patterns we need to incorporate in order to adjust the pathway of our center of mass so that we are maximally efficient change depending upon whether we are walking or running. At slower speeds we are most efficient when our legs are stiff and inflexible but at higher speeds we must increase

the degree of knee and hip flexion in order to improve shock absorption. These findings correlate with the clinical observation that walking feels more comfortable when moving slowly, while running is more comfortable as speeds increase.

To determine exactly which gait pattern is most efficient at a specific speed of locomotion (there are hundreds of options regarding the selection of specific joint movements), scientists from the robotics laboratory at Cornell University published an article in the prestigious journal *Nature* in which they created a computerized mathematical model to evaluate metabolic efficiency associated with every possible type of gait (including odd patterns such as the Groucho gait) (4). As expected, at slow speeds of locomotion, walking was most efficient with the knees relatively stiff and nearly locked (remember the quadriceps are expensive muscles to fuel), while at higher speeds, conventional running with an airborne phase was most efficient (Fig. 3.4, A and B).

Hybrid Running: The Ideal Gait

The most important result of the computerized model created by the Cornell researchers was that walking and running were only used at the extremes of speed: walking at low speeds and running at high speeds. For all in-between speeds, the computer model suggested that people would choose an intermediate gait referred to as "pendular running." In this gait pattern, which I like to call hybrid running, the stride length is significantly shortened, the airborne phase is reduced or absent, and the lower limbs are stiff for brief periods during stance phase (Fig. 3.4, C).

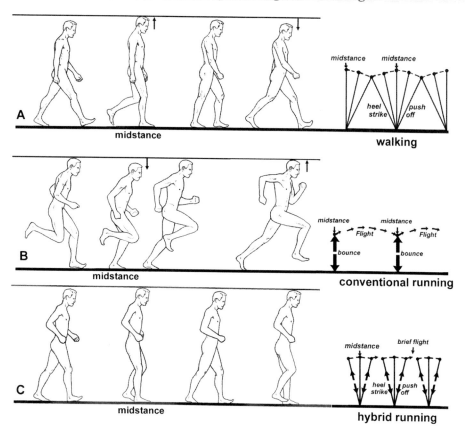

3.4. Pendular or hybrid running. Notice that while walking (**A**), the center of mass is highest during midstance and lowest when both legs are on the ground. When running (**B**), the center of mass is highest during swing phase and lowest during midstance. With hybrid running (**C**), the stride length is shortened, there is minimal to no airborne phase, and knee stiffness prevents excessive up-and-down movement of the center of mass. Notice also that, with hybrid running, ground contact is made with the foot almost directly beneath the pelvis.

Notice that in all of these illustrations, the primary difference between walking and running is that the center of mass is at a low point during midstance when running fast, and at a high point during midstance when walking. The location of the center of mass during midstance is important because it serves as the only accurate indicator to signal when we transition from walking to running. Unfortunately, the overwhelming majority of running researchers

continue to use the presence of an airborne phase as a way to differentiate walking from running. The improper use of the airborne phase to define running was pointed out more than 20 years ago by the Harvard biologist Tom McMahon (5), who noted that slow runners often make contact with their lead foot before their pushoff foot has left the ground; i.e., there is no airborne phase.

Given the popularity of running, it is surprising that except for occasional references to

"Groucho running" and "double-limb support slow running," options other than conventional airborne phase running are rarely discussed. Because it has a brief or absent airborne phase and a shorter stride length, hybrid running is metabolically more efficient than regular running and is the choice of many recreational runners, especially Masters runners. Hybrid running is also a safer way to run because the reduced or absent airborne phase significantly lessens the impact forces associated with contacting the ground. The only problem is that it's hard to run fast with hybrid running.

The various types of gait available during locomotion are made apparent by stepping onto a motorized treadmill and gradually increasing your speed. At first, conventional walking is very comfortable but as you press the acceleration button to increase speed, you're quickly unable to match the speed of the treadmill so you respond by increasing the frequency of your steps (i.e., cadence). Increasing your step frequency is only comfortable for a short time because the metabolic cost of rapidly accelerating and decelerating the lower limbs is too high, so you eventually respond by increasing your stride length. Because each person has a preferred stride length in which they are most efficient, the vast majority of people will increase their cadence before they lengthen their stride. While professional racewalkers are capable of greatly increasing stride lengths by hyperextending their knees and exaggerating pelvic and ankle motions (often achieving walking speeds of 6 minutes/mile), the average person rapidly reaches a length of stride that becomes difficult to maintain. At this point, most people transition into hybrid running. The precise point at which you will transition into a slow, non-airborne phase run varies as each person has his or her own unique transition speed (the average transition to running occurs at a little over 4 mph).

The reason each person has a unique transition speed was the topic of debate until recently. By embedding special sensors into the calf muscles of test subjects while measuring force beneath their forefeet, researchers determined that people transition into a slow run in order to lessen strain on their gastrocnemius and soleus muscles: As our stride length increases, muscles in the back of our calves become so overstretched that they are no longer able to generate sufficient force to push us forward (6). At this point, and it's slightly different for everyone, we immediately transition into slow hybrid running because the shorter stride lengths associated with non-airborne running allow the calf muscles to work in a more midline position. The fact that an overstretched muscle is unable to generate significant force is apparent while attempting to do a pull up: at first, it feels impossible to lift yourself up but when you pass the first few inches, the pull-up seems easier because your biceps are in a more midline position.

Once you've initiated hybrid running, continuing to increase the speed button on the treadmill will force you to increase your stride length and you will quickly go airborne. Impact forces increase and you can feel the strain on your quadriceps as your knees flex to absorb impact forces and flatten the pathway of the center of mass. Although metabolically expensive, running with an airborne phase allows you to increase your speed simply by increasing your stride length. If you were to accelerate into a full-blown sprint, you'd quickly reach an optimal stride length and you would continue to accelerate by increasing your cadence until your maximum speed was achieved. By analyzing all methods of increasing the speed of sprint running (i.e., increasing stride length, cadence and/or shortening the time the swing phase leg is in the air), Weyand and colleagues (7) determined that the fastest sprinters spend less time on the ground and generate more force during stance phase. The combination of reduced ground contact times coupled with greater forces (which increase stride length and cadence) produces the fastest possible sprinting speeds. This interesting research confirms that if you want to run faster, you have to figure out a way to generate more force while spending less time on the ground.

Since the increased aerial phase associated with fast running results in a 5-fold increase in ground-reactive force, the body must immediately choose from several different biomechanical options in order to dissipate these amplified forces. For example, the increased impact forces can be dampened by making initial ground contact with the forefoot, lowering the opposite hip, and/or by excessively flexing the knee and hip. The exact combination of biomechanical options chosen is highly variable as each person has significant differences in strength, bony architecture, and flexibility. Even prior injury may influence which joint movements are incorporated. By experimenting with every biomechanical option, people select a specific running pattern that is metabolically most efficient for them. This explains why runners, unlike walkers, present with such a wide range of running styles. It also explains why any attempt to modify a runner's

self-selected stride length almost always results in a metabolically less efficient gait. According to the exercise physiologist Tim Anderson (42), runners are able to critically evaluate all factors associated with "perceived exertion to arrive at a stride length which minimizes energy cost." It turns out, contrary to what many experts tell you, there is no one perfect way to run.

Because understanding exactly what's going on in the body while running is helpful when trying to understand why we get injured, the following section reviews the more important biomechanical events occurring during the gait cycle.

Stance Phase:

While walking is a relatively simple process in which we strike the ground with our heel and smoothly pole vault over our stance phase limb, running presents a greater challenge because of the significantly amplified impact forces. To emphasize the difference between these two activities, if a 150-pound man were to walk one mile, his stride length would average 2 1/2 feet, impact forces would be 110% body weight and a force of 175 tons would be applied to his feet. If the same man were to run one mile, his stride length would increase to 4 1/2 feet, impact forces would increase to 3 to 5 times body weight and his feet would have to absorb a force in excess of 350 tons.

Dissipating such large forces is no easy task and we learn to incorporate nearly every muscle and joint in the body in order to remain injury-free. Just before we contact the ground, our body aligns itself so the shock-absorbing muscles are in midline positions (muscles are strongest when neither stretched nor shortened) and each joint is ideally aligned to manage the impending impact. While running slowly, our stride length is reduced so we can make initial ground contact directly beneath the pelvis. The first point of contact is almost always along the outer aspect of the heel and to keep our stride short, we bend our knees slightly. Fast running is different because in order to run fast, we have to significantly increase our stride lengths. (Remember, sprinters have stride lengths of up to 16 feet!) To produce these long strides while running full speed, we rotate our pelvis forward, flex our hips and knees through larger ranges of motion and make initial ground contact with the forefoot. By contacting the ground with our forefoot, we can immediately pull the contact leg back to accelerate us forward.

The biomechanics of sprinting and distance running are very different. Sprinters could care less about efficiency and their only concern is achieving top speeds. Conversely, efficiency is everything to a marathon runner. One of the key distinctions between fast and slow distance runners is that while slow runners almost always make initial contact along the outer side of the heel, fast distance runners will strike the ground pretty much anywhere they want: along the heel, midfoot, or forefoot. Although the reason fast runners choose such varied contact points is unclear, it is more than likely influenced by a variety of factors including foot architecture, bony alignment, muscle flexibility, and even prior injuries. The perfect example of how bony alignment can influence strike patterns is the great marathon runner Bill Rogers. In order

to compensate for a large discrepancy in the lengths of his legs, Bill contacts the ground on the forefoot on the side of the short limb and on the heel on the side of the long limb. The asymmetrical contact points level his pelvis and more than likely reduce his risk of low back injury.

The Contact Period

Despite the fact that the vast majority of slow runners instinctively strike the ground with their heels, there is a growing trend among running experts to have recreational runners switch to a more forward initial contact point. Proponents of the more forward contact point suggest that a mid or forefoot strike pattern is more natural because experienced lifelong barefoot runners immediately switch from heel to midfoot strike patterns when transitioning from walking to running. The switch to a more forward contact point is theorized to improve shock absorption (lessening our potential for injury) and enhance the storage and return of energy in our tendons (making us faster and more efficient).

Although appealing, the notion that switching to a mid or forefoot contact point will lessen the potential for injury and improve efficiency is simply not true. Regarding injury, epidemiological studies evaluating more than 1600 recreational runners conclude there is no difference in the incidence of running related injuries between rearfoot and forefoot strikers (8). Advocates of midfoot strike patterns will cite a frequently referenced study showing that runners making initial contact at the midfoot have 50% reduced rates of injuries (9). The problem with this study is that the 16 runners involved were all Division I college runners that self-selected a midfoot strike pattern. While self-selecting a midfoot strike pattern is fine and is often the sign of a high-level athlete, it's the conversion of a recreational heel strike runner into a midfoot strike runner that is problematic. In my experience, the world's fastest runners who self-select midfoot strike patterns tend to be biomechanically perfect, with well-aligned limbs, wide forefeet and neutral medial arches. Over the past 30 years, I've noticed that flat-footed individuals who attempt to transition to forefoot strike patterns tend to get inner foot and ankle injuries (such as plantar fasciitis and Achilles tendinitis), while high-arched runners attempting to transition to a more forward contact point frequently suffer sprained ankles and metatarsal stress fractures.

In a detailed study evaluating the biomechanics of habitual heel and forefoot strike runners, researchers from the University of Massachusetts demonstrate that runners who strike the ground with their forefeet absorb more force at the ankle and less at the knee (10). The opposite is true for heel strikers in that they have reduced muscular strain at the ankle with increased strain at the knee. This is consistent with several studies confirming that the choice of a heel or midfoot strike pattern does not alter overall force present during the contact period, it just transfers the force to other joints and muscles: midfoot strikers absorb the force in their arches and calves while heel strikers absorb more force with their knees. This explains the much higher prevalence of Achilles and plantar fascial injuries in mid and forefoot strikers and the higher prevelance of

knee pain in heel strikers. This research proves that choosing a specific contact point does not alter overall force, it just changes the location where the force is absorbed. This is the biomechanical version of "nobody rides for free."

Foot Strike and Tibial Stress Fractures

While it was originally suggested that the reduced impact loading rates associated with midfoot strike patterns would lessen the potential for tibial stress fractures, recent research suggests that this is not the case. By using CAT scans to design personalized strain gauges that were fitted to the legs of test subjects, researchers performed a step-by-step analysis of joint forces present in the tibia during the first 50% of stance phase as subjects ran with one of three test conditions: a rearfoot strike while wearing running shoes, a forefoot strike while wearing running shoes, and while barefoot running (11). Contrary to expectations, subjects striking the ground with their forefoot had significantly higher strain rates in their tibia compared to subjects striking the ground with their heel. The increased muscular activity in the back of the calf associated with the more forward contact point actually increased strain on the tibia by pulling on the bone with so much force that it began to bend. Rather than lessening the risk of tibial stress fracture, the increased muscular activity necessary to accommodate the forefoot contact point created significantly higher tibial stress than a hard heel strike.

Although this outcome came as a surprise to the researchers, it shouldn't have since it happens elsewhere in the body. For example, rowers tend to fracture their ribs along a line separating the serratus anterior muscle (a shoulder stabilizer) and the external oblique muscle (a core muscle). When vigorously pulling an oar, these two muscles can pull in opposite directions with so much force they crack the ribs that separate them. Muscle-induced fractures also occur in the fibula: because the peroneus longus and brevis muscles perform different actions during the push-off phase while running, the fibula often fractures at the bony interface between these two muscles.

Foot Strike and Metabolic Efficiency

The research suggesting that midfoot strike patterns are more efficient than rearfoot strike patterns is even more spurious than the research suggesting a forward contact point reduces injury rates. In an important paper published in the *Journal of Experimental Biology,* scientists calculated joint torque, mechanical work performed, and muscle activity associated with altering initial contact points at various speeds of walking and running (12). The results of this study confirmed that running with a mid/forefoot contact provided no clear metabolic advantage over heel-first strike pattern. In contrast, walking with a heel-first strike pattern reduced the metabolic cost of walking by a surprising 53%. That's a huge difference in efficiency and it explains why almost all slow joggers (who often run just a little faster than walking pace) make initial ground contact with their heel. While some elite runners are efficient while landing on the forefeet, the overwhelming majority of slower runners are more efficient with a heel-first strike pattern.

The big question is, since the world's fastest runners often strike the ground with their forefeet while slow runners strike with their heels, at exactly what speed do you lose the metabolic efficiency associated with heel strike? In a computer simulated study evaluating efficiency, researchers from the University of Massachusetts showed that while running at a 7:36 minutes/mile pace, heel striking was approximately 6% more efficient than mid or forefoot striking (13). Some experts believe that the 6-minute-mile pace is the transition point at which there is no difference in economy between heel and midfoot strike patterns.

Given the clear metabolic advantage associated with heel striking at all but the fastest running speeds, it's not surprising that when asked to rate comfort between heel and midfoot strike patterns, recreational runners state that a rearfoot strike pattern is significantly more comfortable (14). Improved efficiency also explains why approximately 35% of recreational runners transitioning into minimalist footwear continue to strike the ground with their heels despite the amplified impact forces: heel striking is too efficient to give up (15).

Evolution of the Calcaneus

Our preference for rearfoot strike patterns dates back millions of years, as laser analysis of the 1.5-million-year-old *Homo erectus* footprints found in Ileret, Kenya, revealed that our most efficient hominid ancestor made initial ground contact at the heel (16). The reason for this is simple: 7 million years of evolution have molded the heel bone (aka, the calcaneus) into a shape that is perfectly suited for absorbing the forces associated with heel strike. One of the most important factors making the heel effective at stress dissipation is its size: the average 100-pound human female has a larger calcaneus than a 350-pound gorilla.

Another factor improving its ability to absorb shock is the somewhat incongruous finding that the calcaneus, despite being exposed to large impact forces during contact, possesses an extremely thin outer layer of bone (i.e., the cortical bone is paper thin). The inner supporting bone (trabeculae) is also thin but it is reinforced with an extensive supply of blood vessels that function to assist in the repair of damaged bone. The combination of the thin outer layer of bone and the extensive internal supply of blood vessels results in the formation of a nearly hollow structure that functions like an overblown cushion at heel strike; i.e., the heel expands and contracts like a rubber ball bouncing off the ground. Clinically, the fact that the calcaneus has such a thin layer of cortical bone is helpful when trying to diagnose possible stress fractures in the heel: a light squeeze to the sides of the heel produces significant pain when a stress fracture is present. If the heel's cortical bone were thick (as it is in the vast majority of bones), even a vise-like squeeze would barely be noticed. This simple test can save you or your insurance company about $1400 on an MRI because the squeeze test is extremely accurate for diagnosing calcaneal stress fractures.

The World's Best Shock Absorber

The final factor making the calcaneus effective at stress dissipation is that it is protected by an incredibly well-designed fat pad. Averaging 3/4 inch thick in the typical adult male, the fat pad of the heel is comprised of spiral chambers of sealed fat surrounded by whorls of fibroelastic material (Fig. 3.5). Ultrasound evaluation reveals the fat pad is divided into a deep, thick, highly deformable inner chamber, and a thin, superficial, nondeformable outer chamber. Because it maintains its shape upon compression, the outer chamber functions as a protective cup that serves to contain the inner chamber beneath the heel. In contrast, the inner chamber functions as the major shock absorber, quickly deforming and rebounding with the application of force (Fig. 3.6). The heel pad is remarkably effective at absorbing impact forces and was recently shown to absorb shock 2.1 times better than Sorbothane, which is considered the most

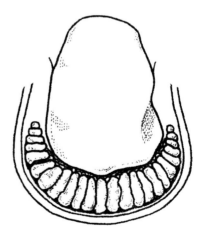

3.5. The calcaneal fat pad.

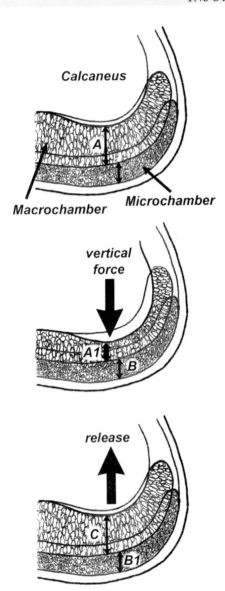

Calcaneus

Macrochamber   **Microchamber**

vertical force

release

3.6. The normal fat pad is composed of a deep macrochamber and a surface microchamber. When exposed to impact forces, the macrochamber compresses significantly (compare **A** and **A1**) while the microchamber remains unchanged (compare **B** and **B1**). When impact forces are removed, the macrochamber springs back to its original shape, returning a significant amount of energy.

effective commercial shock absorber available.

While standing upright, the fat pad functions to reduce peak pressure points beneath the heel by distributing pressure evenly over the entire surface of the calcaneus. The heel pad also plays a role in reducing heat loss to the environment. Although I wouldn't recommend it, if you were to run barefoot in the snow for a period of time, you'd realize the heel pad provides significant insulation and reduces heat loss from the body into the ground. The pad is also unusual in that it retains almost all of its shock absorbing properties even in subzero temperatures. The ability of the heel pad to function in cold environments is due to the higher percentage of polyunsaturated fats present in the pad. Unlike conventional fatty tissue with a polyunsaturated to saturated fat ratio of 2.5:1, the typical human heel pad contains 4.5 times more polyunsaturated fats. The increased prevalence of polyunsaturated fat improves function because it lessens heel pad viscosity allowing the heel pad to be more stable at low temperatures.

Using fluoroscopy and a special optical display, researchers evaluated exactly how the fat pad functions while we walk (17). During initial contact, the fat pad compresses very rapidly to a deformation of about 40%, dissipating approximately 20% of the forces associated with heel strike. Although effective at dampening forces while walking, the 3- to 5-fold increase in vertical forces associated with heel strike while running produces a jarring impact capable of damaging the walls of the heel pad chambers. In a study of heel pad compression in barefoot and shod running, researchers from the Netherlands (18) demonstrate that barefoot running produces a 60% deformation of the heel pad, compared to the 35% reduction when running with running shoes on. The reduction with running shoes is comparable to the 40% deformation associated with walking barefoot (17).

These studies confirm that running while wearing running shoes produces about the same fat pad compression as walking barefoot (an activity the heel pad was designed to tolerate). Conversely, barefoot running, or heel-strike running while wearing minimalist shoes (which often occurs in slow runners) may produce a level of compression capable of permanently damaging the heel pad. Maintaining a healthy heel pad is important because thinning of the heel pad is a proven predictor of chronic heel pain. Because our hominid ancestors rarely lived past the age of 35, and more than likely didn't run that much, maintaining the integrity of the heel pad was not much of a concern to them (they had more pressing things to worry about). Since we're currently expected to live into our late 70s (and runners are expected to live up to six years longer), maintaining a healthy heel pad is extremely important for the long-term health of our feet.

Because the forces of running are so great, the degree of shock absorption provided by the heel pad is helpful but the amplified impact forces associated with running are better managed by our powerful muscles, which actively lengthen to absorb shock. To understand how important muscle lengthening is for absorbing shock, picture yourself catching a fastball with your bare hands: to prevent injury, you reflexively extend your arms while you're about to catch the ball so your elbows can quickly flex while you're in the pro-

cess of catching it. Flexing your elbows allows your triceps to absorb shock and reduce the risk of hand injury. The faster the ball is thrown, the more you flex your elbows. Another great example is an egg-catching contest: the farther an egg is thrown, the more the person exaggerates body motions while trying to catch it to allow muscles more time to reduce impact forces on the egg's shell.

Options for Ground Contact

If you choose the heel as your initial contact point, the muscles in the front of the leg assist in shock absorption by slowly lowering the forefoot to the ground (Fig. 3.7). The tibialis anterior muscle is particularly well-suited for lowering the forefoot because its muscle architecture is arranged in such a way that it is almost impossible to damage even with repeated forceful contractions (19).

If a midfoot strike pattern is selected, the tibialis posterior muscle will slowly lower the inner foot to the ground. This muscle is also specially designed to handle impact forces because its tendon rotates almost 45° before it attaches, allowing it to absorb shock like a spring (20).

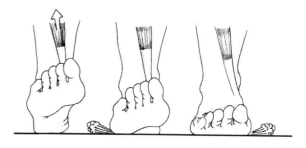

3.7. During the contact period, the muscles in the front of the leg smoothly lower the fore-foot to the ground.

Lastly, if a forefoot strike pattern is chosen, the gastrocnemius and soleus muscles slowly lower the heel to the ground and impact forces are absorbed by the large muscles of the calf. While forefoot contact points are very effective for absorbing shock, the gastrocnemius muscle is not very well-designed for lowering the heel to the ground because it crosses both the ankle and the knee (Fig. 3.8). Several studies have shown that muscles that cross more than one joint are more likely to be damaged while lengthening under tension (19,21). The relative weakness of two-joint muscles explains why heel strikers who switch to forefoot contact points frequently complain of delayed onset muscle soreness in their gastrocnemius muscles. Unlike the tibialis anterior muscle, which can tolerate even the most forceful contractions without being damaged, gastrocnemius is a strong but sensitive muscle and should not be used by slow long distance runners.

Vibrating Bones

Once impact forces pass the ankle, they travel through the leg towards the knee. By embedding special sensors in the tibia, researchers proved that these forces travel at speeds exceeding 200 mph, creating horizontal oscillations that cause the tibia to vibrate at approximately 40 to 50 cycles per second (22). In order to remain injury-free, these potentially dangerous vibrations must be dampened.

In an intriguing study of contact forces in horses, researchers determined that when a galloping horse's leg strikes the ground, the impact causes the horse's leg to vibrate rapidly (23). By evaluating all possible ways that hors-

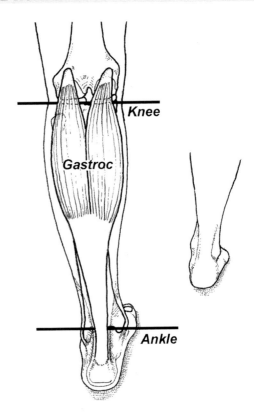

3.8. The gastrocnemius muscle crosses both the knee and ankle, and has no direct attachment to the tibia.

es can dampen these dangerous vibrations, the investigators conclude that the digital flexor muscles play the most important role in dampening the harmful bony vibrations. The ability of this muscle to do anything important came as a surprise, because it was previously believed that this muscle was a useless evolutionary remnant of when horses had toes. Also, because the digital flexor muscle has extremely short muscle fibers and a long, thin tendon, it was believed that this muscle was incapable of producing motion. From an evolutionary point of view, it appeared the digital flexor was slowly disappearing.

It turns out that although useless for creating joint movement, the horse's digital flexor muscle is ideal for dampening bony vibrations, since its short muscle fibers angle sideways to absorb and distribute the bony vibrations that occur upon impact. To understand how this muscle dampens vibration, imagine taking an aluminum baseball bat and striking a metal signpost: the vibrations would be felt through your entire body. Now picture yourself tightly wrapping the bat with a wet towel before hitting the same signpost. The towel would muffle the impact and the vibrations would be significantly reduced. The wet towel in this analogy does the same thing the flexor muscle does in horses; it dampens the dangerous vibrations by absorbing them with its short, angled muscle fibers.

In an attempt to understand which muscles dampen vibration in humans, scientists evaluated bony oscillations while subjects ran on hard and soft surfaces and compared the results to EMG studies evaluating muscle activation patterns when running on different surfaces (24). Using this elaborate technique, the researchers determined that the lateral head of the gastrocnemius and the outer hamstring muscle (biceps femoris) are the major contributors to dampening the lower extremity vibrations associated with heel strike.

Because impact vibrations occur so quickly following ground contact, reflex muscular activation is unable to provide protection and the vibration dampening muscles, to be effective, must be preactivated prior to contacting the ground. This explains research confirming that running on concrete produces the same bony vibrations as running on dirt: your body anticipates the increased impact forces associated with concrete and preactivates muscles to manage the resultant bony oscillations more effectively. Amazingly, animal studies confirm that variation in surface hardness is accommodated with altered muscle function within a single stride length.

The Knee

After impact forces have passed through the tibia, they come upon the knee, which is by far the body's most effective shock absorbing system. While walking occurs with the knee almost completely straight, the impact forces associated with running cause the knee to flex as much as 40°. Excessive flexion of the knee allows the quadriceps to absorb force by slowly lengthening under tension. The degree in which the knee flexes varies from person to person and is often speed dependent: fast runners typically flex their knees more than slow runners. The increased strain placed on the knee while running explains why painful knees are an epidemic in the running community, with nearly 25% of runners developing knee pain annually.

To improve the ability of the knee to absorb shock, the body places a large bone, the patella (aka, the kneecap), directly inside the quadriceps tendon. The patella belongs to a group of bones called sesamoids, which are strategically positioned inside tendons to improve mechanical efficiency by pulling the tendon farther away from the joint's axis of motion (Fig. 3.9). Unlike conventional sesamoid bones, which tend to be small and oval, the patella is broad and flat (patella is Latin for *small plate*). By some estimates, the patella improves efficiency of the quadriceps muscle by more than 50%.

As the knee flexes, contact points on the back of the patella constantly shift (Fig. 3.10). When peak flexion occurs while running, pressure is distributed along the middle portion of the patella, an area possessing the thickest cartilage in the body. To help the quadriceps absorb shock at peak knee flexion, the body actually shifts the knee's axis of motion ten millimeters backward at the precise moment the knee reaches maximum flexion while running (Fig. 3.11). This sudden shifting was proven in an interesting study in which researchers evaluated the knee's axis of motion

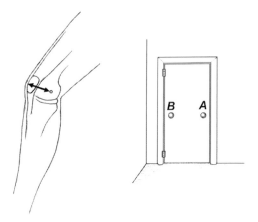

3.9. The patella belongs to a group of bones called sesamoids, which move tendons farther away from their joint's axis of motion (double arrow). Moving the tendon farther away from the axis of motion improves efficiency because the muscle now works through a longer lever arm. The classic example of this is the standard doorknob. Because the typical knob is located farther away from the hinges (**A**), it doesn't take a lot of force to open the door. In contrast, it takes significantly more force to open the door when the doorknob is located close to the hinges (**B**).

as subjects ran through specially designed MRIs (25). The rapid and completely unexpected shift of the knee's axis of motion temporarily increases the quadriceps' lever arm at the exact moment that peak knee flexion occurs while running. Although only reported in one study, this amazing shifting of the axis prevents countless injuries by lessening strain on the quadriceps at just the right time.

The Hip

While not as important as the knee for absorbing shock, the hip, with its powerful muscular support and significant surface area, also contributes appreciably to dampening impact forces associated with running. At slower speeds of running, the gluteus medius muscle plays an important role by smoothly lowering the opposite pelvis to the ground (Fig. 3.12). This method of shock absorption is not that effective and as speeds of running increase, the gluteus maximus muscle plays a more important role in both absorbing shock and providing stability. Interestingly, gluteus maximus is almost completely inactive while walking but fires vigorously while running.

Because gluteus maximus controls movement in all three planes of motion, it functions to prevent lowering of the opposite hip (i.e., assisting gluteus medius), while simultaneously decelerating hip flexion and inward rotation of the thigh (Fig. 3.13). These latter actions are essential for absorbing shock and preventing inward collapse of the knee while running.

Although not essential for shock absorption, the piriformis and lower gluteus medius muscles play a key role in protecting the femoral neck

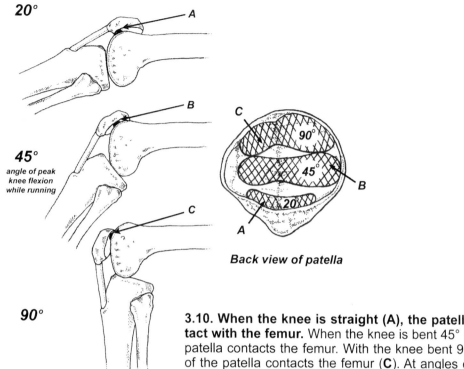

20°

45°
angle of peak
knee flexion
while running

90°

Back view of patella

3.10. **When the knee is straight (A), the patella has minimal contact with the femur.** When the knee is bent 45° (**B**), the center of the patella contacts the femur. With the knee bent 90°, the upper portion of the patella contacts the femur (**C**). At angles greater than 90°, the outer portions of the kneecap contact the femur. Note that the cartilage in area **B**, which is the area of peak knee flexion while running, possesses the thickest cartilage in the body.

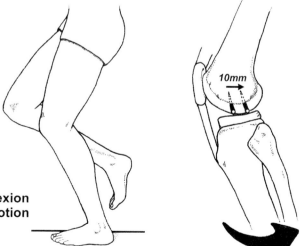

3.11. Just as the knee reaches peak flexion during stance phase, the knee's axis of motion rapidly displaces 10 mm backwards.

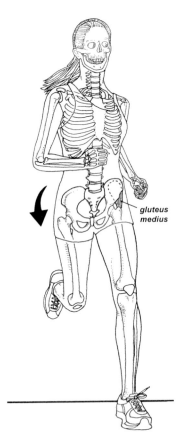

gluteus medius

3.12. At slow speeds of running, gluteus medius improves shock absorption by lowering the opposite pelvis towards the ground (arrow).

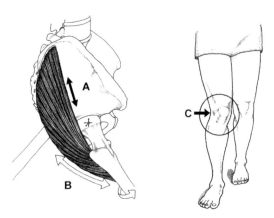

3.13. Because gluteus maximus is such a large muscle, its upper fibers assist the gluteus medius in keeping the pelvis level (A), while its lower fibers prevent the knee from turning inward (B). By limiting inward rotation, gluteus maximus plays an important role in protecting the knee from excessive inward collapse (**C**).

from fracturing. While most orthopedic surgeons claim the piriformis muscle is vestigial and unimportant while running, the paleoanthropologist Owen Lovejoy proved otherwise. After meticulously reconstructing Lucy's pelvis from more than 40 pieces, Lovejoy confirmed the piriformis and gluteus medius muscles function to create a compressive force along the entire femoral neck that prevents it from bending (Fig. 3.14). In fact, these muscles are so effective at reinforcing the femoral neck that modern

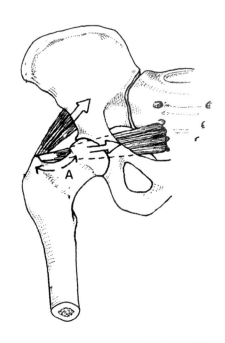

3.14. The piriformis and gluteus medius muscles create a powerful compressive force that prevents the femoral neck (A) from fracturing.

humans possess significantly less cortical bone than either Lucy or a modern chimpanzee (Fig. 3.15). (Lovejoy used this fact to support his theory that Lucy was only occasionally upright.)

Since stress fractures of the upper femoral neck are notorious for progressing into full-blown fractures, maintaining strength in the hip abductors and external rotators is essential for the well being of the hip. After reading Lovejoy's article, I began treating femoral neck stress fractures with the piriformis and gluteus medius exercises illustrated in figure 3.16 and have had great results. Unfortunately, many orthopedic surgeons continue to cut the piriformis muscle

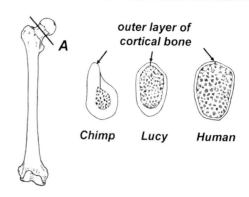

3.15. Cross-sections through the femoral neck (A) in chimpanzees, Lucy, and modern humans. Because the piriformis and gluteus medius muscles in Lucy and in modern humans prevent the femoral neck from bending, the cortical bone in their femoral necks is extremely thin compared to chimpanzees.

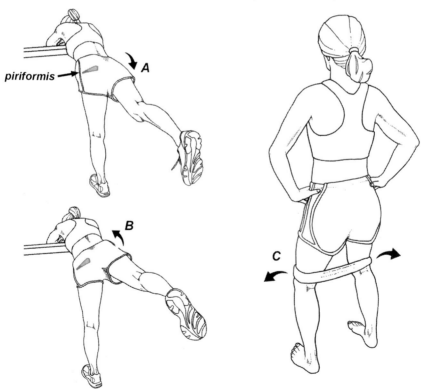

3.16. While standing on the involved leg, use your piriformis muscle to raise and lower the opposite hip (arrows A and B). Another exercise is to wrap a TheraBand around your lower thighs and move your knees in and out (arrows in **C**).

from its attachment in an attempt to reduce compression of the sciatic nerve. (Because the piriformis muscle sits on top of the sciatic nerve, excessive tension in this muscle can cause sciatica in runners.) Surgical sectioning of the piriformis can have disastrous consequences for the long-term health of the femoral neck.

The Sacrum and Lumbar Spine

Once past the hip, impact forces travel through the sacroiliac joints into the sacrum and lumbar spine. Compared to the sacrum of a chimpanzee, the past 7 million years of evolution have formed our sacrum into a keystone shaped structure that becomes more stable with the application of impact forces (Fig. 3.17). The sacrum has also changed in that there has been a marked increase in the surface area of the sacroiliac joint, which allows this joint to assist in shock absorption more effectively (Fig. 3.18). Notice in figure 3.19 that when the foot hits the ground, the pelvis extends backward while body weight causes the sacrum to rock forward. This subtle shifting allows the ligaments of the sacroiliac joint to absorb energy during early stance and uncoil to return this energy when we go into the propulsive period.

To stabilize the sacroiliac joint and assist in the storage of energy, our outer hamstring muscle tenses just before we strike the ground. In addition to reducing bony vibrations, tensing the outer hamstring increases tension on the sacrotuberous ligament, which plays an important role in limiting the degree that the sacrum rocks forward (Fig. 3.20). Recent dissections of this important ligament show that it spirals in a spring-like manner

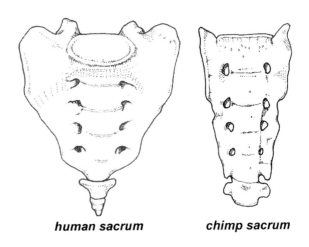

human sacrum   *chimp sacrum*

3.17. Compare the keystone-shaped human sacrum with the rectangular chimpanzee sacrum.

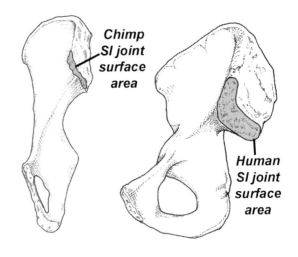

3.18. The surface area of the sacroiliac joint in chimpanzees is greatly reduced compared to the human sacroiliac joint (shaded areas).

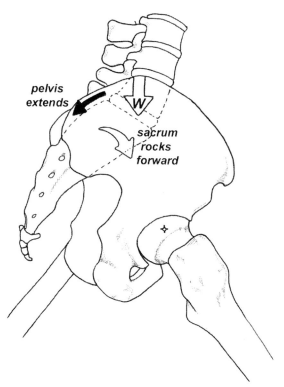

pelvis
extends

W

sacrum
rocks
forward

3.19. When the foot hits the ground while running, the weight of the spine (W) causes the sacrum to rock forward (white arrow) while the pelvis extends back (black arrow). This subtle action is important for shock absorption and protects the lower discs from excessive impact forces.

to effectively control movement of the sacrum.

After being slightly dampened by the sacroiliac joint, impact forces enter the lumbar spine. Just as the sacrum has widened to tolerate forces associated with walking and running, the lumbar spine has also evolved to manage the forces associated with running by becoming gradually wider when moving from top to bottom (Fig. 3.21). The greater surface areas present in the lower vertebrae allow for improved pressure distribution.

To enhance shock absorption following

ground contact, the lumbar spine quickly bends forward allowing the back muscles to absorb shock by lengthening. Comparable to how the quadriceps absorb shock while the knee flexes, decelerating spinal flexion allows the back muscles to dampen impact forces by absorbing energy as they lengthen. In a study in which spinal motions (flexion, rotation, and side bending) were evaluated at different speeds of locomotion, the degree of spinal flexion present following initial ground contact increased in a linear manner with speed, while rotation and side bending remained unchanged (emphasizing the importance of a slight forward bend to the spine following impact) (26).

In a different study evaluating efficiency in runners, researchers determined that the most economical runners made ground contact with the spine flexed forward 5.9°, while the least efficient runners made ground contact with the spine almost vertical (27). Although most coaches suggest you make ground contact with a straight spine (e.g., the Pose Method of Running and Chi Running), maintaining a slightly flexed spine at impact appears to be advantageous, both for improving shock absorption and increasing efficiency.

Contrary to popular belief, the discs of the lumbar spine play almost no role in shock absorption. As discussed in his textbook, *Low Back Disorders: Evidence-Based Prevention and Rehabilitation*, Stuart McGill points out that because intervertebral discs are composed of contained liquid, they are unable to absorb shock because contained fluid does not compress. According to McGill, it is the end plates of the vertebral bodies, not the discs, that absorb shock while running by rapidly bulging inward with the application of

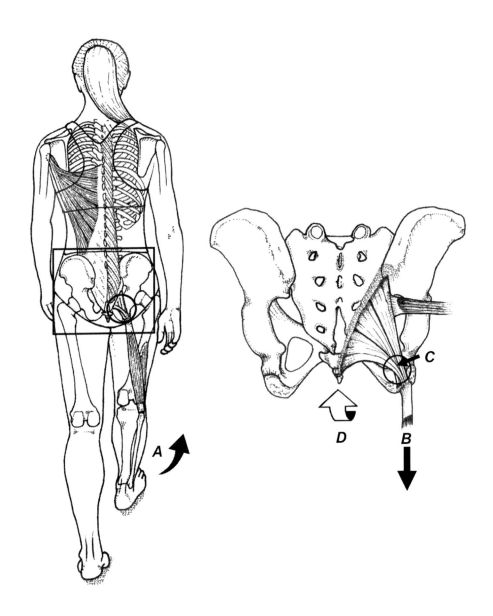

3.20. While walking and running, when the leg swings forward (A), tension in the outer hamstring muscle (B), pulls on the sacrotuberous ligament (C), which stops the sacrum from rocking forward excessively (D).

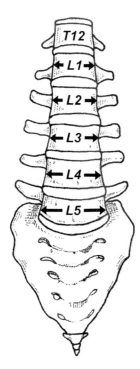

3.21. The lumbar vertebrae become gradually wider when moving towards the bottom of the lumbar spine (L1 to L5).

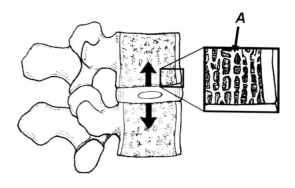

3.22. Side view of lumbar vertebrae demonstrating how the thin vertebral end plates bulge in and out (*arrows*), allowing impact forces to be absorbed by the specially designed bone present inside the vertebral bodies (inset). The bone inside the vertebral bodies contains long vertical supports (**A**) that bend with the application of impact forces.

impat forces. Dissections of vertebral bodies confirm that the end plates are made from extremely thin bone (i.e., less than 0.6 millimeters thick) that rapidly deform with the application of impact forces (Fig. 3.22). The inward bulging allows the upper and lower portions of the vertebral bodies to absorb shock like a trampoline, while the height of the intervertebral discs remains unchanged.

When properly functioning, the lumbar spine is remarkably resistant to the forces associated with running. In fact, McGill claims that it is almost impossible to herniate a disc while running since almost all disc injuries occur when the lumbar spine is flexed forward. I've noticed that if a runner does present with a herniated disc, it is more likely to have occurred while stretching forward to improve flexibility in a yoga class than while running long distances.

The Midstance Period

With forces associated with the contact period absorbed, the runner begins a very brief midstance period. Throughout this period, the body attempts to hold onto the energy absorbed during initial contact in order to return it during the propulsive period. By some estimates, the storage and return of energy during midstance reduces the metabolic cost of running by as much as 40%.

The ITB and a Level Pelvis

In the hip, the iliotibial band (ITB) plays a role in storing energy by preventing the opposite pelvis from dropping (Fig. 3.23, A).

The ITB uses this stored energy to protect the thigh and knee from the bending strains present during midstance: a recently discovered band of connective tissue extends from the ITB to reinforce the femur. This extensive soft tissue support creates a compressive force that stops the femur from bending (Fig. 3.23, B).

Though rarely included in rehab programs, femoral shaft stress fractures in runners should be treated with aggressive strengthening exercises for the gluteus maximus and tensor fasciae latae muscles. By protecting the femoral shaft from bending, the iliotibial band functions in a manner similar to the way the piriformis muscle protects the femoral neck from bending.

Because the ITB crosses the knee, it also creates a protective compressive force that stops the knee from bowing inward (Fig. 3.23, C). The band is so effective at reducing the inward bow of the knee that individuals with inner knee arthritis rarely complain of pain as long as the muscles controlling the ITB are strong.

The Hips as Motors and Legs as Springs

While the ITB plays a role in storing energy and providing stability, the muscles of the hip are really designed to be the body's force generators: they possess long powerful muscle fibers with short inelastic tendons that allow for maximum force generation. In contrast, the muscles of the foot and leg are perfectly designed to store and return energy because they possess short angled muscle fibers and long flexible tendons that stretch with the application of force.

When running, muscles of the hip generate

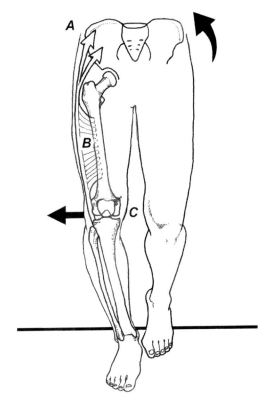

3.23. Different actions of the iliotibial band (see text).

force, while muscles of the foot and leg act like large rubber bands that store and return energy. Prosthetic researchers took advantage of this knowledge when creating the artificial legs used by Paralympic athletes (Fig. 3.24). Because the prosthetic limbs possess the perfect degree of flex, they absorb force generated by the hips by bending during early stance and return the force by springing back during late stance. Creating the perfect limb requires tuning the degree of flex so forces are absorbed and returned at just the right time.

The muscles and ligaments of the human foot and leg are also designed to absorb and return energy generated by the hip. Although

3.24. Prosthetic limbs on Paralympic athlete.

counterintuitive, muscle lengths present in the foot and leg during midstance remain relatively unchanged while the corresponding tendons stretch and rebound back through significant ranges, comparable to the prosthetics used by Paralympic athletes. The nearly isometric contraction of muscles allows tendon elasticity to perform most of the work while muscle activity is significantly reduced (saving precious calories).

By placing special sensors in the muscles and tendons of turkeys and evaluating them as they ran on treadmills, researchers from Brown University confirmed that even though their joints moved through large ranges while the turkeys ran, there was little change in the lengths of the muscles (28). In contrast, the tendons of the turkeys were shown to move through large ranges, stretching and recoiling back to return stored energy. In fact, certain tendons were so efficient that they were able to return 93% of the work performed while stretching them. Interestingly, animal studies also confirm that the capacity of tendons to store and return energy decreases

with age (i.e., running economy is significantly reduced in older adults because muscles are unable to compensate for the stiffer tendons) and in immature tendons (explaining the metabolic inefficiency present in children). The reduced elasticity present in older tendons explains why the perceived effort associated with running increases as we age (and why we slow down so much).

Tendon Resiliency and Energy Return

In humans, for tendons to store and return energy effectively, they must be stretched through very specific ranges. Because excessive stretching can damage a tendon and too little stretching can limit the storage of energy, it is important for a tendon to be moved through a very specific range. Think of the tendon as a rubber band. If you stretch a rubber band too far it will break. Alternately, if you stretch the same rubber band too little, it won't shoot very far.

To determine the ideal degree of tendon stretch necessary to maximize efficiency in runners, a group of exercise physiologists decided to evaluate the precise degree the medial arch lowers while running. Because lowering of the arch stretches tendons, measuring deflection of the arch is an easy way to quantify tendon stretch. It turns out, the typical medial arch lowers 7 to 10 mm while running (29).

A separate study of the effect of surface stiffness on running efficiency proved that this exact distance results in the fastest running times. By having subjects run over experimental tracks made from different materials, researchers determined that an overly flexible track absorbs too much energy, while a rigid track absorbs too little, causing running speeds to be diminished in both situations. In their quest to identify the perfect amount of track flexibility, scientists determined a track that flexes 7 to 8 millimeters vertically will return more than 90% of the energy stored following foot strike, allowing for the fastest possible running speeds. Because this distance is identical to the degree of motion present as our arch flattens, it is suggested that a 7 millimeter lowering of the medial arch stores the perfect amount of energy in the tendons and muscles of the foot and ankle. The authors speculate that when moving through this precise range, the tendons in the arch can return up to 17% of the energy absorbed during early stance.

To evaluate the exact degree of joint motion associated with deflection of the arch, scientists surgically embedded metal pins into nine bones of the foot and ankle while subjects walked and then ran over level terrain (30,31). Not surprisingly, the joints of the midfoot moved through the largest ranges of motion, with the medial cuneiform moving as much as the ankle (Fig. 3.25). What really made these papers interesting was that joint motions were significantly greater in all subjects while walking than during slow running. The clinical implication of this research is that contrary to popular belief, slow running is often easier on the joints of the feet and ankles than walking.

The Flexor Digitorum Brevis Muscle

Although difficulties in quantifying energy storage make it impossible to determine exactly which tissues of the arch are responsible for spe-

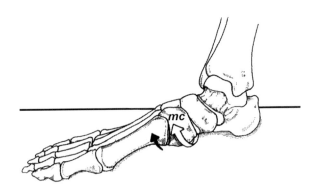

3.25. While walking and running, the medial cuneiform (MC, white arrow), moves upward as much as the ankle. The first metatarsal moves about half that distance (**black arrow**).

cific amounts of energy storage, it is likely that the flexor digitorum brevis muscle (FDB) and the plantar fascia play key roles in storing and returning energy (Fig. 3.26). The FDB is especially important because when utilized properly, this muscle can actually produce a structural change in the height of the medial arch (i.e., convert a low arch into a neutral arch). Increased tone in FDB possibly explains why individuals running in minimalist shoes frequently report a gradual elevation in height of the medial longitudinal arch. The increased muscle activity in response to barefoot activity is theorized to enhance the ability of this muscle to store and return energy. By increasing tone in response to stress, flexor digitorum brevis may behave as a variable-length spring that functions to reduce stress on the plantar fascia if forces become too high. The downside is that this muscle can fire with so much force that it actually results in the formation of a heel spur at the muscle's attachment to the base of the heel.

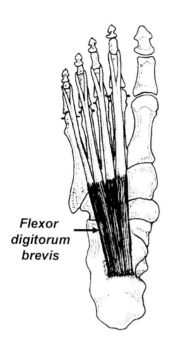

Flexor digitorum brevis

3.26. The flexor digitorum brevis muscle.

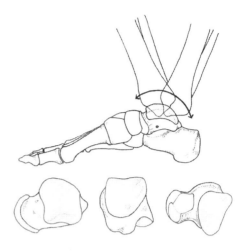

3.27. Because so much of its surface is covered with cartilage (shaded areas), the talus functions like a frictionless ball bearing, allowing the lower leg to glide over its upper surface (arrow).

The Propulsive Period

As midstance phase comes to an end, the leg continues to pivot over the talus and the energy stored in the muscles and tendons is used to propel us forward. The talus is perfectly designed to function as a pivot point because more than 70% of its surface is covered with cartilage, allowing it to function as a nearly frictionless ball bearing (Fig. 3.27). To stabilize the talus during the push-off phase, the muscle that goes to the big toe (the flexor hallucis longus), pulls the fibula downward (Fig. 3.28). Downward motion of the fibula serves to deepen the ankle mortise and protects against lateral ankle sprains. As a result, in addition to conventional ankle exercises, runners with recurrent ankle sprains

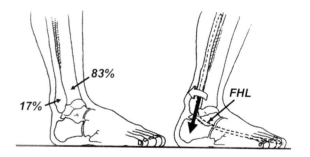

3.28. During early stance, the fibula supports less than 18% of body weight while the tibia supports 83%. The fibula plays a more important role during propulsion, when the flexor hallucis longus muscle (**FHL**) pulls the fibula downward. Pulling the fibula downward deepens the ankle socket and makes the ankle less likely to be sprained.

should consider mobilizing the fibula and/or strengthening flexor hallucis longus muscle (all exercises are reviewed in the next chapter).

The Achilles Tendon

By far, the most important tendon for storing and returning energy is the Achilles. Putting aside its significant length and thickness, the Achilles tendon is uniquely designed to store and return energy because the lower portions of the tendon rotate approximately 90° before attaching to the heel (Fig. 3.29). This extreme rotation allows the Achilles tendon to return more than 35% of the energy used to stretch it.

Surprisingly, research has demonstrated that the gastrocnemius and soleus muscles perform relatively little work during the propulsive period because they isometrically tense just before the initiation of propulsion. Rather than rapidly shortening to propel the body forward (which is how most muscles function to produce movement), it appears the primary role of these muscles while running is to produce an "isometric impulse" that anchors the Achilles tendon so that the tendon itself can store and return energy.

In the previously mentioned study of turkeys forced to run on treadmills, Roberts and colleagues (28) show that when turkeys run at progressively faster speeds, their gastrocnemius muscles remain relatively stationary while their Achilles tendons stretch through large ranges before snapping back to return the stored energy. The nearly isometric contraction of the gastrocnemius and soleus muscles significantly lessens the metabolic expense of running by reducing the

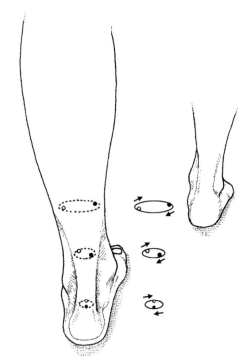

3.29. Rotation of the Achilles tendon. When moving top to bottom, the inner fibers move backward (**black dots**) while the outer fibers move forward (**white dots**). This results in a 90° twisting of the Achilles tendon.

work performed by the muscles (which consume calories, generate heat, and require removal of waste products such as lactic acid). In order to perfectly time the isometric impulse, the gastrocnemius and soleus muscles receive information regarding changes in muscle length and acceleration from an unusual muscle called the plantaris.

Located between the gastrocnemius and soleus muscles (refer back to page 5), the plantaris muscle is too thin to function in force production but it was recently proven to contain a large number of special sensory nerve receptors that provide the central nervous system with detailed information regarding length changes in the gastrocnemius and soleus muscles. The additional sensory information improves our ability to precisely time the exact point the isometric impulse should be applied in order to allow the Achilles tendon to return energy more efficiently.

In addition to propelling the body forward, the rapid return of energy associated with the snapping of the Achilles tendon significantly lessens strain in the hip flexors. As demonstrated by researchers from the Rehabilitation R&D Center in Palo Alto, California, plantarflexion of the ankle during propulsion allows the gastrocnemius muscle to function as a powerful hip flexor by driving the knee up and forward during the initiation of swing phase (32) (Fig. 3.30). By driving the knee up and forward, a strong gastrocnemius muscle will greatly reduce the risk of injuring the hip flexor muscles while running.

Once the heel has left the ground, a considerable amount of stress is transferred directly into the forefoot. To protect the forefoot from the extreme forces present during propulsion, pressure receptors present in the skin beneath the forefoot cause the flexor muscles to tense, creating a stabilizing force in the toes that reduces pressure beneath the metatarsal heads. To determine the exact degree of protection provided by the toe muscles, researchers measured pressure changes beneath the forefoot while using pneumatic clamps to duplicate the effect of toe muscle activity (33) (Fig. 3.31). Strain gauges were also embedded into the metatarsal shafts to evaluate bending forces present in the bone with and without simulated muscle contraction. This elaborate laboratory experiment confirmed that reflex activation of the

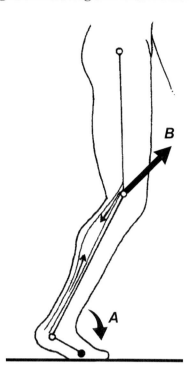

3.30. Because the gastrocnemius muscle crosses both the ankle and the knee, plantarflexion of the ankle during propulsion (A) drives the knee up and forward (B), significantly reducing strain on the hip flexors.

toe muscles markedly reduces pressure beneath the central forefoot and prevents buckling of the metatarsal shafts. The authors of the study state that the toe muscles could play a key role in the redistribution of pressure throughout the forefoot and in the prevention of metatarsal stress fractures.

Sesamoid Bones

In a separate study of forces acting on the foot during propulsion, an orthopedic researcher from Switzerland determined that when you push down with your big toe, you transfer a significant

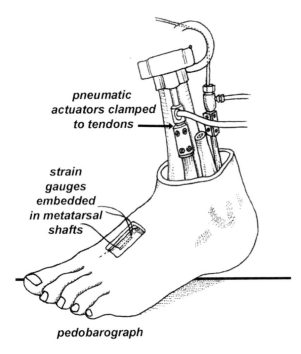

pneumatic
actuators clamped
to tendons

strain
gauges
embedded
in metatarsal
shafts

pedobarograph

3.31. Cadaveric experiment evaluating pressures beneath the forefoot and metatarsal bending strains present during propulsion.

amount of pressure away from the center of the forefoot onto the toe (34). As a result, to avoid developing a range of forefoot injuries (such as metatarsal stress fractures and/or interdigital neuritis), it is very important that runners be capable of generating significant force in the flexor muscles attaching to the big toe. To that end, the body places two sesamoid bones in the tendon of the flexor hallucis brevis muscle (Fig. 3.32). Comparable to the relationship between the kneecap and the quadriceps tendon, the sesamoid bones increase muscular efficiency, thereby stabilizing the big toe during propulsion. Unfortunately, they also become weight-bearing points and can be a chronic source of pain in runners. (Treatment of this condition will be discussed in chapter 7.)

Peroneus Brevis and Running Speed

While the Achilles tendon is important for storing and returning energy, the peroneus brevis muscle plays an important role in allowing us to run faster. In a paper published in the *American Journal of Sports Medicine*, researchers evaluated leg muscle activity as subjects ran at different speeds and concluded that the transition to the faster running speeds was associated with significant increases in peroneus brevis activity, with little change in activity of the gastrocnemius and soleus muscles (35). The peroneus brevis muscle can be exercised by running back and forth on slightly sloped surfaces. Peroneus brevis is important in fast running because it everts the heel, thereby allowing pushoff to occur through the transverse axis of the metatarsal heads (Fig. 3.33). According to the anatomist Bojsen-Moller (36), use of the transverse axis by means of peroneus brevis contraction represents the final evolutionary change in the process of producing a fast, efficient propulsion.

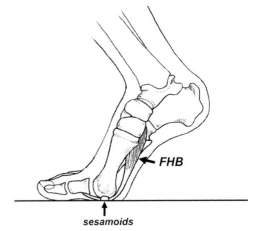

← FHB

sesamoids

3.32. Two sesamoid bones are located in the tendon of flexor hallucis brevis muscle (FHB).

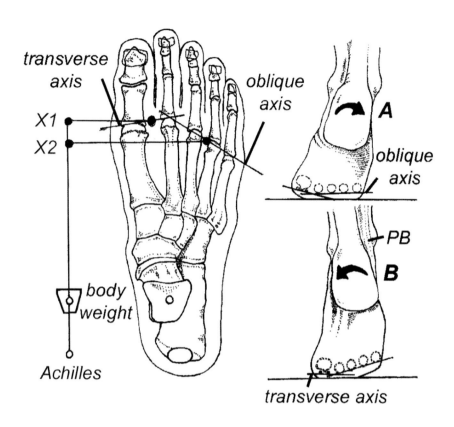

3.33. Because the second metatarsal is longer than the remaining metatarsals, it serves as a pivot point allowing the foot to choose between two different push-off options. When the rearfoot supinates (**A**), push-off occurs through the oblique axis, which has a shorter lever arm to the ankle joint (compare **X1** and **X2**). This lessens strain on the Achilles and is often used when running uphill. Because of the shorter lever arm, use of the oblique axis is called a low gear push-off. When greater force is needed (e.g., sprinting) the peroneus brevis muscle (PB in **B**) everts the rearfoot (**B**) thereby forcing the foot onto the transverse axis. Because of the longer lever arm, use of the transverse axis is referred to as a high gear push-off and this axis is used when faster speeds are required.

Swing Phase:

Once the foot has left the ground, the leg and hip swing forward in anticipation of the next ground contact. To increase stride length, runners rotate their pelvis forward on the side of the swing leg. To counter the forward motion of the pelvis, the upper body and arms rotate in the opposite direction. Because these rotations are equal in magnitude and occur in opposite directions, some coaches suggest that rotational arm motions are necessary to maximize efficiency because they counteract horizontal motions in the pelvis. A few world-class coaches have gone so far as to have their endurance athletes modify the positions of their thumbs while running.

Unfortunately, the belief that arm motions actively counterbalance pelvic motion and are therefore necessary to improve efficiency is incorrect. Recent research confirms that the arms act as passive dampeners that reduce the amount of torso and head rotation, not active force generators necessary to counteract pelvic motions (37). The negligible effect arm motions have on efficiency is supported by the fact that ostriches are among the most efficient bipeds on the planet even though they do not move their wings to counter pelvic rotations. Fortunately for ostriches, they possess long necks that reduce head oscillation without upper extremity involvement.

Arm Motions

Essentially, arm motions in distance runners act in a manner similar to the vibration dampeners placed on the bows of Olympic archers (Fig. 3.34): they dampen bow vibration while having

no effect on the speed of the arrow. The incorrect assumption that arm motions play an important role in improving efficiency while distance running may come from the fact that sprinters incorporate exaggerated forward/backward arm motions to maximize acceleration. Although important for sprinting, endurance runners need to avoid excessive forward/backward motion of the arms and their upper extremities should remain relaxed. Several studies confirm that the most economical distance runners present with low amplitude arm movements (27,38). Exaggerated arm motions should always be discouraged because it takes muscular effort to accelerate and decelerate these motions, which can lessen efficiency.

To improve performance, distance runners should try to incorporate arm motions that minimize wrist excursions and reduce excessive forward/backward motions at the shoulders. They should keep their arms relaxed with their elbows bent in a comfortable position. Because subtle asymmetries in arm motions are not correlated with inefficiency, long distance runners can move their arms through any movement pattern that is comfortable for them, as long as the motions are not excessive.

The fact that making subtle changes in arm motions will not alter efficiency was proven in a study in which subjects were forced to run with their arms folded across their chest and again with their arms moving naturally (37). In both cases, the metabolic cost of running was the same. In the same study, researchers evaluated muscle activity associated with producing arm motions while running and determined that the front and back portions of the shoulder muscles contracted

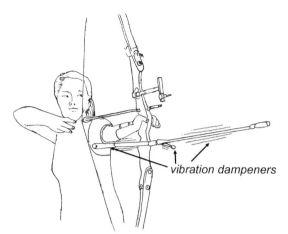

3.34. Vibration dampeners used in archery reduce vibration of the bow while having no affect on arrow speed.

simultaneously, rather than firing alternately to drive the arms. If arm motion played an active role in opposing pelvic rotation, muscles of the right and left shoulders would be alternately pulling and pushing to create the force necessary to counter the opposing pelvic motions.

The questionable significance of making slight changes in arm motions while endurance running is obvious when you look at the world's best runners. In the 2004 women's 10K Olympics in Athens, Xing Huina from China won a gold medal while running with her arms held straight at her side. In contrast, Khalid Khannouchi set a world record in the 1999 Chicago marathon with his hands positioned near his chin. Additionally, the world record holder in the women's marathon, Paula Radcliffe, often runs with her arms abducted and her wrists moving through asymmetric motions. If these asymmetric arm motions were metabolically inefficient, Paula would never have been able to shatter the world record with

a 2:15:25 marathon. Although asymmetric arm motions may occasionally be a sign of a biomechanical problem elsewhere in the body (e.g., a tight left hip can cause the right arm to crossover more), as demonstrated by Paula Radcliffe, subtle side-to-side variation in arm motions in an endurance runner is not always correlated with reduced efficiency and/or biomechanical problems.

The Hamstrings

While arm motions play a relatively unimportant role during swing phase, the hamstrings play a key role in improving efficiency because they isometrically tense just before your foot hits the ground allowing you to store some of the energy used to swing the leg forward. In a study of hamstring activity present while sprinting, researchers noted that during the late swing phase of sprinting, contraction of the hamstring muscles slowed considerably while their tendons lengthened (storing the elastic energy associated with decelerating the forward motion of the foot and leg) (39). Again, the body attempts to reduce the metabolic cost of running by isometrically tensing muscles in a fixed position while the tendons store and later return the free energy. According to some experts, this is a learned response and the ability to store and return energy can improve with practice. As will be discussed later, the incorporation of specific plyometric and agility drills may be the key to optimizing the storage and return of energy.

Until recently, no one could figure out why the outer hamstring, the biceps femoris, was the hamstring muscle that was strained almost exclusively in runners. Different theories were proposed suggesting that because two different nerves innervate the biceps femoris muscle, it is less coordinated than the other hamstring muscles and therefore prone to injury. It turns out that the real reason for the high injury rate in the biceps femoris is that it attaches lower on the leg than the other hamstring muscles. The lower attachment point increases the lever arm the biceps femoris works against, which increases the strain absorbed by this muscle.

By calculating strain associated with the lower attachment point, it was determined that the biceps femoris lengthens 9.5% during late swing phase, while the other hamstrings lengthen less than 8% (40). The amplified strain associated with the lower attachment point increases the potential for injury, but it also improves the ability of the biceps femoris muscle to store and return appreciable amounts of energy. As previously mentioned, this important muscle also plays a key role in dampening bony vibrations following heel strike and helps the sacroiliac joint absorb shock by limiting excessive tilting of the sacrum (refer back to Fig. 3.20).

The Braking Phase

Just before the end of swing phase, the runner begins to rotate the pelvis backward in an attempt to minimize the braking phase associated with making ground contact (Fig. 3.35). The braking phase is that brief period of deceleration that occurs immediately following ground contact. To understand the braking phase, imagine yourself walking across a room while carrying a full bowl of soup: every time your foot strikes the ground, the soup shifts forward. The soup moves because the forward motion of your body is temporarily decelerated when your front foot strikes the ground. Remember Newton's first law: *Bodies in motion tend to stay in motion*. When your foot hits the ground, forward motion of your body is decelerated by the sudden ground contact but the soup continues to stay in motion. While running, the braking phase is often blamed for the development of a wide range of impact related injuries because it can create dangerous shockwaves that travel up the foot and leg. The belief is that running with longer strides amplifies the braking phase, increasing the potential for injury. To dampen the dangerous shockwaves associated with braking, many running experts suggest that you shorten your stride and make initial ground contact with your foot directly beneath you.

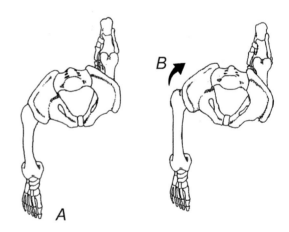

3.35. Immediately following heelstrike (A), the pelvis rotates backward to reduce impact forces (B).

Should You Shorten Your Stride Length?

The problem with shortening your stride to reduce the braking phase is that you have to run with long strides if you want to run fast. While some running coaches claim higher speeds can be accomplished by shortening your stride and increasing your cadence, this statement does not hold up when you evaluate fast runners. In their study of running mechanics as a function of speed, Weyand and colleagues showed that runners can run up to a 6:45 mile pace by increasing their stride length only (7). After that, increases in both stride and cadence are necessary to run faster (with stride length increasing significantly more than cadence). Because the typical runner's leg weighs about 20 pounds, rapidly accelerating and decelerating the lower limb by increasing cadence is metabolically inefficient and the vast majority of recreational runners increase their speed by increasing their stride length.

Rather than increasing your cadence and striking the ground with your foot directly beneath you (which can reduce efficiency), you should develop movement patterns that lessen the deceleration associated with braking while keeping your natural stride length. Although it's an extreme example, sprinters avoid the braking phase completely by striking the ground with their forefoot and immediately pulling back on the stance phase leg. Slower runners making initial ground contact with the heel can reduce their braking phase by smoothly lowering the forefoot to the ground with a lengthening contraction of the tibialis anterior muscle (refer to Fig. 3.7). Another way to dampen the braking phase is to make initial contact on the outer portion of the midfoot and slowly lower the inner foot to the ground using the tibialis posterior muscle.

The Best Way to Reduce the Braking Phase

Although both the hamstring and ankle muscles can effectively reduce the braking phase, nothing compares to using posterior rotation of the pelvis. After evaluating all possible ways to reduce the braking phase, researchers determined that backward rotation of the pelvis during initial ground contact plays the greatest role in limiting the magnitude of the braking phase (41). Apparently, the best runners learn to markedly reduce impact forces associated with the braking phase by pulling their pelvis back at just the right time. While it may occasionally be necessary to strike the ground with the foot directly beneath you in order to avoid injury, the preferred approach would be to run with your naturally selected stride length and learn to efficiently reduce the braking phase by incorporating specific movements of the pelvis, knees, and ankles.

References

1. Saunders JB, Inman VT, Eberhart HT. The major determinants in normal and pathological gait. *J Bone Joint Surg.* 1953;5813:153.
2. McMahon T, Valiant G, Fredrick E. Groucho running. *J Appl Physiol.* 1987;62:2326-2337.
3. Taylor C. Relating mechanics and energetics during exercise. *Adv Vet Sci Comp Med.*1994;38A:181-215.
4. Srinivasan M, Ruina A. Computer optimization of a minimal biped model discovers walking and running. *Nature.* 2006;439:72-75.
5. McMahon T. The spring in the human foot. *Nature.* 1987;325:108-109.
6. Neptune R, Sasaki K. Ankle plantar flexor force production is an important determinant of the preferred walk-to-run transition speed. *J Exp Biol.* 2005;208:799-808.
7. Weyand P, Sternlight D, Belizzi J, Wright S. Faster top running speeds are achieved with greater ground forces not more rapid leg movements. *J Appl Physiol.* 2000;89:1991-1999.
8. Kleindienst F, Campe S, Graf E, et al. Differences between fore- and rearfoot strike running patterns based on kinetics and kinematics. XXV ISBS Symposium 2007, Ouro Preto, Brazil.
9. Daoud A, Geissler G, Wang F, Saretsky J, Daoud Y, Lieberman D. Foot strike and injury rates in endurance runners: a retrospective study. *Med Sci Sports Exerc.* 2012;Jul;44(7):1325-34.
10. Hamill J, Allison H. Derrick G, et al. Lower extremity joint stiffness characteristics during running with different footfall patterns. *European J Sports Sci.* Oct 15, 2012.
11. Altman A, Davis D. Comparison of tibial strains and strain rates in barefoot and shod running. Presentation at American Society of Biomechanics. August 18, 2012.
12. Cunningham C, Schilling N, Anders C et al. The influence of foot posture on the cost of transport in humans. *J Experimental Biology.* 2010;213:790-797.
13. Miller R, Russell E, Gruber A, et al. Foot-strike pattern selection to minimize muscle energy expenditure during running: a computer simulation study. Annual meeting of American Society of Biomechanics in State College, PA, 2009.
14. Delgado **T,** Kubera-Shelton E, Robb R, et al. Effects of foot strike on low back posture, shock attenuation, and comfort in running. *Med Sci Sports Exerc.* 2013;45(3):490-6.
15. Goss D, Lewek M, Yu B, et al. Accuracy of self-reported foot strike patterns and loading rates associated with traditional and minimalist running shoes. Human Movement Science Research Symposium, 2012, The University of North Carolina at Chapel Hill.
16. Bennett M, Harris J, Richmond B, et al. Early hominin foot morphology based on 1.5-million-year-old footprints from Ilieret, Kenya. *Science.* 2009;323:1197-1201.
17. Gefen A, Megido-Ravid M, Itzchak Y. In vivo biomechanical behavior of the human heel pad during the stance phase of gait. *J Biomech.* 2001;34:1661-1665.
18. DeClercq D, Aerts P, Kunnen M. The mechanical behavior characteristics of the human heel pad during foot strike in running: an in vivo cineradiographic study. *J Biomech.* 1994;27:1213–1222.
19. Hasselman C, Best T, Seaber A, et al. A threshold and continuum of injury during active stretch of rabbit skeletal muscle. *Am J Sports Med.* 1995;23:65-73.
20. Roukis T, Hurless J, Page J. Torsion of the tibialis posterior. *J Am Podiatr Med Assoc.* 1995; 85:464-9.
21. Garrett W. Muscle strain injuries. *Am J Sports Med.* 1996; 24(6):S2-8.

22. Lake M, Coyles V, Lees A. High frequency characteristics of the lower limb during running. Proc 18h Congr Int Soc Biomech. (eds. Muller R, Gerber H, Stacoff A) 200-201 (Laboratory for Biomechanics, ETH, Zürich 2001).

23. Wilson A, McGuigan M, Su A, et al. Horses damp the spring in their step. *Nature.* 2001;414:895-899.

24. Wakeling J, Nigg B. Modifications of soft tissue vibrations in the leg by muscular activity. *J Appl Physiol.* 2001;90:412-420.

25. van den Bogert A, Reinschmidt C, Lundberg A. Heilcal axes of skeletal knee joint motion during running. *J Biomech.* 2000;41:1632-1638.

26. Callaghan J, Patla A, McGill S. Low back three-dimensional joint forces, kinematics and kinetics during walking. *Clin Biomech.* 1999;14:203-216.

27. Williams K, Cavanagh P. Relationship between distance running mechanics, running economy, and performance *J Appl Physiol.*1987;63:1236-1246.

28. Roberts, T, Marsh, R, Weyand, P, et al. Muscular force in running turkeys: the economy of minimizing work. *Science.* 1997;275:1113–1115.

29. Ker R, Bennett M, Bibby S, et al. The spring in the arch of the human foot. *Nature.* 1987;325:147-149.

30. Arndt A, Wolf P, Liu A, et al. Intrinsic foot kinematics measured in vivo during the stance phase of slow running. *J Biomech.* 2007;40:2672-2678.

31. Lundgren P, Nester C, Liu A, et al. Invasive in vivo measurements of rearfoot, mid and forefoot motion during walking. *Gait and Posture.* 2008;28:93-100.

32. Neptune R, Kautz S, Zajac F. Contributions of individual ankle plantar flexors to support, forward progression and swing initiation during walking. *J Biomech.* 2001;34:1387-1398.

33. Ferris L, Sharkey N, Smith T, et al. Influence of extrinsic plantar flexors on forefoot loading during heel rise. *Foot Ankle.* 1995;16:464-473.

34. Jacob, H. Forces acting in the forefoot during normal gait: an estimate. *Clinical Biomechanics.* 2001;16:783-792.

35. Reber L, Perry J, Pink M. Muscular control of the ankle in running. *Am J Sports Med.* 1993;21:805-810.

36. Bojsen-Moller F. Calcaneocuboid joint and stability of the longitudinal arch of the foot at high and low gear push off. *J Anat.* 1979;129:165-176.

37. Pontzer H, Holloway J, Raichlen D, Lieberman D. Control and function of arm swing in human walking and running. *Journal of Experimental Biology.* 2009, 212, 523-534.

38. Anderson T, Tseh W. Running economy, anthropometric dimensions and kinematic variables (abstract). *Med Sci Sports Exerc.* 1994;26 (5 Suppl.):S 170.

39. Thelen D, Chumanov E, Best T, et al. Simulation of biceps femoris musculotendon mechanics during the swing phase of sprinting. *Med Sci Sports Exerc.* 2005;37:1931-1938.

40. Thelen D, Chumanov E, Hoerth D, et al. Hamstring muscle kinematics during treadmill sprinting. *Med Sci Sports Exerc.* 2005;37:108-114.

41. Pandy M, Berme N. Quantitative assessment of gait determinants during single stance via a three-dimensional model-Part 1. Normal gait. *J Biomech.* 1989;22:717-724.

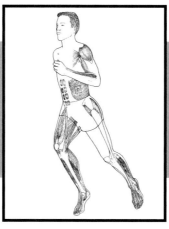

Chapter Four

THE PERFECT GAITS FOR ENDURANCE RUNNING, SPRINTING, AND INJURY PREVENTION

Even though natural selection has relentlessly modified each person's musculoskeletal system for over 7 million years, there is significant individual variation in running skill: Some people are fast and tire easily, while others are slow but can run forever. Moreover, the world's best sprinters are often terrible at long distance running and the best marathoners are relatively slow while sprinting. The following section reviews the specific traits responsible for success in endurance running followed by a list of factors associated with successful sprinting. Although not necessarily associated with improved efficiency, the final section reviews alternate styles of running when your running goal is to remain injury-free.

Endurance Running

1) According to the exercise physiologist Tim Anderson (1), the best male long distance runners tend to be slightly shorter than average while females tend to be slightly taller than average. Females tend to be thin while males tend to be a little more muscular. Elite males and females both present with lower percentages of body fat than sub-elite runners. As previously mentioned, the paleoanthropologist GJ Sawyer notes that sub-Saharan Africans possess increased limb lengths relative to torso volume, which markedly improves efficiency because a smaller torso is easier to move long distances. Although longer limbs relative to torso volume improve efficiency while running, the benefits associated with longer legs are less clear. Despite the fact that walking efficiency improves with longer legs, evaluation of leg lengths in runners provides conflicting results: a study of Olympic level male runners revealed that long distance runners were short-legged, middle-distance runners were long-legged and sprinters were short-legged (2).

In a detailed study comparing metabolic efficiency in runners of different abilities, Williams and Cavanagh (3) found no connection between leg length and efficiency when running.

2) The best long distance runners possess muscular hips, thin legs, and small feet. Runners with muscular hips and relatively thin lower legs are more efficient because accelerating and decelerating heavier legs contributes greatly to the metabolic cost of locomotion. Since the feet and legs have long levers to the hips, even a slight increase in weight applied to the foot will greatly reduce efficiency. To prove this, researchers measured oxygen consumption before and after adding weights to either the foot or thigh of recreational runners and determined that while adding weight to the thighs had little effect on efficiency, the same weight added to the feet more than doubled the metabolic costs of locomotion. Additional studies have confirmed that increasing shoe weight by only two ounces increases the metabolic cost of running approximately one percent. These findings explain why endurance runners with small feet are more efficient than their large-footed rivals (3).

3) Running efficiency *tends* to be associated with less up and down movement of the body's center of mass along with longer stride lengths. In an interesting study of efficiency in middle and long distance runners competing in a 5 km race, researchers from Japan determined that the center of mass in the best runners moved with a vertical displacement of only 6 cm, while the less efficient runners averaged vertical displacements of 10 cm (4). The length of stride between fast and slow runners was also different in that

the average stride length for a good runner was 1.77 m compared to 1.60 m for the less skilled runners. The authors noted that the good runners ran 5,000 meters in 2,825 steps while the poor runners required 3,125 steps. The added work associated with lifting the center of mass the additional 4 cm with each stride produced an increased workload roughly the equivalent to the cost of running up a 50-story building.

While this seems impressive, the notion that increasing stride length will automatically improve efficiency is flawed. Because the less skilled runners generated less force with their shorter strides, the metabolic expense associated with long versus short strides is difficult to compare. Remember that every runner selects a stride length that maximizes efficiency and any attempt to modify an individual's freely chosen stride length invariably increases the metabolic cost of locomotion (5). Additional studies confirm that while skilled runners tend to have longer strides at any given velocity than less skilled runners, elite runners tend to have shorter absolute and relative stride lengths compared to sub-elite runners (5). Apparently, the world's fastest runners are able to determine their maximally efficient stride length and achieve their top speeds by maintaining this stride length while increasing their cadence.

Note that stride length does not correlate with limb length, as tall runners often possess very short strides while short runners frequently have very long strides.

4) Efficient runners plantarflex their ankles 10° less during propulsion, and this reduced movement occurs at a faster velocity (Fig. 4.1) (5,6). The decreased range and increased speed

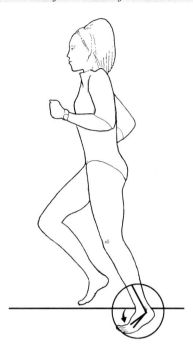

4.1. The best runners plantarflex their ankles more rapidly, through a smaller range of motion.

of ankle plantarflexion is most likely the result of the Achilles tendon rapidly snapping back during early propulsion when it shortens to return stored energy. In a paper published in the *European Journal of Applied Physiology*, world-class Kenyan endurance runners were found to have longer Achilles tendons that more effectively stored and returned energy compared to height-matched control subjects (7). According to the authors, the longer more resilient Achilles tendons present in the Kenyan runners were "optimized to favor efficient storage and recoil of elastic energy." The only flaw with this paper is that the authors compared world-class Kenyans to non-world-class controls. It is likely that all world-class endurance runners have longer, more resilient Achilles tendons compared to controls.

5) While there are no specific arm movements that improve efficiency, inappropriate arm motions may increase the metabolic cost of running. Williams and Cavanagh (3) correlated running efficiency with decreased wrist excursions while Anderson and Tseh (6) confirm that the most economical long distance runners present with the smallest arm movements.

Sprinting

1) According to a classic study published in the *Journal of Applied Physiology*, Peter Weyand and colleagues prove that the fastest sprinters spend less time on the ground and generate significantly more force while they are making ground contact (8). Interestingly, fast and slow sprinters spend about the same amount of time in the air and reposition their swinging limbs at about the same rate. These authors demonstrate that increasing the force applied to the ground by 1/10 body weight will increase the top speed of running by one meter per second. While stride length increases significantly with faster running, each runner has an upper limit to the length of his/her stride, after which continued increases will actually lessen speed. For the 30 sprinters in their study, stride length was maximized at 8 m/s (a 3:20 mile pace) while cadence gradually increased to the maximum speed of 9 m/s (3 minute mile pace). In all of the sprinters, the aerial phase of running continued to increase until the 4:30 mile pace, at which time it decreased slightly until the maximum sprint speed was achieved.

2) Several studies reveal that sprinters have significantly longer muscle fibers in

their gastrocnemius muscles compared with non-sprinters (9,10). The longer fibers might allow the muscles to behave like large rubber bands that store and return energy more effectively than short fibers. The longer fibers can be inherited but more likely result from training, since muscles rapidly adapt to high intensity training by increasing muscle fiber length.

3) The fastest sprinters flex their hips and knees through larger ranges during swing phase, and these motions occur at faster velocities. As a result, the trailing knee of the fastest sprinters is farther forward when the lead foot touches the ground (Fig. 4.2).

According to some experts, recovering the back leg more quickly allows sprinters to immediately pull the lead foot backward upon impact. Excessive knee flexion during swing phase is

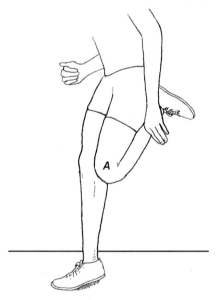

4.2. The best sprinters flex their knees and hips through large ranges of motion and the trail knee is farther forward (A) when the lead foot contacts the ground.

essential to sprint rapidly because flexion of the knee shortens the relative length of the lower extremity, which decreases muscular strain on the hip flexors (the flexed knee has a shorter lever arm to the hip). You can demonstrate this on yourself by placing an exercise band around your ankle and pulling forward: when your leg is straight you can feel the hip flexors strain but when you bend your knee, there's a significant decrease in stress placed on the hip flexors. The world's fastest sprinters take advantage of the reduced lower extremity lever arm associated with knee flexion by pulling their heels up towards their hips as they pull their knees forward. Since marathon runners occasionally need to sprint towards the finish line, the best coaches suggest that endurance runners learn to move their hips and knees like sprinters.

4) In an interesting study of foot shape in sprinters, Lee and Piazza (11) determined the distance from the back of the heel to the center of the ankle is 25% shorter in elite sprinters compared with the non-sprinter controls. Conversely, sprinters possess toes that are almost one centimeter longer than non-sprinter controls. While counterintuitive, the 25% shorter lever arm allows the Achilles to plantarflex the ankle effectively with little change in length occurring in the gastrocnemius and soleus (Fig. 4.3). The reduced lever arm may decrease mechanical efficiency of the Achilles tendon, but it allows the gastrocnemius and soleus to move the ankle with a nearly isometric contraction.

On the opposite side of the fulcrum, the longer toes allow for greater force production in the forefoot because the increased toe lengths provide the toe muscles with significantly longer lever arms that allow for a more powerful push-off. Even though the added metabolic cost of accelerating and decelerating the longer, heavier toes would lessen efficiency while walking and running long distances (which is why evolution has favored shorter toe lengths), the longer toes provide increased force production during propulsion, thereby allowing the elite sprinter to run at the fastest speed possible. The combination of a short Achilles lever arm coupled with long toes is also found in nature; e.g., cheetahs, which are capable of sprint speeds exceeding 70 mph, have shorter heels and longer toes than lions. Although it takes millions of years, natural selection eventually matches form to function with the simplest possible design.

Ideal Running Form to Remain Injury-Free

The specific running form necessary to keep you injury-free is dependent upon the speed and distance you plan on running. Because fast runners have no option but to maintain their self-se-lected stride length and cadence (even slight reductions in stride length have been proven to reduce efficiency), they must develop a running form in which their muscles and joints smoothly absorb the unavoidable high impact forces. In contrast, slow runners are less concerned about speed and efficiency and can lessen their potential for injury by reducing impact forces with subtle manipulations of their stride length, cadence, and/or contact points. To compare impact forces between fast and slow runners, look at a video analysis of the participants in the 2011 Boston Marathon. While the typical recreational runner has a stride of about 3 1/2 feet and a cadence of 175 steps per minute, Geoffrey Mutai set the world record in Boston that year by running with a cadence of more than 180 steps per minute and a stride length of over 7 feet. That stride length and cadence would probably fracture bones in the average runner, but Mutai ran a 4:41 mile pace for the entire marathon with no sign of distress. To manage these large forces and remain injury-free, fast runners must learn to move their joints through very specific motions that

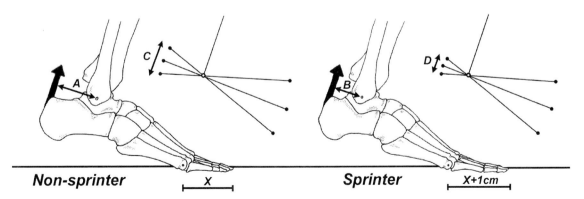

4.3. Because the distance from the Achilles tendon is 25% longer in non-sprinters (compare A and B), the gastrocnemius and soleus must move through larger ranges of motion to plantarflex the ankle (compare C and D). Notice the toes of sprinters are one centimeter longer than non-sprint-ers.

dampen excessive impact loads and maximize efficiency (see Table 1). They must also possess symmetric strength, endurance, and flexibility.

The Best Ways to Absorb Force

To enhance force production and improve form, many runners incorporate specific plyometric drills designed to improve the storage and return of energy. One particular study showed a 6% improvement in running endurance across three different running speeds and a 3% increase in 3 km race performance (12) (Fig. 4.4). The authors attributed the improved performance and speed to an enhanced ability of muscles and tendons to store and return energy following completion of the plyometric drills. By increasing the speed of force production without increasing muscle size (large muscles consume more calories and are therefore less desirable for distance running) plyometric drills may allow athletes to spend less time on the ground while simultaneously pro-

---

1. While recreational runners do well by running with short strides and high cadences, elite runners need to experiment with subtle changes in stride length and cadence in order to achieve the fastest running times. By evaluating stride length and cadence in the world's fastest sprinters, Salo et al. (16) noted that some athletes self-selected excessively long strides with low cadences, while others ran with short strides and high cadences. The authors suggest that the sprinters with the longest strides may have chosen long stride lengths because of an inability to rapidly turn their legs over. Conversely, the sprinters that self-selected high cadences may have done so because of an inability to lengthen their stride. Salo et al. propose that athletes who are overly reliant on long strides should do drills to increase their leg turnover (such as pool running with a high cadence), while athletes dependent upon high cadences should focus on improving flexibility and strength in order to achieve longer strides. By giving the athlete the option of increasing cadence and/or stride length, faster running times may be possible.

2. Video analysis from the side should reveal symmetric knee and hip ranges of motion (both in flexion and extension) and the knees and hips should flex through large ranges of motion during swing phase (refer to figure 4.2).

3. During propulsion, the ankle should plantarflex rapidly through a small range of motion. This movement can be measured with standard video equipment. The speed of ankle plantarflexion can be enhanced by performing agility drills.

4. Practice using the peroneus brevis muscle during propulsion by pronating your rearfoot so you push off with your big toe (refer back to figure 3.33). Also practice gripping with your toes during propulsion. You can evaluate how the different toes distribute pressure by looking at wear patterns on your insoles: in order to remain injury-free, there should be visible wear beneath the toes (especially the big toe) with minimal wear beneath the forefoot.

5. Focus your attention on an external source while training and racing. In a fascinating review of the literature, Dr. Gabriel Wulf (17) repeatedly demonstrates that athletes focusing on external cues perform better than those focusing on internal cues. For example, sprinters who are told to "claw the floor with the shoes" (the floor is an external cue) perform better than sprinters who are told to "increase the speed of foot and leg movements" (which are internal cues). Apparently, excessive internal focus overwhelms the athlete, interfering with performance. Dr. Wulf demonstrates that even a one-or two-word difference in instructions can alter outcomes (e.g., "focus on the finish line" is associated with faster sprint times than "focus on moving your feet").

Table 1. Elite Running Form Checklist.

Gluteals	While walking, lift knee toward chest, raising the body on the toes of the opposite leg.	
Hamstrings	Walk while swinging your leg forward until a stretch is felt in your hamstrings. Keep your toes pointing towards your knee.	
Adductors	While moving forward, raise the trail leg by abducting the hip 90°, while keeping the knee flexed. Move as though you were stepping over an object just below waist height.	
Gastrocnemius	Move forward while alternately walking up and down onto your tiptoes. The aim is to raise your body as high as possible with each step.	
Quadriceps	Rapidly kick heels towards buttocks while moving forward.	
Abductors	Quickly move sidewards alternating one leg in front of the other. Go 15 yards and repeat in opposite direction.	

4.4. Dynamic stretching drills. Modified from reference 12 in Chapter 4. The abductor, or grapevine drills, were not part of the study but they are important for warming up the hip abductors.

ducing greater force. Drills that encourage rapid ankle plantarflexion during propulsion are especially helpful when trying to improve efficiency.

Reducing Stride Length

Unlike fast runners, recreational runners can lessen their potential for getting hurt by simply decreasing their stride length. The easiest way to do this is to make initial ground contact with the foot directly beneath you. It doesn't take much to affect impact forces since shortening stride length by as little as 10% has been shown to reduce impact forces by 20% (13). An alternate method to reduce impact forces is to increase your cadence. While some experts advocate an ideal cadence of 180 steps per minute, this recommendation is unfounded since it is possible to increase cadence without decreasing stride length (look at Geoffrey Mutai's Boston performance). Rather than setting a goal of 180 steps per minute, a better approach is to count your steps per minute while running at a comfortable pace and then slightly increase your cadence. Researchers from the University of Wisconsin prove that a 5% increase over your naturally selected cadence significantly reduces knee strain, while a 10% increase in cadence reduces excessive twisting of the hip (13).

Midfoot Strike to Reduce Knee Pain

Another simple way to reduce impact force is to make initial ground contact with your outer midfoot instead of your heel. While midfoot strike patterns have been shown to lessen efficiency in recreational runners (14), striking the ground with your midfoot greatly reduces strain on the knee. The downside of the midfoot strike pattern is that the reduced knee strain comes at a price, since there is an increased potential for developing plantar fascial, Achilles, and/or gastrocnemius injuries.

In an interesting study in which the degree of muscle damage associated with using different foot strike patterns was evaluated by measuring blood levels of an enzyme called creatine kinase (which leaks from damaged muscles and is an excellent marker for evaluating muscle damage), ultra-marathon runners favoring mid and forefoot strike patterns were found to present with greater creatine kinase levels (14). The elevated enzyme levels most likely resulted from microscopic tears in the gastrocnemius muscle, which crosses two joints and is therefore more susceptible to muscle damage. Even though the forward contact points reduce strain on the knee, recreational runners should use them cautiously because they increase the potential for calf and forefoot injuries. In my experience, calf strains and metatarsal stress fractures are common occurrences in runners switching to mid and forefoot strike patterns.

Choosing the Running Form that is Best for You

Because the best predictor of future injury is prior injury, the most effective way to avoid future injury is to accommodate your prior injuries. For example, runners with a history of knee injury should consider reducing their stride length while increasing their cadence five percent over their self-selected natural cadence. If it's not uncomfortable, runners with a recurrent knee pain should consider switching to a midfoot strike. Conversely, runners with a tendency for developing Achilles tendinitis or plantar fascial injury should almost always strike the ground with their outer heels. The same is true for runners with a history of recurrent ankle sprains, since forefoot contact points increase the risk of inversion ankle sprains. As a general rule, mid and forefoot contact points tend to be more comfortable in runners with neutral arches and wide forefeet, while runners with low arches and narrow forefeet tend to prefer making ground contact along the outer heel.

An important fact to remember is that because runners come in all shapes and sizes, there is no one form that is ideal for everyone and each runner should develop a style of running that suits his or her own specific biomechanical needs. A perfect example of this is how some people naturally run with a toe-out running form. While books on running form such as Pose and Chi Running say that runners should keep their feet straight and aligned, about five percent of the population have a natural twist to their legs (called external tibial torsion) and it's important for these individuals to run with their toes pointing out a little. If individuals with tibial torsion were to run with their feet straight, they would eventually damage their kneecaps since the femurs must twist in to accommodate the forward facing feet (Fig. 4.5). It is also possible to have a slight degree of internal tibial torsion, and these people should run with their feet pointing in slightly. The easiest way to tell if you have internal or external tibial torsion is to sit in a chair with your knees together, your legs straight, and your ankles held at 90 degrees. People with external tibial torsion will have their feet pointing outward, while people with internal tibial torsion will sit with their feet pointing in. Runners with internal tibial torsion should run with a slight toe-in, and runners with external tibial torsion should run with a slight toe-out.

The Anteverted Hip

The most common anatomical alignment that needs to be accommodated while running is the anteverted hip. From the Latin words for "forward twisting," hip anteversion represents a bony alignment in which the femur twists forward more than ten degrees. You can tell if you have anteverted hips by standing up and turning your feet in and out as much as you can. While the typical person can turn their feet in

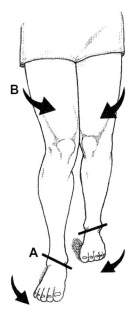

4.5. In order to walk with their feet straight, people with external tibial torsion (A) must force their knees to twist in excessively (B).

and out almost the same amount, people with anteverted hips can turn their feet in almost 90 degrees while barely being able to turn out at all (they make terrible ballerinas). Anteverted hips are often troublesome for runners because they allow the knees to twist inward too far, which greatly stresses the outer kneecaps (Fig. 4.6).

Individuals with anteverted hips often need to strengthen their hips and practice running with their knees straight. A simple test you can do to evaluate your hip strength is to slowly step off a stair while looking down to see if your knee twists in (Fig. 4.7). If your hip drops or your knee twists in while performing this test, you should do the exercises described on page 117.

Unfortunately, exercises alone are often not enough to prevent inward rotation of the hips and it is almost always necessary to practice running while visually observing your lower extremity

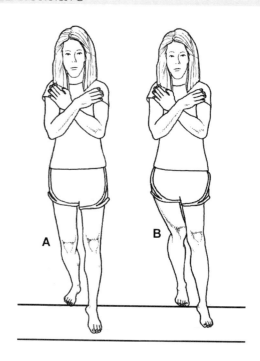

4.7. The forward step-down test. Normally, while stepping off a 4-inch platform, your knees and hips remain straight (**A**). If your hips are weak, the weight-bearing knee often twists inward (**B**).

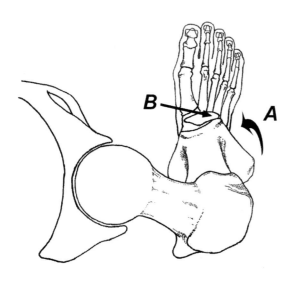

4.6. Anteverted hips often force the knee to twist in excessively (A), allowing the patella to shift sidewards (B). Anteverted hips are more common in women than men.

motions. Running on a treadmill positioned in front of a mirror is the easiest way to evaluate form. You can also evaluate running form by placing a video recorder in front of your treadmill (or run towards the video recorder positioned on a track or road) and evaluate the angles of your hips. In every situation, your knees should flex straight back and forth and there should be no inward or outward twisting. While later chapters review the more common alignment issues that affect the angles of the hips and knees, the only thing you have to remember regarding form is that your knees should always flex in the sagittal plane (i.e., move straight forward and backward).

To help you remain injury-free, Table 2

summarizes the specific joint motions that reduce impact forces and lessen joint strain. The combination of an outer heel strike, shortened stride, reduced knee flexion, and greatly diminished airtime produces a gait pattern very similar to the hybrid running form discussed earlier in the chapter. Although you can't run fast with hybrid running, it's easy on your joints and very efficient. No matter what gait you end up with, your chosen running form should feel smooth and comfortable.

---

1. Slow runners should strike the ground with the outer heel, while faster recreational runners (especially runners with a history of knee pain) should consider making initial ground contact with the outer side of the midfoot. Again, whichever contact point you select, it should be comfortable. The only contact point to avoid is one in which both the inner and outer side of the heel contact the ground at the same time. In a study of 400 recreational athletes followed for one year, the athletes making ground contact along the outer side of the heel had the lowest injury rates, while those making initial contact with a vertical heel had significantly higher injury rates (15).

2. Your knees must always flex in the sagittal plane. This is readily evaluated by running on a treadmill positioned in front of a mirror, or by placing a video camera in front of you on a track or treadmill. It is also helpful to have a running friend inform you if your knees are starting to twist inward. Surprisingly, the help of a knowledgeable friend has been proven to modify gait more effectively than home exercises.

3. During contact, runners with a history of patellar pain should flex their knees as little as possible and try to develop a relatively stiff-legged gait. While this method of running can increase stress on the bones, running with your knees nearly straight greatly reduces pressure beneath the patella. It is possible to generate force while running with this style of gait by using your hips in a scissors-like action to propel you forward. You'll learn to compensate for the reduced knee motion by using your ankles more. Although difficult to run fast, running with your knees nearly straight is an effective way to avoid injury.

4. Runners with a history of stress fractures should focus on absorbing shock as smoothly as possible. This is best accomplished by flexing the knees and rotating the pelvis backward at heel strike. The stiff-legged gait described in number 3 above may be effective for people with kneecap disorders, but this style of running is associated with slower running speeds and can stress the ankles and hips. To remain injury-free, individuals with a tendency for stress fractures must learn to utilize knee flexion, which is the single best method for absorbing shock.

5. Try to keep your hips almost level during midstance, since excessive up and down motion of the hips correlates with the development of tibial stress fractures and iliotibial band friction syndromes. You can practice running with your hands on your hips in order to maintain a level pelvis. In all situations, the hip should be close to level and your knees should move straight back and forth. The best way to evaluate form is to run on a treadmill positioned in front of a mirror.

6. Slow runners should evaluate their most comfortable cadence by counting the number of heel strikes per minute. Increasing cadence 5% over your self-selected rate will significantly lessen knee pressure, while increasing cadence 10% will lessen knee and hip pressure (13).

Table 2. Recreational Running Form Checklist.

References

1. Anderson T. Biomechanics and running economy. *Sports Med.* 1996;22:76-89.
2. Tanner J. The Physique of the Olympic Athlete. London: Allen and Ulwin, 1964.
3. Williams K, Cavanagh P. Relationship between distance running mechanics, running economy, and performance. *J Appl Physiol.*1987;63:1236-1246.
4. Miyashita M, Miura M, Murase Y, et al. Running performance from the viewpoint of aerobic power. In: Folinsbe L (ed.) Environmental Stress. New York: Academic Press, 183-193.
5. Cavanagh P, Pollock M, Landa J. A biomechanical comparison of elite and good distance runners. *Ann NY Acad Sci.* 1977;301:328-345.
6. Anderson T, Tseh W. Running economy, anthropometric dimensions and kinematic variables (abstract). *Med Sci Sports Exerc.* 1994;26 (5 Suppl.):S 170.
7. Sano K, Ishikawa M, Nobue A, et al. Muscle–tendon interaction and EMG profiles of world class endurance runners during hopping. *European Journal of Applied Physiology.* Dec. 11, 2012.
8. Weyand P, Sternlight D, Belizzi J, Wright S. Faster top running speeds are achieved with greater ground forces not more rapid leg movements. *J Appl Physiol.* 2000;89:1991-1999.
9. Abe T, Fukashiro S, Harada Y, et al. Relationship between sprint performance and muscle fascicle length in female sprinters. *J Physiol Anthropol.* 20:141-147.
10. Kumagai K, Abe T, Brechue W, et al. Sprint performance is related to muscle fascicle length in male 100-meter sprinters. *J Appl Physiol.* 2000;88:811-816.
11. Lee S, Piazza S. Built for speed: musculoskeletal structure and sprinting ability. *J Exper Biol.* 2009;212:3700-3707.
12. Turki O, Chaouachi D, Behm D et al. The effect of warm-ups incorporating different volumes of dynamic stretching on 10-and 20-M sprint performance in highly trained male athletes. *J Strength Cond.* 2012;26: 63-71.
13. Heiderscheit B, Chumanov E, Michalski M, et al. Effects of step rate manipulation on joint mechanics during running. *Med Sci Sports Exerc.* 2011;43:296-302.
14. Hoffman M, Kasner M, Wren J. The Western States 100-mile endurance run: participation and performance. Pre-publication.
15. Willems T, De Clercq D, Delbaere K, et al. A prospective study of gait-related risk factors for exercise-related lower leg pain. *Gait & Posture.* 2006;23:91-98.
16. Salo A, Bezodis I, Batterham, A, et al.. Elite sprinting: Are athletes individually step-frequency or step-length reliant? *Med Sci Sports Exerc.* 2011;43:1055-1062.
17. Wulf G. Attentional focus and motor learning: a review of 15 years. *International Review of Sport and Exercise Psychology.* 2013;6:77-104.

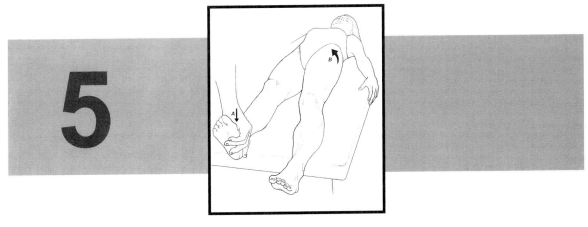

Chapter Five

RISK FACTORS PREDISPOSING
TO RUNNING INJURIES

Even with perfect running form, odds are that sooner or later you're still going to get injured. In many situations, the cause of an injury can be traced back to a specific training error (e.g., running more than 40 miles per week is a proven predictor of injury). Other times, running injuries can be related to problems with bony alignment, flexibility, strength, and/or prior injury. In many cases, the potential for developing an injury (or reinjury) can be greatly reduced with specific rehabilitative techniques. The classic example of this is hamstring injuries. With an annual reinjury rate of more than 70%, hamstring injuries are considered one of the worst soft tissue injuries a runner can get. However, a recent study published in the *Journal of Orthopedic and Sports Physical Therapy* shows that when certain rehabilitative exercises are performed, the annual reinjury rate for hamstring strains drops from 70% to 7.7%

(1). If these exercises were performed routinely by all runners, the potential for developing hamstring strains could be significantly reduced.

Another modifiable risk factor for developing running injuries is tightness in the gastrocnemius muscle. In a clever paper in which ankle range of motion was related to a variety of mid and forefoot injuries, researchers demonstrated that individuals with tight gastrocnemius muscles were three times more likely to develop metatarsalgia, plantar fasciitis, and metatarsal stress fractures (2). The authors suggest that tightness in the gastrocnemius muscle causes the heel to leave the ground prematurely, transferring a greater percentage of force into the forefoot (Fig. 5.1). If runners would routinely lengthen the gastrocnemius muscle by performing straight leg calf stretches, they could reduce their potential for developing a range of serious

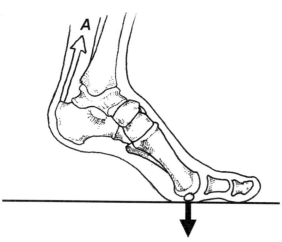

5.1. Tightness in the gastrocnemius muscle (A) causes a premature lifting of the heel, driving the forefoot into the ground with more force (arrow).

injuries. The remainder of this chapter reviews the causes and treatments for the more common biomechanical factors associated with injury.

Height of the Medial Longitudinal Arch

A long-held belief in the running community is that arch height predicts injury. The basic premise is that low-arched runners tend to pronate, or roll in excessively, and this excessive inward rolling has been blamed for the development of a variety of injuries, ranging from bunions to low back pain (Fig. 5.2). Conversely, high-arched runners don't pronate enough and the lack of inward rolling predisposes them to ankle sprains and stress fractures. To protect themselves from the perils of pronation and supination, runners have spent millions on running shoes and custom orthotics designed to lessen their potential for developing injury.

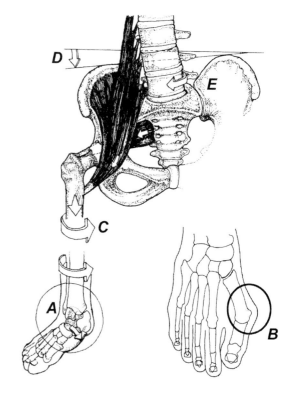

5.2. Injuries theoretically associated with excessive pronation. Excessive inward rolling of the foot (**A**), is often blamed for the development of bunions (**B**). Because pronation causes the leg to twist inward (**C**) and drop downward (**D**), excessive pronation has been blamed for the development of hip flexor tendinitis and external rotator strain. The downward drop associated with excessive pronation has also been implicated in the development of low back pain (**E**).

While the correlation between arch height and foot function is clear to the average sports medicine practitioner with more than a few years of experience (and even the average salesperson in a running shoe store), the respected researcher Benno Nigg published a paper in 1993 suggesting that arch height and pronation/supination are in no way correlated (3). By using calipers to measure height of the medial arch, Nigg and his colleagues performed three-dimensional imaging on 30 subjects and found no connection between arch height and foot function: individuals with high arches frequently pronated excessively, while low-arched individuals often supinated excessively. Even though it was published more than 20 years ago, Dr. Nigg's research continues to be referenced in mainstream literature. *The New York Times* recently published an article in which Dr. Nigg was quoted as saying "arches are an evolutionary remnant, needed by primates that gripped trees with their feet. Since we don't do that anymore, we don't really need an arch" (4). The main point of the article was that since arch height does not correlate with altered movement, there is no need to correct the "perceived biomechanical defect" of being flat-footed with an arch support or a running shoe.

A major shortcoming with the belief that arch height does not affect function is that it's based on the findings from one study. While Dr. Nigg used very sophisticated machinery to measure motion, he and his team of researchers made a very basic error in that they identified people as having high or low arches with store-bought calipers, and the resultant arch measurements were never checked against true arch height as determined with weight-bearing x-rays. If they had, they would have found that because each person's arch has a unique curve, it's impossible to pick the precise point along the curve of the arch that actually correlates with true arch height. Because their caliper measurements did not accurately identify true arch height, Dr. Nigg's research provided little insight into the connection between arch height and motion.

In 2001, the controversy regarding arch height and three-dimensional motion was finally resolved. By using the highly reliable method of quantifying arch height by creating a ratio between the length of the foot and the top of the arch (which is extremely reproducible and has been proven to correlate with x-ray measurements of arch structure), Williams and McClay (5) performed three-dimensional motion analysis on high- and low-arched runners and conclusively demonstrated that arch height and foot function are indeed correlated: people with low arches pronate more rapidly through larger ranges of motion, while people with high arches hit the ground harder and pronate through very small ranges.

In a follow-up study using the same measuring techniques (6), the authors determined that arch height was also predictive of injury: low-arched runners exhibited more soft tissue injuries and a greater prevalence of injuries along the inside of their leg (especially at the knee and ankle); while high-arched runners had a greater prevalence of bony injuries (e.g., they had twice as many stress fractures). High-arched runners also had more injuries along their outer leg (e.g., iliotibial band friction syndrome and ankle sprains were particularly common). Overall, the low-arched runners had a much greater tendency for inner foot injuries (such as injuries to the sesamoids beneath the big toe), while the high-arched runners had a greater tendency for outer forefoot injuries (such as stress fractures of the fifth metatarsal).

Combined, these two papers confirm what everyone in the sports community has always known: arch height not only predicts whether your foot pronates or supinates excessively, it also predicts the location of future injuries. One of the nicest things about this research is that the measuring technique used to identify arch height is simple to perform and can be done at home (Fig. 5.3).

Arch Height and the Potential for Injury

While the arch height ratio illustrated in figure 5.3 provides information regarding the location of potential injuries, it does not predict the probability of sustaining an injury. To evaluate the relative risk of injury with different arch heights, researchers from Denmark measured arch height in 927 novice runners before beginning a one-year running program (7). At the end of the year, 33% of the runners with very low arches and 25% of the runners with very high arches were injured. Runners with slightly high arches and neutral feet suffered the same injury rate, around 18%, while only 13% of runners with slightly low arches were injured. In addition to a lower injury rate, the runners with slightly low arches suffered fewer overall injuries, suggesting that a little bit of pronation may actually be protective, probably because slightly low arches are excellent shock absorbers. This research is important because it shows that only runners with excessively high and low arches have an increased potential for being injured. Runners with extremely low arches are especially injury-prone, as not one of the runners classified with very low arches was able to run more than 186 miles during the entire year. That's fewer than 4 miles per week before the low-arched runners had to drop out of the study due to injury.

If you happen to have very low or very high arches, there are a few simple things you can do

to decrease your potential for injury. Because low arches distribute more pressure to the inner side of the foot, it is important that the muscles of the arches remain strong. The easiest way to strengthen the arch muscles is with the exercises described at the end of this chapter. An alternate method to strengthen the arch muscles is to wear minimalist shoes while performing daily activi-

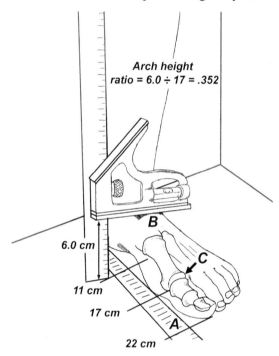

5.3. The Arch Height Ratio. This ratio is determined by measuring the length of the foot to the tip of the big toe (**A**). This number is divided by two and the height on the top of the foot is measured at this point (**B**). The arch height ratio is determined by dividing the height at the top of the foot by the length of the foot measured at the base of the big toe (**C**). It is usually easy to find the base of the big toe by feeling for a small bump at the end of the metatarsal head (**arrow**). If the resultant number is less than .275, the arch is characterized as low. Runners with high arches present with an arch height ratio greater than .356.

ties. While not recommended for long distance running because lightweight running shoes are notorious for producing plantar fasciitis in low-arched individuals, minimalist shoes allow the toes to move through larger ranges of motion and can very effectively strengthen muscles of the arch when worn routinely throughout the day.

Orthotics

The most popular method for treating flat feet is to wear either over-the-counter or custom orthotics. Although the precise reason for their success remains obscure (i.e., you will continue to pronate the same amount whether or not you wear orthotics) several studies have shown orthotics can reduce your potential for being injured. In a paper recently published in the *American Journal of Sports Medicine*, researchers performed a randomized controlled trial of 400 military recruits during basic training and determined that the trainees wearing orthotics specifically designed to reduce pressure points along the bottom of their feet were 49% less likely to develop overuse injuries compared to the control group that did not wear orthotics (8).

Despite the fact that orthotics do not appreciably alter range of motion, they may lessen your potential for injury by distributing pressure away from the heel and forefoot into the arch. Increased skin contact with the edges of the orthotic may also reduce your potential for injury by enhancing sensory feedback, which is thought to improve balance.

An alternate theory to explain why orthotics may lessen your potential for injury is that even though they don't alter the overall range of pronation, they reduce the velocity of the pronating joints (9). According to some experts, the speed of pronation is more likely to produce injury than the overall range of pronation. The most effective way to reduce the speed of pronation is with medial or varus posts (Fig. 5.4). These posts are usually added to the bottom of a custom or prefabricated orthotic but they can also be placed directly beneath the insole of your running shoe. Varus posts have been proven to reduce strain on the plantar fascia (10) and are an inexpensive treatment option for a variety of running-related injuries.

Unlike flat-footed runners, high-arched runners rarely require orthotics (why support an already elevated arch?). Since high-arched runners are prone to injuries along the outside of their legs and feet, many sports injury experts recommend that high-arched runners attach over-the-counter

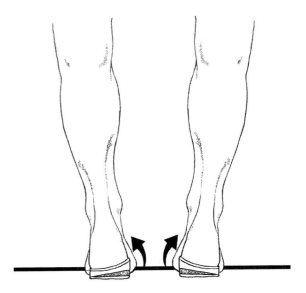

5.4. Varus posts elevate the inside of the feet.

valgus posts to the outer side of their insoles (Fig. 5.5). Stock posts can be purchased online and are sometimes referred to as lateral posts. Felt is a common material and they usually have a self-stick backing to make them easier to apply.

Because high-arched runners are forced to manage large impact forces, they should avoid minimalist shoes and wear running shoes with cushioned heels. An alternate way for high-arched runners to reduce impact forces is to switch to a midfoot strike pattern. In every situation, runners with high arches should be discouraged from making initial ground contact with the forefoot, because this contact point increases the potential for ankle sprain. Regardless of how they strike the ground, ankle sprains are so prevalent in high-arched runners that runners with high arches should consider using ankle rock boards to preventively strengthen their ankles. One study from the Netherlands showed the regular use of a balance board reduced the frequency of ankle sprains by 47% (11).

Arch Height and Balance

Besides increasing range of motion and strengthening the muscles of the leg, ankle rock boards can also improve balance. In an interesting evaluation of balance in people with high and low arches, researchers from the University of North Carolina at Chapel Hill determined that, compared to people with neutral arches, people with high and low arches have impaired balance, but for different reasons (12). People with high arches have poor balance because the bottom of their feet make less contact with the ground

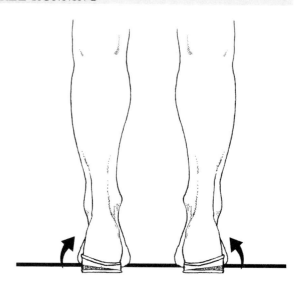

5.5. Valgus posts elevate the outside of the feet.

and the pressure receptors located in the skin supply less information regarding the distribution of pressure (see Fig. 7.9 on page 146). The reduced sensory feedback associated with lessened contact with the ground makes it difficult for high-arched runners to balance themselves. Low-arched runners were also shown to have impaired balance, possibly because their overall joint laxity makes it harder for their muscles to control the rapid and often extreme joint movements. As a result, ankle rock board exercises can be helpful for both high- and low-arched runners.

Pronation and Low Back Injuries: A Questionable Connection

An important point regarding the effect of high and low arches is that pronation and supination are more likely to injure the foot and/or ankle than injure the hip and/or back. As a rule, the farther you get away from the foot, the less likely pronation and supination are responsible for producing an injury. For example, while low arches have frequently been blamed for the development of low back pain, a recent study proves that excessive pronation and low back pain are in no way connected (13). In my opinion, as with running injuries in general, slightly low arches may actually protect the hip and low back because a little extra pronation improves shock absorption.

Until recently, it was believed that excessive pronation caused the leg to twist inward an excessive amount, transferring the rotation up the entire lower extremity. The belief that exaggerated pronation causes the knee and hip to rotate excessively is related to a mitered hinge analogy developed over 60 years ago. In this model, which is still taught in medical schools, pronation of the foot is converted into inward rotation of the leg with a 1:1 movement ratio; e.g., 8° of pronation causes the leg to twist in 8° (Fig. 5.6).

Since low-arched people pronate more, it makes perfect sense that they would have greater ranges of leg rotation. However, evaluation of three-dimensional motion shows that this is not the case: the legs of low-arched pronators rotate inward the same degree as the legs of high-arched supinators (14). The equal ranges of leg rotation present in low- and high-arched runners explains why orthotics produce more consistent outcomes when treating foot and ankle injuries than when treating knee and hip injuries.

Recent research confirms that the mitered hinge analogy is all wrong. Even though low-arched people pronate through larger ranges of motion, the joints of their feet absorb most of

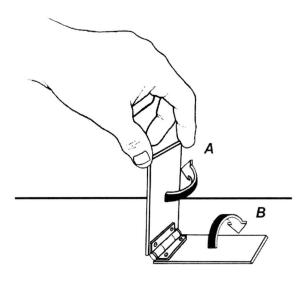

5.6. Mitered hinge analogy. If you twist the top of a mitered hinge (**A**), the bottom of the hinge will twist the same amount (**B**).

this motion and they transmit less rotation into their legs. Conversely, high-arched individuals pronate less but their feet transfer a greater degree of rotation into their legs. The end result is that both high- and low-arched runners transmit the same rotation into their legs even though they pronate different amounts. This is nature's way of accommodating variation in arch height so the structures above the ankle are not affected by the different degrees of pronation.

The bottom line is that while arch height may predispose runners to certain injuries (especially in the feet), slightly high or low arches rarely require treatment unless an injury is present. On the other hand, to deal with the stresses associated with high mileage running, experienced runners frequently wear orthotics to lessen their potential for injury regardless of their arch height. As mentioned, orthotics do not work by altering the overall range of pronation; their effectiveness is more than likely related to their ability to distribute pressure, decelerate joint movements, and improve balance. These are good things whether you have high, neutral, or low arches.

Rather than investing in expensive custom orthotics right off the bat, you should first try running with a pair of over-the-counter orthotics. Even though custom orthotics have been shown to distribute pressure more effectively than over-the-counter orthotics (15), there is no evidence that custom orthotics are superior to prefabricated orthotics for injury prevention (16). Nonetheless, lifelong orthotic users often prefer custom orthotics because of their durability (graphite orthotics can last up to 15 years) and versatility (any of a dozen different modifications can be added to an orthotic). Over time, despite their initial cost, custom orthotics eventually become less expensive than over-the-counter orthotics because they are replaced so infrequently.

Limb Length Discrepancy (LLD)

Surprisingly, almost everyone has legs that are within a few millimeters of being the same length. In a study of limb symmetry in rural Jamaica, researchers determined that while arm length differs markedly from side to side, only one in 1,000 people have leg length discrepancies greater than one centimeter (17). The authors attribute the reduced frequency of lower extremity limb length discrepancies to natural selection favoring lower limbs of equal lengths; i.e., because the muscles on the side of the long limb work harder while walking and running, individuals with large limb length discrepancies have to spend more calories getting around. As a result, they would have less energy left for reproduction and would therefore be quickly removed from the gene pool.

While moderate LLDs rarely cause problems in the general population, even small limb length discrepancies can injure a runner. To dramatize this point, the podiatrist Steve Subotnick came up with the threefold rule: Because the forces associated with running are three times greater than the forces associated with walking, a four millimeter discrepancy in the legs of a runner (which is present in about 30% of the population) produces the same symptoms as a 12 millimeter discrepancy in a non-runner (which is present in about one in 2,000 people).

Structural versus Functional Discrepancies

An important factor to consider is that many runners possess functional limb length discrepancies in which tightness in certain muscles and/or asymmetric pronation can make limbs that are of equal length appear to be different (Fig. 5.7). This is a significant distinction because functional discrepancies, unlike structural discrepancies, are not treated with heel lifts since the bones of the lower extremity are the same length. When a functional discrepancy is the result of muscle tightness, stretching the affected muscles is the appropriate treatment. Conversely, asymmetric pronation is treated with arch supports.

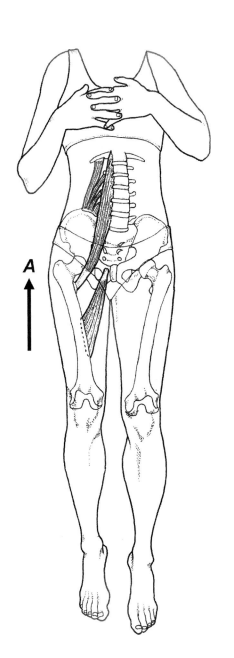

5.7. Functional limb length discrepancies. Tightness in certain muscles can pull the limb up on one side (**A**), causing one leg to appear shorter than the other.

The Long Limb and Stress Fractures

When a true limb length discrepancy is present and there is a short tibia and/or femur (referred to as a structural LLD), the longer limb is much more likely to develop stress fractures because it is exposed to greater impact forces (18). This is consistent with a study of Norwegian military recruits showing that 73% of the recruits fractured a bone on the side of the long limb, 16% on the side of the short limb, and only 11% of stress fractures occurred in recruits with equal limb lengths (19). The long limb hip is also prone to injury. In a study of 100 patients presenting for total hip replacement, 84% of the patients had arthritis on the side of the long limb (20).

The hip abductors on the side of the long limb are especially prone to injury. Because the short limb has a longer distance to fall while walking and slow running, people often attempt to modify their gait by slowly lowering the shorter limb to the ground by using their long leg hip abductors. This frequently results in chronic strain of the gluteus medius muscle and may cause injury to the lumbar spine, since the lumbar vertebrae tilt sideward towards the long limb (Fig. 5.8). Long before symptoms develop, the runner presents with increased tightness in the gluteus medius muscle on the long limb side.

In addition to stress fractures and hip injuries, the patella on the structurally long limb side is also more likely to be injured. Because the most effective way a runner can level the pelvis is by flexing the long limb knee, the knee on that side is subjected to greater force and therefore prone to breaking down. Individuals with limb length discrepancy often walk with the long knee flexed, which strains both the patella and the quadriceps tendon.

The Short Limb

While the majority of injuries occur on the side of the long limb, it is also possible for a runner to get injured on the side of the short limb. In an attempt to stabilize against the tendency to drop sideways towards the short limb, some runners turn their leg out prior to making ground contact. Although this protects you from falling towards the side of the short limb, it increases the potential of a fibular stress fracture because running with your foot pointing out increases the transfer of forces through the fibula (21). This is consistent with Friberg's study of military recruits: Although the long limb tibia was more prone to developing stress fractures, the fibula on the side of the short limb was more likely to fracture (19).

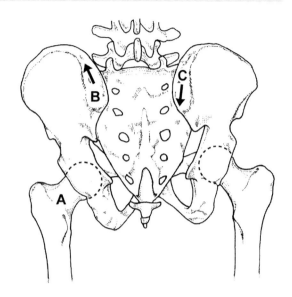

5.9. Pelvic compensation for a limb length discrepancy. To keep the spine vertical, the pelvis on the side of the short limb (**A**) tilts forward (**B**), while the pelvis on the side of the long limb tilts backward (**C**) (51).

An alternate pattern of compensation for a short limb occurs when the runner hyperextends the knee on that side. While this movement may be helpful in bringing the heel closer to the ground during late swing phase, hyperextension of the knee impairs the quadriceps ability to absorb shock, possibly explaining why runners more frequently develop knee arthritis on the side of the short limb.

The sacroiliac joint is also prone to injury on the side of the short limb as, in an attempt to level the sacrum, the pelvis tilts forward on that side (Fig. 5.9). Because of the limited range of motion available to this joint, the compensatory tilting greatly stresses the sacroiliac joint, possibly impairing its ability to absorb shock. This may explain why the sacroiliac joint on the side of the short limb shows earlier and more extensive arthritis than the sacroiliac joint on the side of the long limb (22).

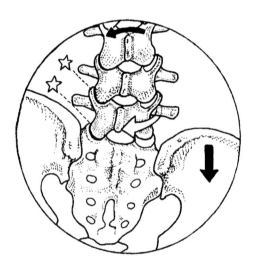

5.8. The lumbar spine tilts away from the side of the short limb, rotating and compressing the joints in the low back (stars).

Evaluating Limb Length Discrepancies

Given the clear association between structural limb length discrepancy and injury, it is important for runners to know whether or not their limbs are the same length. Because functional and structural limb length discrepancies are treated differently, it is important to differentiate a true structural limb length discrepancy (in which the bones are of different lengths) from a functional limb length discrepancy (which most often results from asymmetric muscle tightness). An experienced rehab specialist can easily differentiate structural and functional discrepancies by measuring the distance between the outer pelvis and the inner ankle with a tape measure (Fig. 5.10). While some experts claim CAT scans are necessary to identify true asymmetry in bony limb length, a recent study comparing tape measurements to CAT scans confirms that the tape measurement is 98% as accurate as the expensive and dangerous CAT scans (23) (CAT scans emit ionizing radiation, a proven carcinogen).

Consulting a Specialist

Before casually incorporating a heel lift based upon information obtained from a single measurement, your sports specialist should have fully evaluated respective tibial and femoral lengths in a variety of positions, checked for soft tissue contracture that might be twisting the pelvis, and carefully evaluated foot function to determine whether asymmetric arch height is contributing to a functional limb length discrepancy (Fig. 5.11). Prior to wearing a heel lift, you can perform a simple test on yourself to confirm the presence of a structural limb length discrepancy. Shift your weight back and forth between your right and left leg for about 30 seconds and then stand on the leg that feels more comfortable. When a structural limb length discrepancy is present, the pelvis levels when you stand on your short limb, so 99% of runners with true limb length discrepancy will stand on their short limb. If you find it's more comfortable to stand on what has been diagnosed as your long limb, you should think twice about

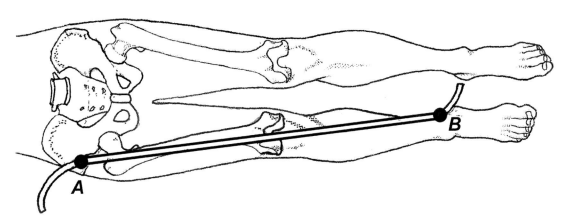

5.10. Measuring limb length discrepancies. By running a tape measure from the ASIS of the pelvis (**A**) to the medial malleolus of the ankle (**B**), it is possible to evaluate limb lengths very accurately.

wearing a heel lift. This test is surprisingly accurate and runners with true limb length discrepancies stand on the short limb with almost no hesitation.

If you do have a structural LLD, the height of the lift is determined by placing lifts of various sizes beneath the short limb and evaluating alignment. The ideal lift will level the iliac crest and, more importantly, bring the lumbar spine closer to vertical. Because of conflicting research regarding the degree of discrepancy necessary to justify treatment, the use of a lift should be based upon physical examination and the runner's symptoms; e.g., strain of the right gluteus medius muscle responds well to a left heel lift, while right sacroiliac pain responds well to a right heel lift.

When a limb length discrepancy is clear upon gait evaluation and the location of the symptoms match with the side of the discrepancy, it is suggested that runners with limb length differences greater than 4 millimeters be treated with the appropriate lift. On occasion, high mileage runners often do well with lifts as small as two millimeters. Since the pelvis compensates for structural limb length discrepancies by tilting back on the side of the long limb and forward on the side of the short limb (51), individuals with structural limb length discrepancy should perform the stretches illustrated in figure 5.12. Because of the effect they have on the entire body, runners with structural limb length discrepancies often respond best to a comprehensive program that includes specific stretches, exercises, and/or chiropractic adjustments to restore symmetric flexibility.

Flexibility

In 1986, Rob DeCastella set a course record by running the Boston Marathon in 2:07:51, just 39 seconds off the world record. A few days before the race, I saw Rob in my office and when I checked his hamstring flexibility, I was shocked to see he could barely raise each leg 30° off the table (even tight runners can raise their legs 60°). Having never seen hamstrings that tight, I asked Rob if he ever stretched and he responded: "When I run, that's as far as my legs go forward so that's as far as I want them to go forward."

At the time, it was just assumed that runners had to stretch to run fast and remain injury-free, but here was one of the world's fastest runners who not only didn't stretch regularly, he avoided

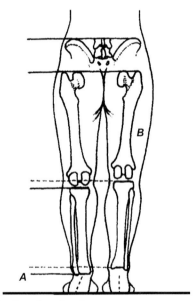

5.11. Evaluation for limb length discrepancies. A functional limb length discrepancy on the left, which is secondary to asymmetric pronation (**A**), coupled with a structural limb length discrepancy of the right femur (**B**), gives the appearance of symmetric limb lengths.

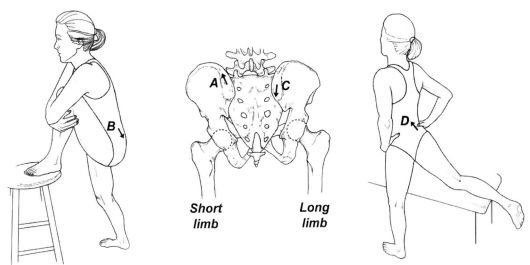

5.12. Home stretches to correct soft tissue imbalances associated with limb length discrepancy. Because the pelvis on the side of the short limb tilts forward (**A**), you should pull your knee towards your chest on that side (**B**). Because the pelvis on the side of the long limb tilts back (**C**), you should stretch the hip flexors on that side by extending the hip back (**D**). The stretches should be held for 20 seconds and performed five times per day.

stretching altogether. According to conventional wisdom, I should have encouraged Rob to stretch, but I didn't. Besides being one of the world's fastest runners, Rob DeCastella knew a lot about exercise physiology and I trusted his judgment.

Years later, research appeared suggesting that tight runners were metabolically more efficient than flexible runners. This is what DeCastella intuitively knew: tight muscles can store and return energy in the form of elastic recoil just like a rubber band can stretch and snap back with no effort. Because tight muscles provide free energy (i.e., the muscle fibers are not shortening to produce force so there is no metabolic expense), stiff muscles can significantly improve efficiency when running long distances.

Anatomy of a Muscle Fiber

To understand why muscles are able to store and return energy, just take a look at how muscles are made. To protect individual muscle fibers from developing too much tension and to assist in the storage and return of energy, muscle fibers and fibrils are surrounded with special soft tissue envelopes called the peri and endomysium. These envelopes contain thousands of strong cross-links that traverse the entire muscle (Fig. 5.13). These cross-links are essential for injury prevention because they distribute tension generated on one side of the tendon evenly throughout the entire muscle.

If these cross-links were not present, or if they were excessively flexible, the asymmetric tendon force would be transferred through the muscle fibers only on the side of the tendon being pulled.

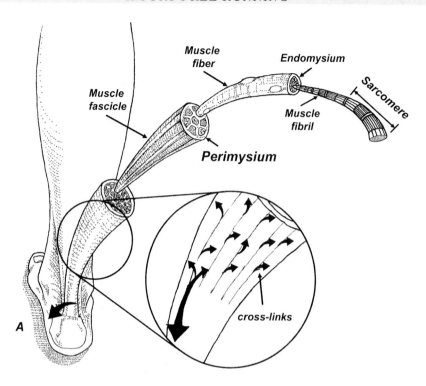

5.13. The components of a muscle. When the foot pronates (**A**), excessive tension is placed on the inner side of the Achilles tendon (**arrow**). Small cross-links present in the perimysium distribute pressure generated on one side of the tendon evenly throughout the entire muscle.

Because fewer muscle fibers would be tractioned, the involved fibers would be more prone to being injured because the pulling force would be distributed over a smaller area. The muscle itself would also be less able to store and return energy simply because fewer fibers would be stretched (the more fibers being pulled, the greater the return of energy). The tight cross-links present in the soft tissue envelopes act as powerful reinforcements that distribute force over a broader area.

Given the improved efficiency associated with tightness, you would think that the world's fastest runners would all be extremely stiff. This isn't the case. Compared to the mid-to-late 80s, today's elite runners are significantly more

flexible. The reason for this is that even though tight muscles can make you more efficient, they are easily strained and are more likely to produce delayed onset muscle soreness after a hard workout (24). Because the best runners currently run more than 130 miles per week with grueling track workouts, increased delayed onset muscle soreness would interfere with their ability to tolerate their rigorous training schedules and would more than likely increase their potential for injury.

To prove that tight muscles are more prone to injury, researchers from Lenox Hill Hospital in New York classified subjects as either stiff or flexible before having them perform repeat hamstring curls to fatigue (24). Following the workout, the stiffer subjects complained of greater muscle pain and weakness. The enzyme marker for muscle damage (CK) was also significantly higher in the stiff group after working out. The authors of the study state that because flexible people are less susceptible to exercise-induced muscle damage, they are able to exercise at a higher intensity for a greater duration on the days following heavy workouts. The catch-22 to muscle tightness is that while a certain degree of tightness increases the storage and return of energy, excessive tightness can increase your potential for injury.

Muscle Tightness and Injuries: a U-shaped Curve

While excessively tight runners are injury prone, excessively loose runners are also prone to injury because their muscles have to work harder to stabilize joints that are moving through larger ranges of motion. Flexible muscles are also less able to store energy in their epi and perimysium so their muscles have to work harder to generate the same force. The end result is that overly flexible runners are just as likely to be injured as stiff runners. It turns out that if you make a graph of injuries associated with different degrees of flexibility, it forms a U-shaped curve with the tightest and the loosest runners being injured (25) (Fig. 5.14).

Evaluate Your Flexibility

Because runners in the middle of the graph are typically not prone to flexibility-related injuries, the goal of a rehab program should be to get yourself away from the extreme ends of the curve. A simple test you can do to quickly

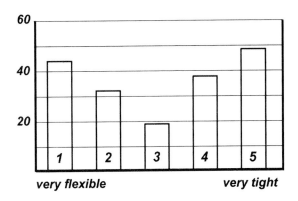

5.14. U-shaped curve of injuries versus flexibility. The vertical axis of the graph represents cumulative injury incidence as a percentage. There were the same number of people in each of the five groups.

evaluate flexibility is to bend your thumb back towards your wrist and measure the distance (Fig. 5.15). Checking the range of motion in your thumb is one of the easiest ways to evaluate overall flexibility because thumb flexibility is a marker for whole body flexibility (just as grip strength is a marker for whole body strength). If you are overly flexible, consider lifting weights to strengthen your muscles and incorporating agility drills to improve coordination.

In contrast, if you happen to fall on the tight side of the spectrum and would like to lessen your potential for injury, consider incorporating specific stretches into your daily routine (Fig. 5.16). Keep in mind that improving flexibility is not that simple. Some great research has shown that when done for just a few weeks, stretching does not alter the ability of a muscle to absorb force because the muscle fibers respond by lengthening slightly to give you the illusion that they're more flexible (26). It's as if the muscle is getting bored with you trying to stretch it so it

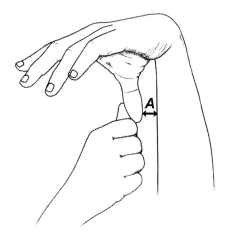

5.15. The thumb to radius index. Excessive flexibility is present when the thumb can be positioned within 2 cm of the forearm (**A**).

just separates a few muscle fibers so you'll leave it alone: you haven't changed the muscle architecture at all, you've just relaxed the muscle a little. Unfortunately, it's still the same muscle and its ability to absorb force has not been altered.

The inability of short-term stretches to improve flexibility explains why there are so many studies showing that stretching does not change injury rates. Because of compliance issues and time constraints, almost every study on stretching and injuries has evaluated stretches over a short duration (probably because so few people would stick with a long-term stretching regimen). That being the case, it's not surprising that while some great research shows that tight muscles are more likely to be injured (24), relatively few studies have ever shown that stretching alters your potential for injury.

In order to produce real length gains, some experts suggest it is necessary to stretch regularly for four to six months. In theory, when a muscle is repeatedly stretched for several months, cellular changes take place within the muscle allowing for a permanent increase in flexibility. Animal studies have shown that the increased flexibility associated with repeat stretching results from a lengthening of the connective tissue envelope surrounding the muscle fibers (especially the perimysium) and/or an increased number of sarcomeres being added to the ends of the muscle fibers (27) (refer back to Fig. 5.13).

To Stretch or Not to Stretch?

Before considering a long-term commitment to stretching, you should be sure it's worth your time and effort. While slower recreational runners running less than 15 miles per week may not want to invest the time, high mileage runners almost always benefit from regular stretching because it improves their ability to tolerate heavy workouts. Also, runners who are asymmetrically tight should consider committing to a long-term stretching program. To determine if you're asymmetrically tight, perform the stretches illustrated in figure 5.16 and compare muscle flexibility on your right and left sides. If one muscle doesn't move as far as the same muscle on the other side, you should definitely stretch the tighter side. Asymmetrical muscle tightness has recently been shown to correlate with the development of future injuries (28).

Assuming you decide to begin a long-term stretching routine, determining the ideal frequency and duration that a stretch should be maintained is the subject of debate. Different studies have recommended anywhere from one to 20 stretch repetitions with each stretch held for anywhere from

10 seconds to 10 minutes. The amount of force used during a stretch is also a subject of debate, as some studies recommend stretching to the point of discomfort while others recommend stretching the muscle only to the point where tension is felt.

To identify the ideal stretch frequencies and duration, researchers from Duke University placed rabbits on special machines designed to evaluate improvements in muscle flexibility following 10 consecutive 30-second stretches (29). Using this elaborate technique, the authors determined that the majority of length gains associated with stretching occur in the first 15 seconds of a stretch, and that after the fourth 30-second stretch, no appreciable length gains were achieved. This research confirms it is better to perform a few 30-second stretches throughout the day than to spend an extended period of time stretching a specific muscle. (Although if you are pressed for time, stretching just once a day for 30 seconds has been shown to effectively increase range of motion [30].)

Improving Tendon Flexibility

While muscle length gains diminish after four 30-second stretches, some interesting research suggests that it is possible to lengthen tendons by performing gentle stretches that are held for up to 10 minutes (31). Improving tendon flexibility is important not only for returning energy but also for preventing injuries. Years ago, Uta Pippig asked me to write an article on stretching for her website. When I gave her the article, which reviewed the research showing that stretching does not alter injury rates, she was surprised by the lack of scientific evidence supporting stretching. Uta felt that holding certain yoga poses for long periods not only helped her get over several chronic injuries, the prolonged stretches also improved her efficiency. Uta Pippig figured out on her own something few researchers were aware of: prolonged stretching can improve tendon flexibility. According to the exercise physiologist Robert Griffiths (32), a more flexible tendon acts as a physical buffer that absorbs stretch forces that would otherwise be channeled into the muscle. Improving flexibility of the Achilles tendon with prolonged static stretches may significantly lessen your potential for developing calf strains.

Trigger Points

Perhaps the most effective way to lengthen a muscle is to massage specific trigger points before stretching the muscle for 30 seconds. Trigger points are localized areas of muscle contracture that tend to occur near muscle-tendon junctions. Figure 5.17 illustrates the more common locations for trigger points in runners. Because trigger points are more sensitive to pressure than regular muscle fibers, the easiest way to find them is to take a foam roller or a massage stick and scan through individual muscles. When you find an uncomfortable point, massage that specific spot in the muscle for a few minutes before holding a 30-second stretch. If you are on the right spot, the muscle lengthens dramatically following the massage. Several studies have shown that massaging a muscle before you stretch it results in more rapid length gains than conventional stretching alone (33, 34).

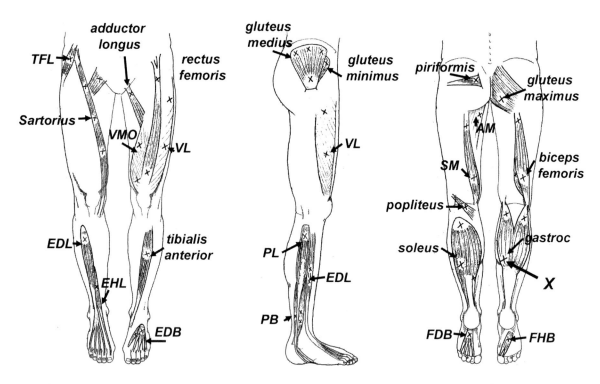

5.17. Common locations of trigger points. These points should be massaged by hand or with a foam roller/massage stick prior to stretching. The trigger point located in the inner gastrocnemius muscle (**X**) is especially important to loosen prior to stretching. Abbreviations: **TFL**-tensor fasciae latae, **VMO**-vastus medialis obliquus, **VL**-vastus lateralis, **PL**-peroneus longus, **PB**-peroneus brevis, **EDL**-extensor digitorum longus, **EHL**- extensor hallucis longus, **EDB**-extensor digitorum brevis, **FDB**-flexor digitorum brevis, **FHB**-flexor hallucis brevis, **gastroc**-gastrocnemius.

Illustration 5.16, A through S, reviews static stretches for all of the major muscle groups used while running. You should perform these stretches on both sides and note any asymmetry in tension. If you are asymmetrically tight in a specific muscle, stretch the tighter side more often. If you have time, spend a minute or two massaging suspected trigger points prior to performing the stretches.

Notice that in all of these illustrations, there are no stretches in which the lumbar spine is actively flexed. Although frequently recommended by coaches and yoga instructors, flexing the lumbar spine while stretching increases the potential for disc injury and should almost always be avoided. The classic example of this is standing toe touches, the plow, and seated toe touches. There are better ways to stretch muscles without hurting your low back. According to the spine researcher Stuart McGill (35), a healthy disc can only be flexed through so many cycles in a lifetime before it ruptures, so you should flex your lumbar spine only when you absolutely have to.

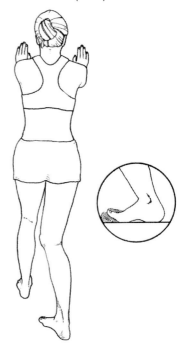

B) Tibialis posterior and inner soleus stretch.
Rotate the back leg inward while slightly flexing the knee. To stretch the deep flexors, place a rolled-up towel beneath the toes (inset).

A) Gastrocnemius stretch.
Keep the knee straight with the hip extended behind you. To stretch the inner fibers of this muscle, rotate the involved leg inward. To stretch the soleus, bend the knee slightly.

D) An alternate way to stretch the anterior compartment muscles is to squat down on all fours with a pillow placed beneath the forefeet.

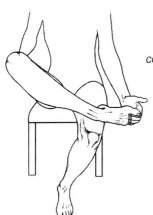

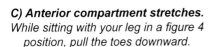

C) Anterior compartment stretches.
While sitting with your leg in a figure 4 position, pull the toes downward.

E) Peroneus longus stretch.
Place a tennis ball beneath your inner forefeet and slightly flex your knees.

5.16. Common stretches for runners.

F) Short adductor stretch.
*Known as the frog pose in yoga, get down on all fours with
your hips abducted. Move your pelvis forward and backward
so you can stretch all of the adductor muscles (**arrow**).*

G) Long adductor stretch.
*Gracilis and portions of adductor magnus
are stretched by placing your heel on an elevated surface positioned at your side. By
rotating your leg in and out, you can stretch
all of the adductor muscles.*

H) Hamstring stretch.
*Place your heel on an elevated surface while keeping a
slight arch in your low back. By pivoting forward at the hips
(**arrow**), you will feel tension in your hamstrings. The outer
hamstrings are stretched by rotating the leg in, while the
inner hamstrings are stretched by rotating the leg out. By
repeating the stretch with the knee flexed 30°, 45°, 90°,
you can isolate specific areas of tightness in the upper and
lower hamstrings.*

I) Rectus femoris stretch.
*This section of the quadriceps muscle
is stretched by pulling your heel
towards the back of your hip while
maintaining a pelvic tuck (**arrow**).*

J) Hip flexor stretch.
*While kneeling on one leg, shift your weight forward until you
feel slight tension in the front of the groin. The hip flexors can
be isolated by moving the ankle out slightly (**arrow**).*

5.16. Common stretches for runners, cont.

L) Tensor fasciae latae stretch.
*The involved leg is positioned behind you while you shift your pelvis towards the wall (**A**). Your spine should be kept in a midline position while performing this stretch.*

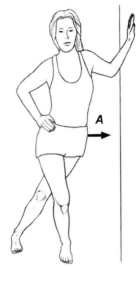

K) Standing hip flexor stretch.
An alternate way to stretch the hip flexors is to extend the straight leg behind you while maintaining a neutral pelvis.

M) Gluteus medius stretch.
*The leg you are stretching is positioned behind you, while the hand on that side is resting against a wall (**A**). To stretch the gluteus medius muscle, move your hip towards the wall (**B**).*

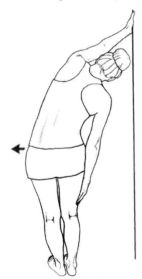

O) Alternate quadratus lumborum stretch.
*Kneel back so your hips are over your heels and pull your upper body to the right to stretch the left quadratus lumborum (**arrow**).*

N) Quadratus lumborum stretch.
*With your feet touching, grab the side of a door jam and shift your pelvis away from the door (**arrow**). By grabbing the door at different points while bending forward slightly, specific fibers of the quadratus lumborum can be lengthened.*

5.16. Common stretches for runners, cont.

Q) Piriformis muscle energy stretch.
*To stretch the left piriformis muscle, the hip is flexed 45° while the opposite leg hooks over the knee (**A**). You then lightly tense the piriformis muscle by pushing the left knee into resistance provided by the right leg. After five seconds, the left piriformis is relaxed and the right leg pulls the left knee inward, stretching the piriformis.*

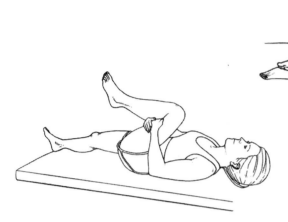

P) Gluteus maximus stretch.
Clasp your hands behind your knee and pull the involved thigh towards your shoulder. To stretch the piriformis muscle, pull knee towards the opposite shoulder.

R) Lumbar rotational stretch.
Lie on the ground with your knees and hips flexed with your arms positioned for stability. Gently rock your knees from side to side, moving through gradually larger ranges of motion. Spend about three seconds rocking in each direction for a total of 60 seconds.

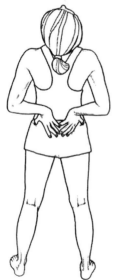

S) Standing hyperextension.
Place your hands over the base of the spine and arch back. Your pelvis should remain still while your lumbar spine extends comfortably.

5.16. Common stretches for runners, cont.

Active Dynamic Running Drills

Rather than slowly stretching each muscle statically, many runners prefer active dynamic warm-ups. Popular with elite and sub-elite runners, these drills allow you to warm up specific muscles while simultaneously stretching them. The dynamic drills illustrated in figure 4.4 (page 71) were recently proven to improve performance in sprinters. Compared to a control group, runners who performed either one or two sets of 14 repetitions of each of the exercises were able to run significantly faster sprint times (36).

Because dynamic stretches can be difficult to master and are time-consuming, slower recreational runners can either incorporate gentler versions of these dynamic stretches or just consider warming up by running slowly with a high cadence and a short stride length. Since older runners tend to be stiffer, the length of time you spend warming up is age-dependent: 30 to 40-year-old runners should consider warming up for 5 to 10 minutes, while the 50 and older group should run slowly for up to 15 minutes. Each person is different so the length of time you spend warming up is up to you.

In the largest randomized control study of stretching to date, Daniel Pereles and colleagues recently proved that runners intuitively know whether or not they should stretch (37). These authors randomly assigned 2,729 recreational runners to either a stretching or a non-stretching pre-run routine. Not surprisingly, there was no significant difference in injury rates between the runners who stretched versus the runners who didn't stretch. However, if a runner who routinely stretched was assigned to the non-stretch protocol, he/she was nearly twice as likely to sustain a running injury. As with almost everything regarding running-related injuries, you are the best judge of choosing which pre-exercise warm-up is right for you.

Strength Training

In the 100th running of the Boston Marathon, Tegla Loroupe was in first place for most of the race with a comfortable lead over Uta Pippig. At about mile 23, Tegla's back began to hurt and she later said that her left leg felt like it was "dead." Despite the pain, Tegla somehow managed to finish in second place, just 85 seconds behind Uta. She didn't know it at the time but Tegla developed small stress fractures in the base of her spine during the downhill portion of the race. Later that same year, Tegla attempted to run the New York Marathon but the stress fractures hadn't completely healed and this time her back pain became severe. An MRI after the race revealed that she had a fracture in the base of her spine called a spondylolysis. Frequently present in gymnasts, this type of fracture occurs when the lower lumbar vertebrae repeatedly extend through large ranges of motion, fracturing a section of bone near the spinal joints. To immobilize the spinal fracture, Tegla was fitted with a special brace designed to stop her low back from moving. Unfortunately, the brace compressed a nerve located near the top of her pelvis, causing a decrease in sensation along the outer portion of her thigh.

Core Weakness and Chronic Injury

Because of the progressive loss of feeling in her outer thigh and her continued low back pain, Tegla came to see me for an evaluation. The sensory nerve injury was relatively minor and gradually resolved once the brace was removed. Tegla's real problem became apparent with a test called Vleeming's test. Developed by a leading spine specialist from the Netherlands, this simple test accurately identifies weakness in the abdominal core muscles. You can do Vleeming's test on yourself by lying on a comfortable surface. With your arms at your side, raise one leg in the air and have a friend push down on the raised ankle (Fig. 5.18). When the abdominal core muscles are strong, the pelvis remains horizontal. In Tegla's case, the opposite side of her pelvis lifted right off the table.

Core weakness played a huge role in the chronic nature of Tegla's injury because the core muscles function to lock the vertebrae of the low back together, creating a compressive force that stabilizes the entire lower spine while running. Adequate core strength is especially important while running downhill, because the braking phase associated with initial ground contact allows the lower lumbar vertebrae to shift forward upon heel strike (Fig. 5.19). If the core muscles are weak, this forward shifting is unopposed and the excessive forward motion of the lower lumbar vertebrae creates a shear force in the low back capable of producing a stress fracture. Fortunately, it doesn't take a lot of core strength to prevent injury because the core muscles fire with very low intensities while running.

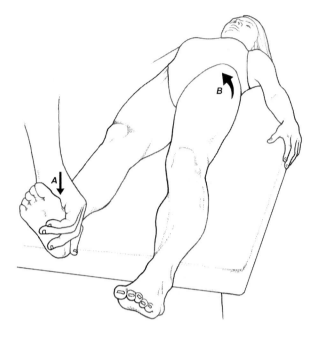

5.18. Vleeming's test. When the core muscles are weak, pushing down on the elevated leg (**A**) will cause the opposite pelvis to lift off the table (**B**).

Based on her exam results, Tegla was treated with soft tissue manipulation to reduce entrapment of the sensory nerve, stretches to improve the flexibility of her hip flexors and abductors (tight hips can cause the back to arch excessively while running), and gentle mobilization of the stiff spinal joints located above the fracture site. The most important component of Tegla's treatment was an intensive program of core exercises. While many rehabilitation experts recommend complex core strengthening exercises in which special machines are used to provide feedback regarding the successful recruitment of the deep core muscles, recent

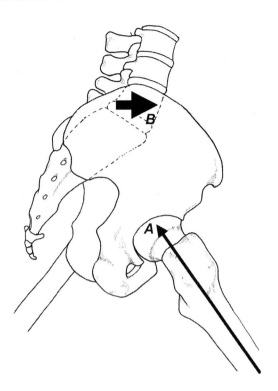

5.19. The braking phase associated with striking the ground (A) causes the lower lumbar spine to shift forward (B).

research confirms that simple home exercises are just as effective as the expensive and complicated core training protocols that require special training and access to high-tech machinery (38).

Tegla was consistent with her stretches and home strengthening exercises and five months later, she set the course record in Rotterdam with a 2:22:07 marathon. She continued with her exercises and the following year Tegla broke the world record by running a 2:20:47 at Rotterdam. One year later, her chronic low back pain finally resolved, and she set another world record at the Berlin Marathon.

Strengthening Exercises

Like many runners, Tegla has always disliked strengthening exercises. People tend to be drawn to things they're good at and while most runners are willing to tolerate intensive track workouts and grueling long distance runs, many of them avoid tedious strengthening exercises. This is unfortunate because several studies have shown that weak runners are prone to injury. For example, weakness of both core and hip abductor muscles have both been proven to predispose to knee injury, while plantar fasciitis and metatarsal stress fractures often result from toe weakness.

Maintaining adequate hip strength is especially important in injury prevention. In an interesting study published in *Arthritis and Rheumatism*, researchers determined that people with strong hip abductors are much less likely to develop osteoarthritis in their knees (39). Apparently, in addition to preventing inward rotation of the thigh, the hip abductors also function to create a compressive force on the outside of the knee that prevents the knee from collapsing inward (Fig. 5.20). In their 18-month study of the progression of knee arthritis in people with bowed legs, the authors noted that there was a reduced progression of knee arthritis in individuals with strong hips, regardless of age, sex, and most importantly, the degree in which their legs bow inward. This research is significant because it demonstrates that strength can protect you from injury even if you are poorly aligned. To increase your strength, the following illustrations review a range of the most effective home exercises (Fig. 5.21, A-Y).

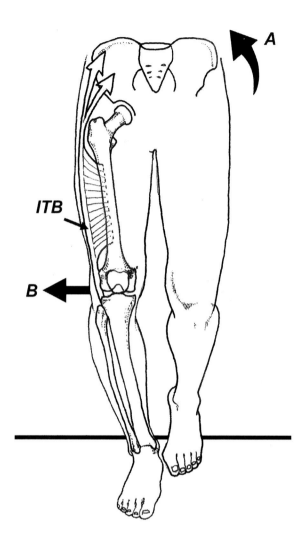

5.20. In addition to keeping the pelvis level (A), the hip abductors pull on the iliotibial band (ITB), creating a compressive force that stops the knee from shifting sidewards (B).

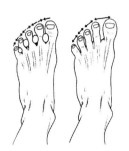

A) Foot intrinsic exercises.
Small corks or rubber tubes are positioned between your toes while you alternate between squeezing and separating the toes.

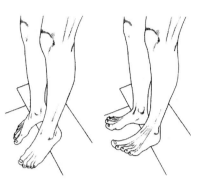

B) Anterior compartment exercises.
Stand with your heels supported on the edge of a stair and alternately raise and lower your forefeet through a full range of motion.

C) Flexor digitorum exercise.
*While seated, place a piece of TheraBand beneath your heel and forefoot, running directly under the toes. Create tension in the band by grabbing the opposite end with your hand and stabilize it near your knee. Flexor digitorum is exercised by pushing downward against resistance provided by the TheraBand (**arrow**). To strengthen flexor hallucis longus, place the band directly beneath the big toe only.*

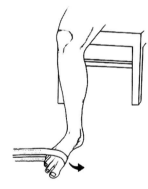

D) Tibialis posterior exercise.
*With a TheraBand anchored to a fixed object (the leg of a table works well), keep your heel in a fixed position while you pull your forefoot inward (**arrow**).*

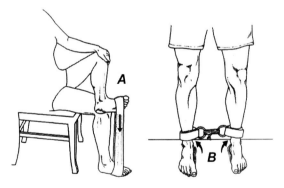

E) Alternate tibialis posterior exercises. *Place the involved foot over the opposite knee with a TheraBand wrapped between the forefeet (**A**). Tibialis posterior is exercised by raising and lowering the upper forefoot. An alternate tibialis posterior exercise is to wrap a series of TheraBand tubes between ankle cuffs and alternately raise and lower your arches (**B**).*

5.21. Strengthening exercises.

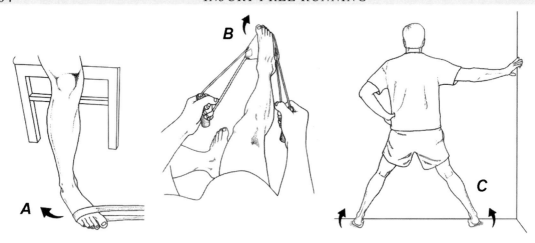

F) Peroneus brevis (A) and longus (B and C) exercises.

*Peroneus brevis is exercised by pulling your forefoot outward against resistance provided by an anchored piece of TheraBand (**A**). Peroneus longus is exercised by pushing down with the inner side of your forefoot against resistance provided by an elastic band (**B**). A more advanced peroneus longus exercise is to stand with your hips separated and knees slightly bent, while alternately raising and lowering your heels (arrows in **C**). You can perform this exercise with a weighted backpack to increase resistance.*

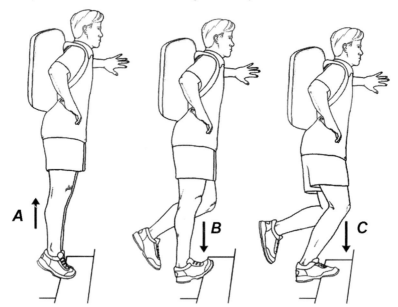

G) Gastrocnemius and soleus eccentric exercises.

*Because these muscles are so strong, these exercises are performed wearing a weighted backpack while standing on the edge of a stair with your heels unsupported. To strengthen the gastrocnemius, lift upward with both legs simultaneously (**A**), and then slowly lower yourself on one leg (**B**). Three sets of 15 repetitions are performed on each side. To strengthen the soleus muscle, this exercise is repeated with the knee flexed (**C**). Redrawn from Alfredson (50).*

5.21. Strengthening exercises, cont.

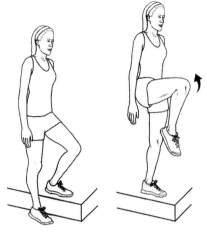

H) Single leg cone touch.
While standing on one leg on an unstable surface (such as the AirEx Balance Pad), pivot forward at the hip so you touch the top of a cone placed in front of you. Immediately jump up and repeat the cone-touch on a neighboring cone.

I) Lateral step ups.
*To strengthen the inner quad, stand next to a 6-inch platform and raise the opposite knee (**arrow**). You can do this exercise with a weighted backpack to increase resistance.*

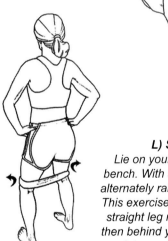

L) Sidelying hip abduction.
Lie on your side near the edge of a workout bench. With a weight placed around your ankle, alternately raise and lower the straight upper leg. This exercise can be performed by repeating the straight leg raises with the hip first in front, and then behind you. Performing the exercise behind you lets you isolate the gluteus minimus muscle.

J) Dynadisc lunge.
A conventional lunge can be performed on an unstable surface to enhance coordination. Be very careful while performing this exercise. At first, make sure you have something to grab onto, should you lose your balance.

K) Standing gluteus medius exercise.
*Stand with your knee slightly flexed and your hips slightly abducted with a TheraBand placed just above your knees. While keeping your feet in place, alternately move your knees in and out (**arrows**).*

5.21. Strengthening exercises, cont.

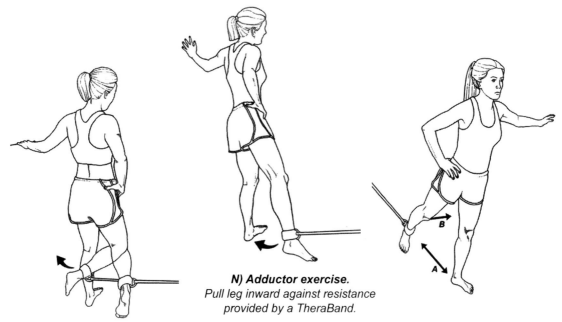

N) Adductor exercise.
*Pull leg inward against resistance
provided by a TheraBand.*

M) TheraBand piriformis exercise.
*Stand with your hip and knee slightly flexed with
a TheraBand wrapped around your ankle. While
keeping your thigh in a fixed position, pull the ankle
inward (**arrow**).*

O) Hip flexor exercise.
*Move the straight leg forward against resistance
provided by a TheraBand. This exercise should
be repeated with the knee straight (**A**)
and flexed (**B**).*

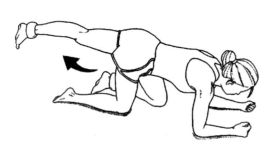

P) Glute Max kickbacks.
*To strengthen the gluteus maximus, get on all fours
and kick the involved leg out against resistance
provided by an ankle weight.*

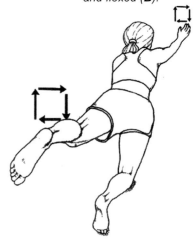

Q) Bird dog exercise.
*Get on all fours and extend opposite arm and leg.
In this position, move each extremity through 4-inch
squares.*

5.21. Strengthening exercises, cont.

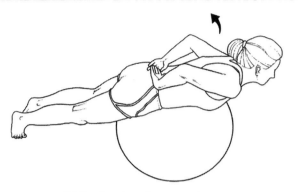

R) Back extension exercise.
With feet slightly separated for stability, lie facedown on a 65 cm physioball and gently arch your back upward (**arrow**). Hold this position for five seconds and repeat 10 times. If you feel even slightly unstable while performing this exercise, you can use a workout bench instead of a physioball.

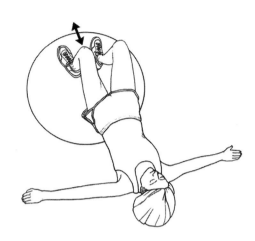

S) Hamstring rollout.
With your arms positioned at your side place, place your feet on a 65 cm physioball with your knees bent and your spine straight. While maintaining a straight spine and pelvis, push and pull the physioball by alternately straightening and flexing your knees. The stronger you become, the farther you can push and pull the physioball.

T) Upper hamstring exercise.
Stand with your weight on the leg to be exercised while the toes of the opposite foot lightly touch the ground. While maintaining a slight arch in your low back, bend forward, pivoting at the hip. It is important to maintain a slight curve in your back while performing this exercise. In order to isolate outer hamstring, tilt slightly away from the involved leg (e.g., the left outer hamstring is isolated by tilting slightly to the right).

U) Lower hamstring exercise.
The lower hamstrings are exercised by standing with your hands resting on a stable surface with a weight placed around your ankle. Alternately raise and lower the leg, slightly flexing the knee and hip.

5.21. Strengthening exercises, cont.

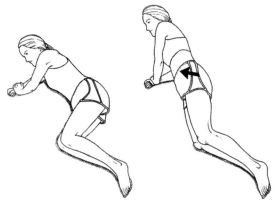

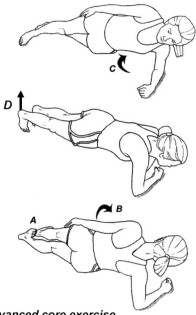

V) Beginner core exercise.
*Because conventional core exercises require a fair amount of strength, an alternate method for strengthening the core is to rest on the floor with your hips and knees flexed while your upper body is supported on your flexed elbow. While maintaining ground contact with the legs and the down knee, the pelvis is lifted up and forward as if rising from a chair (**arrow**).*

W) Advanced core exercise.
*With the upper heel touching the toes of the downside leg (**A**), a sidelying plank is maintained for 20 seconds. You then rotate 90° (**B**), placing your forearms side-by-side with your toes touching the ground. This position is held for 20 seconds before rotating another 90° (**C**), performing a sidelying plank on the opposite side. The cycle is repeated three times. This exercise can be made more difficult by raising one leg at a time while in the plank position (**D**).*

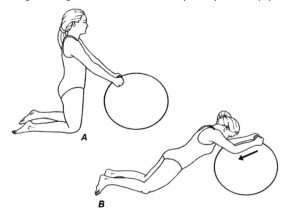

X) Supine bridge with knee extension. *Perform a conventional bridge with knees bent 90° and your pelvis elevated. While maintaining a perfectly level pelvis, alternately raise and lower one leg at a time.*

Y) The rollout abdominal exercise.
Kneel beside a physioball with your fists contacting the ball. Lean forward, rolling your forearms against the physioball while maintaining a straight spine. Pull yourself back and repeat. This exercise was proven to be one of the best ways to recruit the rectus abdominus.

5.21. Strengthening exercises, cont.

Repetitions and Sets

To strengthen a muscle as quickly as possible, various authors recommend different exercise intensities, sets, repetitions, and weekly frequencies. Some experts claim you should perform three sets of 12 repetitions three times per week, while others claim that two sets of 5 repetitions produces the fastest strength gains.

To resolve the controversy, a group of physiologists reviewed the literature and concluded the ideal number of repetitions and amount of resistance necessary to improve strength is determined by the individual's level of fitness: unfit individuals respond best to 4 sets of 12 repetitions performed to failure 3X/week, while fit individuals respond best to 4 sets of 8 repetitions performed to failure 2X/week (40). ("Performed to failure" means that you are so tired after your final repetition that you cannot perform another one.)

Interestingly, unlike the improved flexibility associated with stretching, the strength gains associated with resistance training are more long-term, lasting months after you stop strength training. I tell runners who dislike strengthening exercises to perform them for just three months each year. The strength gains achieved during this short period of time can keep you strong throughout the year.

Strength Asymmetries

Because strength asymmetries can predict future injury, it is important to do the exercises on each side and look for subtle differences in strength. If you notice you are weaker on one side, correct the asymmetry by using the resistance necessary to fatigue your weaker side while exercising the weak and the strong side. At first, the strong side won't be getting much of a workout. Over a six to eight week period of time, strength gradually becomes symmetric and you can increase resistance on both sides. Right to left strength differences commonly occur following prolonged injury. For example, runners with chronic Achilles tendinitis and/or tibial stress fractures frequently present with significant weakness of the calf muscles on the injured side. The weakness is made apparent by repeating heel raises on each side: the injured side is unable to do the same number of repetitions as the uninjured side. Surprisingly, the injured runner is almost always unaware of the strength difference. Correcting the asymmetry is necessary to prevent injury.

Concentric versus Eccentric Contractions

Besides altering the number of repetitions and sets, strength training can also be modified by emphasizing either concentric or eccentric muscle contractions. Concentric contractions occur when a muscle is shortening while producing force. In contrast, eccentric contractions occur when the muscle is lengthening while producing force. For example, when you are lifting yourself up while performing a pull-up, the biceps muscles are shortening and are therefore concentrically contracting. When you lower yourself, the biceps are eccentrically contracting since they are lengthening while producing force.

Differentiating eccentric and concentric contractions is important because exercises are 100% mode specific: If you exercise a muscle only concentrically, it will become strong only when contracting concentrically. Conversely, if you exercise a muscle eccentrically, it is strengthened only during the eccentric component of a contraction. There is no overflow from one type of contraction to the other. This is essential for runners since many exercises emphasize only one type of contraction. The best example of this occurs while wet vest running in a pool to recover from injuries. Although effective for staying fit while rehabilitating injuries such as stress fractures, pool running almost always results in hamstring injury because resistance from the water forces the hamstrings to fire concentrically only: when you're pulling your leg forward, your quads and hip flexors concentrically contract to overcome resistance provided by the water, and when you pull the leg back, the hamstrings also contract concentrically, again to overcome resistance from the water. Rehabilitating the hamstring with concentric contractions only is dangerous because the hamstrings work eccentrically while running to decelerate the forward motion of the swinging leg. When you only tense the muscle concentrically in a pool, the hamstrings become eccentrically weak during your rehabilitation and as soon as you begin running fast, the hamstrings are easily strained since they are no longer able to control the forward swinging leg.

To reduce your potential for injury, muscles should be exercised in the same manner they are used while running. Almost always, both the eccentric and concentric components of an exercise should be included.

Neuromotor Coordination

This is one of the most important criteria for injury-free running because runners with well-coordinated muscles can tolerate high mileage training whether they are flat-footed, bow-legged, knock kneed, or hypermobile. In addition to smoothly absorbing impact forces, coordinated muscles work in unison to level your pelvis while keeping your hips and knees moving in a straight line. Coordinated muscles are capable of smoothly decelerating joint motions even if the muscles themselves are relatively weak. In contrast, uncoordinated muscles allow your joints to move rapidly through large ranges of motion, which almost always results in injury and/or altered form.

Motor Engrams

The most common cause of impaired neuromotor coordination is prior injury. To protect you from further injury, the central nervous system essentially rewires itself by creating an alternate pattern of muscle recruitment to avoid stressing the damaged soft tissues. Referred to as a motor engram, the altered pattern of muscle recruitment persists long after the injury has healed. The perfect example of a faulty motor engram occurs following an ankle sprain. Laboratory evaluation of muscle activity confirms that immediately following an ankle sprain, the peroneal muscles on the outside of the leg pretense with greater force just before your foot hits the ground (41). Pretensing the peroneal muscles protects the damaged ligament by keeping the rearfoot in a stable position during initial ground contact.

Although usually helpful, all too often the motor engrams created are damaging. For example, while increased activity in the peroneal muscles following an ankle sprain is protective, ankle sprains have also been shown to impair recruitment of the gluteus maximus muscle on the side of the sprain. While the exact mechanism responsible for producing inhibition is unclear, the decreased activation of gluteus maximus results in impaired stabilization of the hip and knee. The resultant hip weakness frequently produces a gait pattern in which the knee is allowed to twist in excessively. As previously mentioned, inward collapse of the knee is associated with the development of a wide range of running injuries.

Faulty motor engrams also occur following knee injury. Even minor knee injuries produce inhibition of the inner quadriceps muscle (the VMO) that persists after the knee itself has healed. Without proper stabilization from the inner quadriceps, the patella drifts towards the outside of the knee, often resulting in chronic pain. In one of the more interesting motor engrams I've seen, an Olympic Trials Marathon runner compensated for an outer hamstring injury by switching from a heel to a forefoot strike pattern on the injured side. She also began running with the injured leg turned out almost 35°. Until her uneven shoe wear was pointed out, the runner had no idea that she was striking on her forefoot on one side and her heel on the other. This specific motor engram developed because the forefoot contact point reduced her stride length on the injured side. The reduced stride length lessens strain on the hamstrings because these muscles decelerate forward motion of the swing phase leg: the shorter the stride, the less the hamstring strain. The toe-out gait pattern also reduced strain on the hamstring muscles because it allowed her to use her hip abductors to decelerate forward motion of the swinging leg. Long after the hamstring healed, she continued to run with this faulty running style.

Identifying Faulty Motor Engrams

To help identify faulty motor engrams, a series of functional tests have been developed that test your ability to recruit muscles in a smooth and coordinated manner. These tests are easy to perform and can be done at home. Note that on some occasions, faulty movement patterns are the result of compensating for arthritic joints. Hip and knee arthritis are notorious for producing faulty motor engrams in older runners. Unfortunately, it is often not possible to fully correct a faulty movement pattern associated with arthritis and runners with arthritis should develop a running form that lessens stress on the arthritic joint; e.g., switching to a midfoot strike pattern and/or shortening the length of stride. In all situations, the joint responsible for causing the faulty movement pattern should be stretched and strengthened. While this occasionally requires a visit to your local sports chiropractor or physical therapist, it is possible to maintain symmetric strength and flexibility with the previously described stretches and exercises. Following is a list of the more common functional tests used to identify faulty motor engrams.

The Modified Romberg's Test

Developed in the 60s to assess balance after an ankle sprain, the inability to perform this test is a better predictor of future ankle injury than the degree of ligament damage present on MRIs. Because there is a risk of falling during this test, make sure you are standing near a wall or in a corner so you can catch yourself if you start to lose balance. To begin with, stand on one foot with your eyes open and spend about 30 seconds getting your balance. Once you feel secure, close your eyes and count in seconds how long it takes before you feel unstable. The first time you try this you may lose your balance pretty quickly but after a few attempts, you should be able to maintain your balance for at least 20 seconds. If you are unable to balance with eyes closed despite several attempts, you have impaired muscular stabilization. The reason closing your eyes affects balance is that when your eyes are open, you are relying on visual cues to maintain balance, but as soon as you close your eyes, you are forced to rely on sensory information provided by the muscles, ligaments, and even the skin on the bottom of your weight-bearing foot.

When everything is working properly, the sensory cues from your foot and ankle cause your muscles to immediately tense to stop you from swaying too far in any one direction. The ability to balance with eyes closed is essential while running because you're not looking down while you're running. When your foot hits the ground, subtle changes in terrain cause the foot and ankle to tilt rapidly in a variety of angles, and sensory fibers in the muscles, ligaments, and skin provide

immediate information that allow you to adjust. The inability to maintain your balance while standing on one foot with your eyes closed confirms that there is a glitch in the sensory/motor system. The culprit may be a damaged ligament that is failing to provide your central nervous system with information regarding changes in length and/or an injured muscle that fails to react to the sensory information by tensing rapidly. Either way, the impaired balance needs to be corrected.

The easiest way to improve balance is to routinely practice standing on one leg with your eyes closed. After a week or two, you can usually balance for more than 20 seconds. Once your balance has improved, you can practice shifting your weight slightly forward, sideward, and backwards until you feel stable in all positions. An alternate method to improve balance is with an ankle rock board device (Fig. 5.22). Because these boards force your ankle to move through a full range of motion, the rock board essentially duplicates the position of a potential sprain and forces you to move out of the high-risk position. The resultant movement pattern eventually becomes wired into your system and a faulty motor engram associated with your prior injury is replaced with a safer movement pattern. While performing ankle rockboard exercises, always make sure you have something to catch on to just in case you lose your balance.

Training on unstable surfaces has been proven to improve coordination and reduce injury rates. In a study of high school football players considered high-risk for future ankle sprain (they had a history of prior ankle sprain), researchers from the Nicholas Institute of

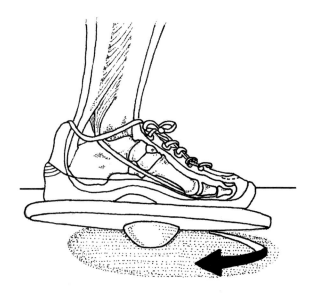

5.22. Ankle Rockboard.

Sports Medicine (42) confirmed that 5 minutes of balance board training performed 5 times a week for 4 weeks resulted in a 77% reduction in the frequency of subsequent ankle sprains.

To improve balance as quickly as possible, consider placing a strip of Kinesiotape along your outer leg and heel prior to performing your rock board exercises. While the rock board is forcing you to move through a full range of motion, the tape gently pulls on your skin providing your nervous system with additional information regarding the position and movement of your ankle. This improved awareness allows for a more effective muscular response. In a study evaluating the length of time necessary to restore balance with ankle rock boards, taped subjects returned to baseline values of balance within six weeks of training, compared to eight weeks with balance board training alone (43).

Sidelying Hip Abduction Test

Designed to evaluate the coordination of your hip abductors and core muscles, this test is performed by lying on your side with your pelvis vertical and your legs straight. With one arm folded beneath your head and the other resting comfortably at your side, try raising your upper leg towards the ceiling while keeping your knee straight and your pelvis perpendicular to the table (Fig. 5.23, A). When the core and hip abductor muscles are working properly, it's relatively easy to lift your leg while maintaining alignment between your torso and leg (Fig. 5.23, B). However, when your hip abductors and core muscles are not working in synchrony, your pelvis rotates out of alignment when you raise your leg (Fig. 5.23, C). A recent study confirmed that

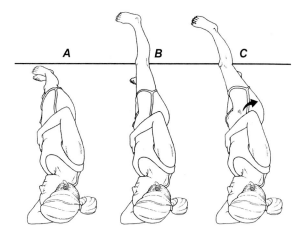

5.23. The sidelying hip abduction test. Lie on your side (**A**) and raise your upper leg straight towards the ceiling (**B**). When your hip abductors are working properly, the pelvis remains vertical while you raise your leg. When your core and hip abductors are not working properly, the pelvis rotates forward or backward (**C**).

if you are unable to smoothly raise your leg in a straight line while maintaining your pelvis in a vertical position, you are six times more likely to suffer low back pain while standing for long periods of time (44). I've been using this test for several years and have noticed that it also predicts low back and hip problems in runners.

If you fail this test and your hip tilts forward or backward while raising your leg, the first step is to practice performing the test itself while maintaining a vertical pelvis. If necessary, raise the top leg only a few inches until you feel stable. Over time, you should be able to move the upper leg through a full range of motion without twisting the pelvis. Once you can do three sets of 15 repetitions with a stable pelvis, you can progress to a sidelying plank performed while alternately raising and lowering the top leg. Rotating from side plank to full plank and back to opposite side plank while raising the upper leg is a very effective exercise to improve coordination between your core and hip abductors (Fig. 5.21, W). In all cases, the pelvis must always be vertical. If you continue to rotate your pelvis out of alignment, go back to the simpler version of the exercise in which you just lie on your side and practice raising your straight leg towards the ceiling while keeping your pelvis perpendicular to the table. Remember, your goal is to correct a faulty motor engram and failure to maintain perfect form will reinforce the faulty movement pattern.

The Star Excursion Balance Test

This test is performed by placing a tape measure on the floor, angled 45° backwards away from your weight-bearing foot. While balancing on one leg, reach back with your toe and touch the farthest point on the ruler you can without losing your balance (Fig. 5.24). Repeat this measurement on both sides and compare the differences. According to a recent study, runners with reach differences greater than four centimeters are 2.5 times more likely to sustain an injury (45).

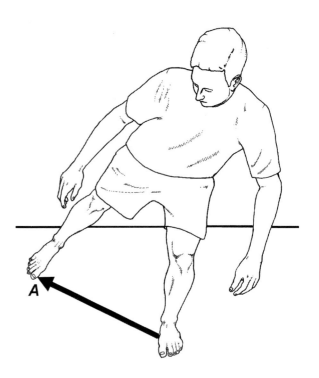

5.24. The star excursion balance test. Place a cloth tape measure on the floor angled 45° back. While standing on one foot, reach back as far as you can without touching the ground. Note the farthest distance you can reach on the tape measure without losing balance and compare right and left sides. You may need a friend to spot the contact point on the tape measure or you can place a small box on top of the tape and push it back while maintaining balance. Redrawn from Hertel (45).

The best way to improve your reach distance is to strengthen your knees and hips with the single-leg cone-touch exercise (Fig. 5.21, H). Once you feel stable, you can perform the cone-touches while standing on an unstable surface, such as *The AirEx Balance Pad*. An alternate way to improve your reach distance is to perform lunges on a Dynadisc (www.performbetter.com) (Fig. 5.25). To perform this exercise, place the Dynadisc close to you and do a small range of motion lunge. Until you are confident in your ability to balance, Dynadisc lunges should only be performed while standing near a wall or some stable structure that you can quickly take hold of if necessary. When you initially perform this

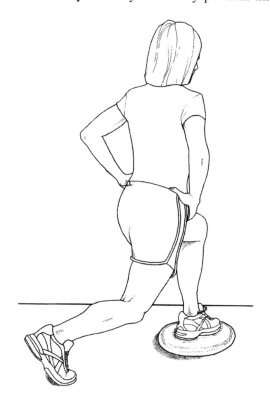

5.25. The Dynadisc lunge exercise.

exercise, even a slight problem with coordination will cause your knee and hip to shift rapidly back and forth. Because the supporting disk is unstable, you quickly learn to tense your hip abductors and rotators in order to stabilize yourself. Over time, this movement pattern becomes more natural and the improved muscle function allows you to run with a more stable running form. Recent research suggests that balancing on unstable surfaces allows you to rewire your movements without conscious thought, and the reflexive corrections are more permanently engrained (46).

The Forward Step-down Test

This is my favorite test to evaluate coordination in runners. Besides identifying very specific altered movement patterns, laboratory studies have proven that this test reliably predicts delayed recruitment times in the hip abductor muscles (47). Identifying delayed recruitment times is necessary for injury prevention because muscles need to tense rapidly in order to provide stability while running. Even a slight delay in when a muscle begins to contract will allow for potentially dangerous movement patterns. A delayed recruitment time is the muscular equivalent of closing the barn door after the horse is out: the muscle tenses too late to provide adequate protection.

To perform this test, stand on a 4-inch high platform positioned in front of a mirror and slowly step down. When the hip abductors are working properly, the pelvis, spine, and weight-bearing leg remain aligned while you are stepping down (Fig. 5.26, A). When the hip abductors are weak and uncoordinated, the step down occurs with the opposite hip dropping towards the floor excessively or with the weight-bearing knee rotating inward. The faulty form associated with a positive test often carries over into running: runners who step down with the recruitment patterns illustrated in figure 5.26 C often run with an uneven pelvis, while the movement pattern illustrated in D is almost always associated with an excessive inward collapse of the knee while running. **Regardless of how you compensate for your weak hips, the** faulty movement pattern should be corrected.

As with the star excursion balance test, **the first step in fixing the inappropriate movement is to strengthen the involved muscles.** The exercises illustrated in figure 5.27 target the hip abductors, extensors, and rotator muscles. Balance exercises on unstable surfaces are helpful to improve coordination (see figures 5.21, H and J) and the agility drills listed in figure 4.4 have been proven to improve muscular reaction times.

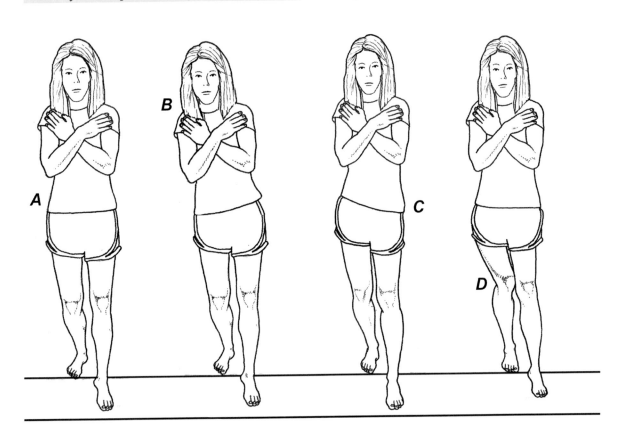

5.26. The Forward Step-down test. When the hip abductors are working properly, the leg, pelvis, and spine remain well-aligned while stepping off a 4-inch platform (**A**). When the core muscles are weak, the runner performs the step down by tilting his or her upper body to the side (**B**). When the hip abductors are weak, the runner lowers the opposite hip excessively (**C**). When the hip external rotators are weak, the knee twists in excessively (**D**).

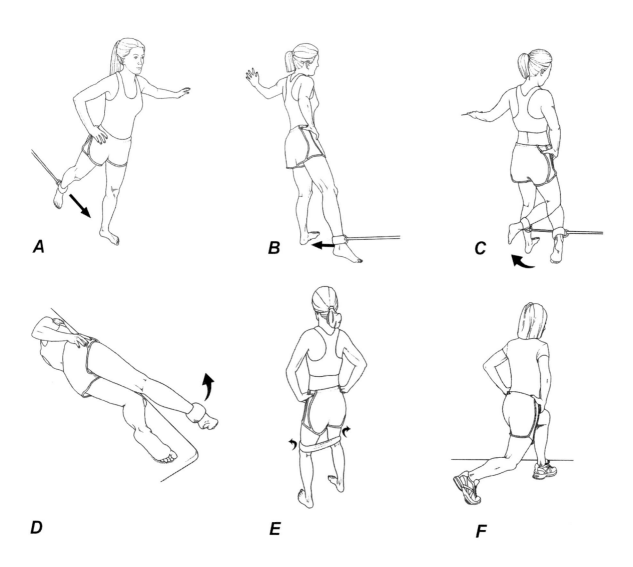

5.27. Hip and knee strengthening exercises. A and **B**) TheraBand exercises performed by rotating body in all 4 directions (hamstring pull and hip abduction not illustrated); **C**) Piriformis exercise; **D**) Sidelying gluteus medius exercise; **E**) Standing hip abduction/external rotation; **F**) Lunge.

Because strengthening exercises alone do not correct faulty movement patterns, it is important to modify form consciously, both while performing your exercises and while running. Focusing on form is essential for injury prevention because a strong muscle can still fire inappropriately. In order to change the movement pattern, you have to consciously rewire how the newly strengthened muscle fires. The inability of strengthening exercises alone to correct faulty running form was demonstrated in a recent study in which researchers measured strength and performed three-dimensional gait evaluations on 10 runners with excessive inward collapse of the knees (48). The runners were all prescribed specific strengthening exercises targeting the hip abductors and external rotator muscles. Six weeks later, the strength and gait evaluations were repeated and while hip strength increased by almost 50%, there was absolutely no change in the faulty running style. The runners' knees continued to collapse inward in spite of the significant strength gains. The inability of strengthening exercises to alter movement emphasizes an important point in rehabilitation: you can't just make a muscle stronger, you have to retrain the muscle to interact in synchrony with other muscles.

Gait Retraining: The Role of Visual Feedback

To correct faulty movement patterns, in addition to strength, balance, and agility training, runners need to incorporate specific gait retraining techniques. Although it may sound complicated, gait retraining can be as simple as running on a treadmill positioned in front of a mirror while deliberately modifying a faulty movement pattern. The most common glitch in running form that needs to be corrected is excessive inward twisting of the knees. While running, focus on keeping your knees moving straight back and forth with no inward rotation. By consciously focusing on improving a specific movement pattern, you can teach your muscles how to fire properly and the movement pattern is eventually memorized by your nervous system. In a thorough review of the literature evaluating the best ways to prevent knee injuries in athletes, the respected researcher Tim Hewett notes that injury prevention is best accomplished by coupling balance exercises with agility drills, strength training, and visual feedback (49). Dr. Hewett emphasizes that an important way to reduce the potential for injury is by recruiting the help of a knowledgeable friend who can inform you when your form begins to falter.

References

1. Sherry M, Best T. A comparison of 2 rehabilitation programs in the treatment of acute hamstring strains. *J Orthop Sports Phys Ther.* 2004;34:116.

2. DiGiovani C, Kuo R, Tejwani N, et al. Isolated gastrocnemius tightness. *J Bone Joint Surg.* 2002;(84A):962-971.

3. Nigg B, Cole G, Nachbauer W. Effects of arch height of the foot on angular motion of the lower extremities in running. *J Biomech.* 1993;26:909-916.

4. Gina Kolata. Close look at orthotics raises a welter of doubts. *The New York Times.* January 17, 2011.

5. Williams D, McClay I. Measurements used to characterize the foot and the medial longitudinal arch: reliability and validity. *Phys Ther.* 2000;80:864-871.

6. Williams D, McClay I, Hamill J. Arch structure and injury patterns in runners. *Clin Biomech.* 2001;16:341-347.

7. Nielsen R, Buist I, Parner E, et al. Foot pronation is not associated with increased injury risk in novice runners wearing a neutral shoe: a 1-year prospective cohort study. *Br J Sports Med.* Published online June 13, 2013 as 10.1136/bjsports-2013-092202.

8. Franklyn-Miller A, Wilson C, Bilzon J, McCrory P. Foot orthoses in the prevention of injury in initial military training : a randomized controlled trial. *Am J Sports Med.* 2011;39:30.

9. MacLean C, McClay I, Hamill J. Influence of custom foot orthotic intervention on lower extremity dynamics in healthy runners. *Clinical Biomech.* 2006;21,623-630.

10. Kogler G, Veer F, Solomonidis S, Paul J. The influence of medial and lateral placement of orthotic wedges on loading of the plantar aponeurosis. *J Bone Joint Surg Am.* 1999;81:1403-1413.

11. Verhagen E, van der Beek A, Twisk J, et al. The effect of proprioceptive balance board training for the prevention of ankle sprains. *Am J Sports Med.* 2004;32:1385-1393.

12. Tsai L, Yu B, Mercer V, Gross M. Comparison of different structural foot types for measures of standing postural control. *J Orthop Sports Phys Ther.* 2006;36:942-953.

13. Brantingham J, Adams K, Cooley J, et al. A single-blind pilot study to determine risk and association between navicular drop, calcaneal eversion, and low back pain. *J Manip Physiol Ther.* 2007;30:380-385.

14. Williams D, McClay I, Hamill J, Buchanan T. Lower extremity kinematic and kinetic differences in runners with high and low arches. *J Applied Biomech.* 2001;17:153-163.

15. Redmond A, Lumb P, Landorf K. The effect of cast and noncast foot orthoses on plantar pressures and force during gait. *J Am Podiatr Med Assoc.* 2000;90:441-449.

16. Landorf K, Keenan AM, Herbert R. The effectiveness of foot orthoses to treat plantar fasciitis: a randomized trial. *Arch Intern Med.* 2006;166:1305-1310.

17. Trivers R, Manning J, Thornhill R, et al. Jamaican symmetry project: long-term study of fluctuating asymmetry in rural Jamaican children. *Human Biology.* 1999;71:417-430.

18. Perttunen J, Antilla E Sodergard J et al. Gait asymmetry in patients with limb length discrepancy. *Scand J Med Sci Sports.* 2004;14:49-56.

19. Friberg O. Leg length asymmetry in stress fractures: a clinical and radiographic study. *J Sports Med Phys Fitness.* 1982;22:485-488.

20. Tallroth K, Ylikoski M, et al. Preoperative leg-length inequality and hip osteoarthritis: a radiographic study of 100 consecutive arthroplasty patients. *Skeletal Radiol.* 2005;34:136-139.

21. Wang Q, Whittle M, Cunningham et al. Fibula and its ligaments in load transmission and ankle joint stability. *Clin Orthop Related Research.* 1996;330:261-270.

22. Giles type L., Taylor J. The effect of postural scoliosis on lumbar apophyseal joints. *Scand J Rheumatol.* 1984;13:209-220.

23. Neely K, Wallmann H, Backus C. Validity of measuring leg length with tape measure compared to CT scan. *J Orthop Sports Phys Ther.* 2013;43: A113.

24 Malachy P, McHugh M, Connolly D, et al. The role of passive muscle stiffness in symptoms of exercise-induced muscle damage. *Am J Sports* Med. 1999;27:594.

25. Jones B, Knapik J. Physical training and exercise-related injuries: surveillance, research and injury prevention in military populations. *Sports Med.* 1999;27:111-125.

26. La Roche D, Connolly D. Effects of stretching on passive muscle tension and response to eccentric exercise. *Am J Sports Med.* 2006;34:1000-1007.

27. Kubo K, Kanehisa H, Kawakami Y, Fukunaga T. Influence of static stretching on viscoelastic properties of human tendon structures in vivo. *J Appl Physiol.* 2001;90:520-527.

28. Radwan A, Buonomo H, Tataevic E, et al. Evaluation of intrasubject difference in hamstring flexibility in patients with low back pain: an exploratory study. *J Orthop Sports Phys Ther.* 2013; 43:A85.

29. Taylor D, Dalton J, Seaber A, et al. Viscoelastic properties of muscle-tendon units-the biomechanical effects of stretching. *Am J Sports Med.* 1990;18:300-309.

30. Bandy WD, Irion JM, Briggler M. The effect of time and frequency of static stretching on flexibility of the hamstring muscles. *Phys Ther.* 1997;77:1090-1096.

31. Kubo K, Kanehisa H, Kawakami Y, Fukunaga T. Influence of static stretching on viscoelastic properties of human tendon structures in vivo. *J Appl Physiol.* 2001;90:520-527.

32. Griffiths R. Shortening of muscle fibers during stretch of the active cat medial gastrocnemius muscle: the role of tendon compliance. *J Physiol.* 1991;436:219-236.

33. Loghmani M, Warden S. Instrument-assisted cross fiber massage accelerates knee ligament healing. *J Orthop Sports Phys Ther.* 2009;39:506-514.

34. Hopper D, Deacon S, Das S, et al. Dynamic soft tissue mobilization increases hamstring flexibility in healthy male subjects. *Br J Sports Med.* 2005;39:594-598.

35. McGill S. Low Back Disorders: Evidence-Based Prevention and Rehabilitation. Champaign, IL: Human Kinetics Publishing 2002.

36. Turki O, Chaouachi D, Behm D et al. The effect of warm-ups incorporating different volumes of dynamic stretching on 10-and 20-M sprint performance in highly trained male athletes. *J Strength Cond.* 2012;26: 63-71.

37. Pereles D, Roth A, Thompson D. A large, randomized, prospective study of the impact of a pre-run stretch on the risk of injury on teenage and older runners. USATF Press Release 2012.

38. Fritz JM, Cleland JA, Childs JD. Subgrouping patients with low back pain: evolution of a classification approach to physical therapy. *J Orthop Sports Phys Ther.* 2007;37:290-302.

39. Chang A, Hayes K, et al. Hip abduction moments and protection against medial tibiofemoral osteoarthritis progression. *Arth Rheum.* 2005;52:3515-3519.

40. Rhea M, Alvar B, Burkett L, Ball S. A meta-analysis to determine the dose response for strength development. *Med Sci Sports Exerc.* 2003:456-464.

41. Delahunt E, Monaghan K, Caulfield B. Altered neuromuscular control and ankle joint kinematics during walking in subjects with functional instability of the ankle joint. *Am J Sports Med.* 2006;34:1970-1976.

42. McHugh M, Tyler T, Mirabella M, et al. The effectiveness of balance training intervention in reducing the incidence of noncontact ankle sprains in high school football players. *Am J Sports Med.* 2007;35:1289.

43. Matsusaka N, Yokoyama S, Tsurusaki T, et al. Effect of ankle disk training combined with tactile stimulation to the leg and foot on functional instability of the ankle. *Am J Sports Med.* 2001;29:25.

44. Nelson-Wong E, Flynn T, Callaghan J. Development of active hip abduction as a screening test for identifying occupational low back pain. *J Orthop Sports Phys Ther.* 2009;39:649.

45. Hertel J, Braham R, Hale S, Olmsted-Kramer L. Simplifying the star excursion balance test: analysis of subjects with and without chronic ankle instability. *J Orthop Sports Phys Ther.* 2006;36:131-137.

46. McNevin NH, Wulf G. Attentional focus on suprapostural tasks affects postural control. *Hum Mov Sci.* 2002;21:187-202.

47. Crossley K, Zhang W, Schache A, et al. Performance on the single-leg squat task indicates hip abductor muscle function. *Am J Sports Med.* 2011;39:866.

48. Noehren B, Scholz J, Davis I. The effect of real-time gait retraining on hip kinematics, pain and function in subjects with patellofemoral pain syndrome. *Br J Sports Med.* 2011;45:691-696.

49. Hewett T, Ford K, Myer G. Anterior cruciate ligament injuries in female athletes: part two, a meta-analysis of neuromuscular interventions aimed at injury prevention. *Am J Sports Med.* 2006;34:490.

50. Alfredson H, Pietila T, Jonsson P, et al. Heavy-load eccentric calf muscle training for the treatment of chronic Achilles tendinosis. *Am J Sp Med.* 1998;26:360-6.

51. Cummings G, Scholz J, Barnes K. The effect of imposed leg length difference on pelvic bone symmetry. *Spine.* 1993;18:368-373.

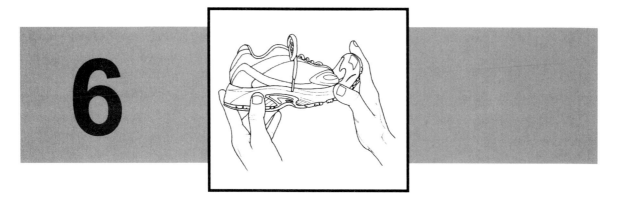

Chapter Six

SELECTING THE IDEAL RUNNING SHOE

Given the potential for lacerations, abrasions, and/or thermal injury, it seems odd that for almost all of our seven-million-year history as bipeds, we got around the planet barefoot. Although we perceive our feet as being delicate structures in need of protection, when barefoot from birth, the human foot is remarkably resilient. In a study comparing lifelong shod feet with the feet of people who have never worn shoes, researchers from Belgium confirm that the unshod forefoot is 16% wider than the shod forefoot (1). The increased width allows for improved distribution of pressure while walking and running. In their analysis of pressure centered beneath the forefoot in lifelong shod versus unshod individuals, the authors confirm that regular shoe use is associated with significantly more pressure being centered directly beneath the middle of the forefoot. When barefoot from birth, your toes become so strong

that they push down with more force, distributing pressure away from the center of the forefoot towards the tips of the toes. This is consistent with an analysis of skeletal remains dating back 100,000 years, confirming that people who are barefoot from birth get less forefoot arthritis because their strong toes distribute pressure more effectively (2). To enhance protection against perforation, the skin of an unshod foot becomes extremely tough and is remarkably similar to leather. These features allowed the feet of our earliest ancestors to effectively manage the stresses associated with moving around sub-Saharan Africa.

Surprisingly, our unshod feet could even handle the extremely cold temperatures and jagged mountainous terrain associated with traversing Eurasia, as evidence suggests that we did not begin routinely using protective footwear until 30,000 years ago. This means that for 80,000 years following our exodus from Africa, we crossed the Swiss and Italian Alps and quickly spread through the harsh climates of Europe and Asia without protective shoe wear.

The First Evidence of Shoe Use

Determining the exact date that we began routinely using shoes has been difficult, since the early shoes were made of leather, grass, and other biodegradable materials that left no fossil evidence. Although Neanderthals and *Homo erectus* were suspected of occasionally using insulated foot coverings, the first direct evidence of shoe use dates back to only 3,500 years ago (Fig. 6.1). While primitive sandals and moccasins discovered in Oregon and Missouri have been carbon-dated to 10,000 years ago, the actual time period that our ancestors first introduced protective shoe wear remains a mystery.

To get around the fact that ancient shoes rapidly decayed leaving no evidence of use, Trinkaus and Shang (3) decided to date the initiation of shoe wear by searching for changes in the shapes of the toes of our early ancestors. Because regular shoe use lessens strain on the toe muscles, the authors theorized that habitual shoe use would be associated with the sudden appearance of a thinning of the proximal phalanges (the bones at the base of our toes). By precisely measuring all aspects of toe shape and composition, the authors discovered a marked decrease in the robusticity of the toe bones during the late Pleistocene era, approximately 30,000 years ago (Fig. 6.2). Because there was no change in overall limb robusticity, the anatomical inference is that

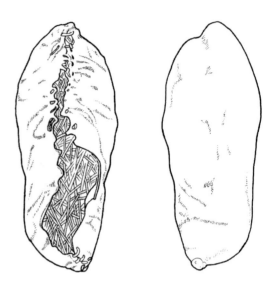

6.1. The earliest shoes resembled stitched leather bags.

shoe gear eventually resulted in the development of narrower toes. The authors state that because there is no evidence of a meaningful reduction in biomechanical loads placed on human lower limbs during the late Pleistocene era (e.g., reduced foraging distances), the logical conclusion is that the thinner toes could only have only resulted from the use of shoes. The authors evaluated numerous skeletal remains from different periods and concluded that based on the sudden reduction in toe diameter, the use of footwear was habitual sometime between 28,000 and 32,000 years ago.

The first shoes were most likely similar to the shoes discovered in the Armenian cave, in that they were simple leather bags partially filled with grass to insulate the foot from cold surfaces. Because shoe gear varied depending on the region,

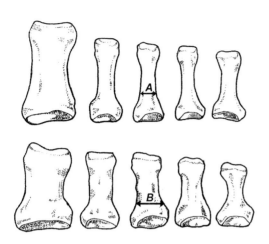

6.2. Compare the width of the toe bones from the early (bottom row) and late (top row) Pleistocene era. Trinkaus and Shang (3) claim that the decreased strain on the toes associated with regular shoe use produced bony remodeling with a gradual narrowing of the toe bones (compare **A** and **B**).

the earliest shoes worn in tropical environments were most likely similar to the 3,000-year-old sandals recently found in Israel. Once discovered, use of protective shoe wear quickly spread. The early Egyptians were believed to be the first civilization to create a rigid sandal, which was originally made from woven papyrus leaves molded in wet sand. Affluent citizens even decorated their sandals with expensive jewels.

While wealthy Greeks and Egyptians had separate shoes/sandals made for their right and left feet, the practice of wearing different shoes on each foot was short-lived and throughout the Dark and Middle Ages, shoes were made to be worn on either foot. Improvements in manufacturing techniques before the American Civil War changed that. By modifying a duplicating lathe used to mass produce wooden gunstocks, a Philadelphia shoemaker was able to manufacture mirror-image lasts that allowed for the production of separate shoes for each foot. (Lasts are three-dimensional foot models used for the manufacturing of shoes.) Using this new technology, the Union Army supplied over 500,000 soldiers with matching pairs of right and left leather shoes.

The First Athletic Shoes

Leather continued to be the most popular material used for making shoe gear until the late 1800s, when Charles Goodyear accidentally dropped rubber into heated sulfur creating vulcanized rubber. Prior to his serendipitous discovery, rubber was a relatively useless material because it melted at relatively low temperatures. The newfound resiliency of this material would have numerous applications, including the production of the first athletic shoe. Although alternate names for the new foot wear include tennis shoes, trainers and runners, the term sneaker became the most popular, and its origin can be traced back to an 1887 quote from The Boston Journal of Education (4): "It is only the harassed schoolmaster who can fully appreciate the pertinency of the name boys give to tennis shoes--sneakers." Apparently, the soft rubber soles allowed schoolchildren to sneak up quietly on unsuspecting teachers.

Spalding manufactured one of the earliest athletic shoes: the Converse All-Star. Used by athletes at Springfield College to play the newly invented game of basketball, the All-Star was immediately popular. Since their introduction in 1908, more that 70 million pairs of Converse have been sold worldwide. In 1916, the U.S. Rubber Company introduced Keds, an athletic shoe made with a flexible rubber bottom and canvas upper comparable to the Converse All-Star. The first orthopedic athletic shoe was developed by New Balance shortly before the Great Depression. New Balance continues to be the world's largest manufacturer of athletic shoes made with different widths. The German shoemaker Adi Dassler formed Adidas in the 1930's, while his brother Rudi formed Puma in the 1940's. Adidas was the more popular company and was the dominant manufacturer of sneakers until the 1960's, when Phil Knight and Bill Bowerman created Blue Ribbon Sports. Renamed Nike Inc. in 1978, after the Greek goddess of victory, this company has remained the world's largest producer of athletic shoes and sporting apparel for more than 40 years, with 2009 revenues exceeding $19 billion (5).

The design of the first sneaker manufactured specifically for running was simple: a thin rubber sole was covered with a canvas upper, providing nominal cushioning and protection. The next generation of running shoes were built with thicker midsoles possessing large medial and lateral heel flares designed to improve stability. Unfortunately, the lateral heel flares were quickly proven to increase the potential for injury as they provided the ground with a longer lever for pronating the rearfoot during heel strike (Fig. 6.3). To make matters worse, many of the early running shoes also had plastic reinforcements built around the heel counters, which also increased the initial velocity of pronation, making them more likely to cause injuries than prevent them.

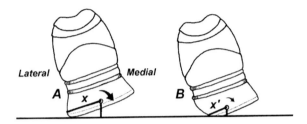

6.3. The first running shoes were made with large lateral flares (A), which provided ground-reactive forces with a longer lever arm (X) for pronating the rearfoot at heel strike. This feature produces significant increases in the initial range and velocity of pronation. Note that a midsole with a negative flare (**B**) provides ground-reactive forces with a shorter lever arm (**X'**) for pronating the rearfoot.

Modern Running Shoes

In contrast to the poorly built early models that were designed around a static model of foot function, modern running shoes are made with foam midsoles shaped with negative flares and toe springs that allow your feet to move more naturally (Fig. 6.4) The outsoles are made from synthetic rubber that effectively resist abrasion and improve traction while the uppers are made from an open mesh material that improves ventilation.

To accommodate different foot shapes, running shoes are manufactured with straight, semi-curved, or curved lasts (Fig. 6.5). To determine which shape is right for you, take a look at your footprint when you're leaving the shower: the angle between the forefoot and rearfoot in your running shoe should match the angle in your footprint.

The upper, in addition to providing space for the toes, also possesses an elaborate lacing

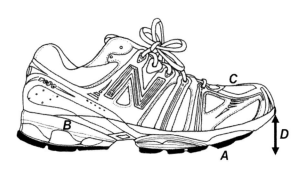

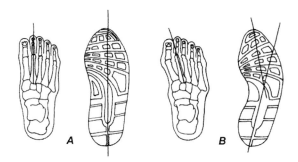

6.4. The modern running shoe. Although every manufacturer has proprietary differences in construction, the typical running shoe is manufactured with a carbon rubber outsole (**A**), a foam midsole (**B**), and a nylon mesh upper (**C**). Notice how the front of the running shoe angles upward (**D**). This upward angulation is referred to as the toe spring. The toe spring allows the foot to move in a more natural manner and reduces strain on the Achilles and plantar fascia.

6.5. Straight and curve-lasted sneakers. The last refers to the foot-shaped mold that a running shoe is constructed around. A straight-lasted shoe is well-aligned in the forefoot and rearfoot and is recommended for individuals with straight feet (**A**). Curve-lasted shoes are angled inward at the forefoot and are typically worn by high-arched runners whose forefeet tilt inward (**B**).

system that has the ability to modify motion (Fig. 6.6). In their detailed analysis of foot motion and pressure distribution in runners wearing the same type of running shoe tightened with different lacing techniques, Hagen and Hennig (6) demonstrate that the high 7-eyelet lacing pattern secured with moderate tension produced significant reductions in peak pressure beneath the heel and outer forefoot, along with reduced loading rates and pronation velocities. (Remember that it is the speed of pronation that correlates with injury, not the range.) The authors claim that because this technique creates a firm foot-to-shoe coupling that lessens loading rates and pronation velocity, the firm 7-eyelet lacing pattern may play an important role in reducing the risk of running injuries.

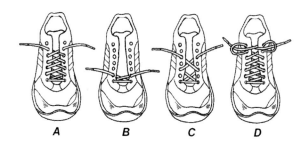

6.6. Variation in lacing patterns. (**A**) Standard 6-eyelet lacing, which may be tightened various degrees; (**B**) low lacing, in which only the first and second eyelets are tightened; (**C**) alternate lacing of the first, third, and fifth eyelets; (**D**) high lacing with all seven eyelets used. In this lacing pattern, the laces are pulled from outside the sixth to the seventh eyelet on the same side, and then to the resulting loop formed between the sixth and seventh eyelet on the opposite side. Redrawn from Hagen and Hennig (6).

The Midsole

Although lacing may favorably modify impact forces and the speed of initial pronation, the most functional portion of a running shoe is the midsole, which is made from a variety of foams and gels to enhance shock absorption and durability. Polyurethane (PU) is the most resilient of these materials. The typical polyurethane midsole can tolerate up to 700 miles of running before it needs to be replaced. Ethylene vinyl acetate (EVA) is another common midsole material. Despite its tendency to deform rapidly with repeated impacts, EVA is a popular material because it is inexpensive to produce and easy to mold. Other materials have recently been incorporated into midsoles, such as *Adiprene*, which is made from urethane polymers cured with special chemicals to enhance strength and resilience. The new midsole materials are lightweight, durable, and are designed to store and return a greater percentage of impact energy.

Because the vast majority of runners strike on the outside of their heels, running shoe manufacturers incorporate duo-density midsoles in which the outer portion of the midsole is significantly softer than the inner portion. The softer material on the outer side lessens impact forces and decreases the initial velocity of pronation, while the firmer material on the inner side provides protection against excessive pronation (Fig. 6.7). To protect the outer heel from breaking down, the outer sole is reinforced with high-density carbon rubber that effectively resists abrasion.

Another important attribute of a midsole is its overall stiffness. In my experience, the stiffness

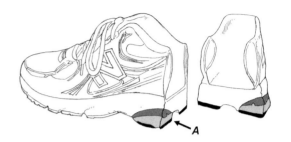

6.7. The duo-density midsole (A).

of a running shoe midsole is the most important factor associated with comfort and injury prevention. You can easily evaluate midsole stiffness by twisting it in several directions while grabbing the heel and forefoot. There is a surprising amount of variation in midsole stiffness as running shoes will bend with anywhere from 5 to 50 pounds of force (Fig. 6.8). The best running shoes will bend with very little pressure allowing your feet to move freely in all directions. Unfortunately, manufacturers rarely provide information regarding overall stiffness and it is important for runners to know the precise degree of running shoe stiffness that is most comfortable for them. High-arched runners tend to be drawn to extremely flexible midsoles while low-arched runners usually prefer a slightly stiffer midsole. The extremely stiff midsoles are almost universally uncomfortable.

The thickness of the midsole beneath the heel and forefoot is also important in injury prevention. Because thick midsoles absorb shock so well, you might think wearing the thickest possible midsole would reduce the potential for injury. Although logical, thick midsoles have never been proven to prevent injury. Research dating back more than 25 years has repeatedly shown that excessive

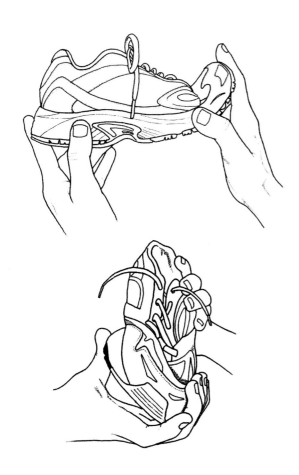

6.8. Evaluating midsole stiffness.

midsole cushioning interferes with your ability to balance by reducing sensory feedback from the bottom of your feet. In the 1980s, Robbins and Hanna performed a simple test by having subjects walk across a 4-inch balance beam while wearing running shoes manufactured with different midsole thicknesses. In every situation, subjects wearing the thicker midsoles had greater difficulty balancing. Robbins went on to publish several additional papers confirming that excessive midsole thickness increased the potential for injury (7-9).

Besides interfering with balance, an additional problem with excessive midsole cushioning is its weight. Because a running shoe is located so far from your hip, it has a very long lever arm to the hip musculature, forcing these muscles to work harder to accelerate and decelerate the added weight. Researchers have proven that increasing shoe weight by 100 grams (3.5 ounces) increases the metabolic cost of running by one percent. The increased exertion associated with accelerating and decelerating a heavy midsole can be extremely fatiguing when worn over the course of a marathon.

The Cost of Cushioning

Given the fact that excessive midsole cushioning can impair balance and reduce efficiency, it might seem that the best midsole would be no midsole at all. While this is often suggested by advocates of barefoot running, the complete removal of a midsole may result in chronic injury because some degree of midsole cushioning is necessary to protect the heel and forefoot fat pads from trauma. As pointed out previously, researchers from the Netherlands have proven that barefoot running results in a 60% deformation of the calcaneal fat pad, while running with running shoes with conventional midsoles results in only a 35% deformation of the fat pad (10). When repeated tens of thousands of times over your running career, the 60% deformation may permanently damage the walls of your protective fat pads, resulting in chronic heel and/or forefoot pain.

In addition to extending the lifespan of your heel pads, recent research proves the typical running shoe midsole is capable of storing and returning energy, offsetting the reduced efficiency associated with its added weight. By studying oxygen consumption while runners ran either barefoot or with running shoes having ten millimeter thick midsoles, researchers from the University of Colorado prove that despite the added midsole weight associated with wearing running shoes, there is no difference in efficiency when running barefoot or with heavy midsoles (11). The authors state "the positive effects of shoe cushioning counteract the negative effects of added mass, resulting in the metabolic cost for shod running approximately equal to that of barefoot running."

One of the more intriguing results of this study was that the researchers also evaluated efficiency as runners ran on specially designed treadmills fitted with 10 and 20 millimeters of midsole material attached directly to the treadmill belt. Interestingly, the treadmill fitted with 10 millimeter thick midsole material produced the same improvement in efficiency as the treadmill fitted with 20 millimeters of midsole material. Apparently, just as flexible running tracks providing 7 millimeters of deflection allow for the fastest running times (refer back to page 51), 10 millimeters of midsole cushioning provides the ideal amount of energy return with less weight and only a minimal reduction in sensory perception.

To provide adequate cushioning without reducing efficiency with unnecessary weight, most running shoes are made with a little more than 10 millimeters of midsole material placed beneath the forefoot. To protect the heel pad from trauma, the midsole beneath the rearfoot is usually 6 to 12 millimeters thicker (Fig. 6.9). Referred to as the heel-toe drop or heel-toe

6.9. The heel-toe drop. Most manufacturers provide information regarding the thickness of the midsole along its outer margins (**A** and **B**), not beneath the center the forefoot and rearfoot (**C** and **D**). Measurements of midsole thickness taken directly beneath the foot are much different. In the above New Balance 860, which was cut into pieces, the manufacturer's listed thickness of the rearfoot and forefoot as 38 and 26 mm, respectively. In reality, the measured thickness beneath the heel and forefoot is 22 mm and 11 mm, respectively, providing a heel-toe drop of 11 mm.

differential, the difference in midsole thickness between the rearfoot and midfoot is an important factor for both comfort and injury prevention. The majority of recreational runners who are heel strikers typically prefer about ten to twelve millimeters of heel-toe drop. More experienced heel strike runners favor the reduced weight associated with a six millimeter heel-toe differential. Conversely, fast runners who strike the ground with their midfoot do not need extra cushioning placed beneath the heel and prefer the reduced weight associated with a zero-drop midsole.

As with midsole stiffness and weight, the heel-toe differential is an important factor associated with improved comfort and you should experiment with different models until you find the midsole that feels best to you.

Arch Height and Running Shoe Prescription

Because runners with different arch heights are prone to different injuries, running shoe manufacturers have developed motion control, stability, and cushion running shoes that are specifically designed for low, neutral, and high-arched runners, respectively (Fig. 6.10). To control the excessive pronation present in low-arched individuals, motion control running shoes possess duo-density midsoles with additional midsole material placed

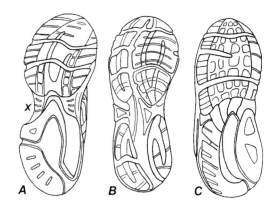

6.10. Bottom view of the 3 basic types of running shoes. Cushion running shoes (**A**) are made for individuals with high arches. They are slightly curved to match the shape of the typical high-arched foot and possess flexible midsoles with significantly less bulk in the midfoot region (**X**). The reduced midsole material in the midfoot gives the shoe an hourglass appearance when viewed from below. Stability sneakers (**B**) are made for individuals with neutral foot types. They are straighter and have slightly more midsole material reinforced beneath the arch. In contrast, motion control sneakers (**C**) are very straight and are strongly reinforced throughout the midfoot with extra-thick midsole material. Because of the additional midsole material, motion control sneakers are extremely stiff.

beneath the center of the arch. Motion control running shoes are also made with straight lasts to match the shape of the typical pronated foot.

On the other side of the spectrum, cushion running shoes are made for runners with high arches and are manufactured with a curve-lasted shape designed to fit the typical high-arched foot. The midsoles in cushion running shoes are significantly softer in order to improve shock absorption. To fit runners with neutral feet, stability running shoes are made with semi-curved lasts and only a moderate amount of midsole cushioning.

For the past 30 years, the prescription of motion control, stability, and cushion running shoes for runners with low, neutral, and high arches was believed to reduce injury rates and increase comfort. However, some recent research disputes this theory. In one of the largest studies done to date, Knapik et al. (12) divided 1,400 male and female Marine Corps recruits into two groups: an experimental group in which running shoe recommendation was based on arch height, and a control group that wore neutral stability running shoes regardless of arch height. After completing an intensive 12-week training regimen, the authors concluded that prescribing running shoes according to arch height was not necessary, since there was no difference in injury rates between the two groups.

In another study evaluating the value of prescribing running shoes according to arch height, Ryan et al. (13) categorized 81 female runners as supinators, neutral, or pronators, and then randomly assigned them to wear neutral, stability, or motion control running shoes. Again, the authors concluded that there was no correlation between foot type, running shoe use, and the frequency of reported pain. One of the more interesting findings of this research was that the individuals classified as pronators reported greater levels of pain when wearing the motion control running shoes. This is consistent with the hypothesis that excessive midsole thickness may dampen sensory input, amplifying the potential for injury.

Supporting the belief that running shoe prescription should continue to be based on arch height, several high-quality laboratory studies have shown that the different types of running shoes actually do what they are supposed to do: motion control running shoes have been proven to limit pronation, and cushion running shoes have been proven to improve shock absorption. To prove this, researchers measured arch height and evaluated impact forces, tibial accelerations, and the range and speed of pronation after high and low-arched runners were randomly assigned to wear cushioned and motion control running shoes (14). The detailed analysis confirmed that motion control running shoes do, in fact, control rearfoot motion better than cushioned running shoes, and cushioned running shoes attenuate shock better than motion control running shoes.

In another study evaluating the effect of motion control versus neutral shoes on over-pronators, Cheung and Ng (15) used electrical devices to measure muscle activity as subjects ran ten kilometers. The authors noted that when wearing motion control shoes, runners who pronated excessively reported reduced muscular fatigue in the front and sides of their legs. In a separate study of excessive supinators, Wegener et al. (16) evaluated pressure along the bottom of the foot when high-arched individuals wore

either cushioned running shoes or a control shoe. The authors confirmed that the cushioned running shoes more effectively distributed pressure and were perceived as being more comfortable than the control running shoe. The results of the previously listed studies suggest that the practice of prescribing running shoes based on arch height has merit, particularly for people on the far ends of the arch height spectrum.

Selecting the Perfect Running Shoe

When you look at all of the research evaluating running shoe prescription and injury, it becomes clear that the most important factors to consider when selecting a running shoe is that it fits your foot perfectly (both width, length, and shape) and the midsole is comfortable. The size is determined by matching the widest part of the forefoot to the widest part of the toe box, and there should be a few millimeters of space between the tip of the longest toe and the end of the running shoe. Also, the shoe's upper should comfortably fit the shape of your foot.

If you have unusually wide or narrow feet, consider testing the fit of a few New Balance running shoes. This company has been making athletic shoes for people with different widths since the 1920s. You should also make sure the last matches your foot shape by comparing your footprints to the bottom of the running shoe.

The midsole should also be selected in part by your running style: heel strikers often need additional cushioning beneath the rearfoot, while midfoot strikers typically prefer zero-drop midsoles. In almost all situations, even extremely flat-footed runners should think twice about wearing heavy motion control running shoes because they may dampen sensory input from the foot and their extreme stiffness often results in ankle and/or knee injuries. In order to identify the midsole that is right for you, experiment with a range of running shoes until you find just the right thickness, stiffness, and downward slope.

Though rarely discussed, one of the most important qualities to look for in a running shoe is that the heel counter securely stabilizes the rearfoot. Besides supporting the sides of the fat pad (which prevents the pad from bottoming out), a well-formed heel counter has the ability to lessen impact forces, decrease activity in the quadriceps and calf musculature, and improve efficiency (17). For a brief period, Reebok manufactured a running shoe with an air pump in the tongue that inflated the sides of the heel counter. Because it took too long to inflate with each run, the running shoe was modified so it could be filled with a replaceable gas chamber. Possibly because of the expense of replacing the chamber or the hassles of filling the heel counter, the customizable heel counter was short-lived. Nonetheless, a tight fitting heel counter continues to be one of the most important and underrated aspects for finding the right running shoe. Modern running shoes are made with lined foam heel collars to stabilize and protect the heel. Because each running shoe has a slightly different heel collar, you will have to try on a few different models to find the specific running shoe that fits your heel the best.

Minimalist Shoes

Another option available to runners is to try wearing **minimalist shoes**. Inspired in part by the popular book *Born To Run* by Christopher McDougal, these athletic shoes have been specifically designed to mimic barefoot running (Fig. 6.11). According to the paleoanthropologist Daniel Lieberman, to protect their heels from injury, barefoot runners naturally switch to a more forward contact point, which theoretically improves the storage and return of energy and more effectively dampens impact forces (18).

While the possibility of improved energy return and dampened impact forces sounds appealing, it is necessary that runners wearing minimalist shoes actually switch to the more forward contact point in order to obtain these benefits. Unfortunately, this is not always the case. In a recent study of runners transitioning to minimalist shoe wear, 35% of the runners

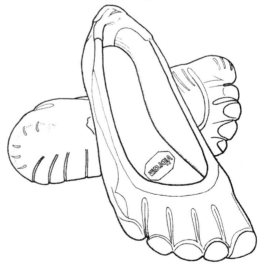

6.11. The Vibram 5-finger running shoe is designed to mimic barefoot activity.

continued to make ground contact with their heels in spite of wearing the minimalist shoes for more than two years (19). Although runners with midfoot strike patterns may benefit from minimalist shoes, slow runners who continue to strike the ground with their heels are more likely to be injured, since vertical loading rates beneath the heel are nearly 40% higher when rearfoot striking with a minimalist shoe (20). Furthermore, research showing that a 10 millimeter thick midsole does not reduce efficiency because it improves the storage and return of energy suggests that even fast runners can afford the protection provided by conventional midsoles (11).

Another problem with minimalist shoe wear is that you are more likely to be injured while breaking them in. In a recent study published in *Medicine and Science in Sports and Exercise,* researchers from Brigham Young University noted that 10 out of 19 runners transitioning into minimalist shoes became injured, compared to only one out of 17 runners in the control group wearing conventional running shoes (21). In my experience, runners with narrow forefeet are much more likely to be injured while wearing minimalist shoes. This is especially true for runners with low arches and/or tight calves.

The final factor to consider is that "barefoot running" with minimalist shoes produces a running style that is very different from true barefoot running. As pointed out by Altman and Davis (22), running while actually barefoot causes you to strike the ground with your midfoot nearly horizontal. In contrast, runners wearing minimalist shoes often strike the ground with their ankles pointing down more, which increases activity in the soleus muscle and greatly increases bending strains in the tibia (potentially increasing the likelihood of a tibial stress fracture). Apparently, in order to get the benefits of barefoot running, you really have to be barefoot.

Despite its questionable value for reducing injuries and improving efficiency, minimalist running is an effective way to strengthen the muscles of the arch. Running short distances with minimalist shoes is also an excellent gait retraining tool, because these shoes force you to shorten your stride and increase your cadence. Although almost always associated with reduced running speed, these simple gait alterations markedly lessen impact forces, making them useful for treating a wide range of running-related injuries.

When worn recreationally while walking or slow jogging, minimalist shoes favorably stimulate muscles of the arch without overloading them, often resulting in an increased arch height when worn regularly. After an appropriate break-in period, runners should consider doing speed workouts on grass or soft dirt as a way to increase tone in their arch muscles. In spite of their questionable value for improving performance, minimalist shoes are an excellent addition to your training routine. While I wouldn't recommend them for long distance training, the improved strength gains associated with recreational use makes minimalist shoes well worth the initial investment.

References

1. D'Aout K, Pataky T, DeClerq D, Aerts P. The effects of habitual footwear use: foot shape and function in native barefoot walkers. *Footwear Science.* 2009;1(2):81–94.
2. Zipfel B, Berger L. Shod versus unshod: the emergence of forefoot pathology in modern humans? *Foot.* 2007;17:205-213.
3. Trinkaus E, Shang H. Anatomical evidence for the antiquity of human footwear: Tianyuan and Sunghir. *J Archeol Sci.* 2008;35:1928-1933.
4. Crisp Sayings. New York Times, September 2, 1887.
5. Nike 2009 10-K, Item 6, page 21.
6. Hagen M, Hennig E, Effects of different shoe-lacing patterns on the biomechanics of running shoes. *J Sports Sci.* 2008;Dec 24:1-9.
7. Robbins SE, Gouw GJ, Hanna AM. Running-related injury prevention through innate impact-moderating behavior. *Med Sci Sports Exerc.* 1989;21:130-139.
8. Robbins S, Hanna A. Running-related injury prevention through barefoot adaptation. *Med Sci Sports Exerc.* 1987;Vol.19:148-156.
9. Robbins S, Waked E. Balance and vertical impact in sport: role of shoe sole materials. *Arch Phys Med Rehab.* 1997;78(5):463-7.
10. DeClercq D, Aerts P, Kunnen M. The mechanical behavior characteristics of the human heel pad during foot strike in running: an in vivo cineradiographic study. *J Biomech.* 1994;27:1213–1222.
11. Tung K, Franz J, Kram R. A test of the metabolic cost of cushioning hypothesis in barefoot and shod running. American Society of Biomechanics Annual Meeting. Gainesville, FL. August 2012.
12. Knapik J, Trone D, Swedler D, et al. Injury reduction effectiveness of assigning running shoes based on plantar shaped in Marine Corps basic training. *Am J Sports Med.* 2010;38:1759-1767.
13. Ryan M, Valiant G, McDonald K, Taunton J. The effect of three different levels of footwear stability on pain outcomes in women runners: a randomized control trial. *Br J Sports Med,* published online June 27, 2010.
14. Butler R, Davis I, Hamill J. Interaction of arch type and footwear on running mechanics. *Am J Sports Med.* 2006;34:1998.
15. Cheung R, Ng G. Motion control shoe delays fatigue of shank muscles in runners with overpronating feet. *Am J Sports Med.* 2010;38:486.
16. Wegener C, Burns J, Penkala S. Neutral-cushioned running shoes on plantar pressure loading and comfort in athletes with cavus feet: a crossover randomized controlled trial. *Am J Sports Med.* 2008;36:2139.
17. Jorgenson J. Body in heel-strike running: the effect of a firm heel counter. *Am J Sports Med.* 1990;18:177.
18. Lieberman D, Venkadesan M, Werbel W, et al. Foot strike patterns and collision forces in habitually barefoot versus shod runners. *Nature.* 2010;463:Jan 28.
19. McCarthy C, et al. Like barefoot, only better. ACE Certified News; September 2011:8-12.
20. Goss D, Lewek M, Yu B, Gross M. Accuracy of self-reported foot strike patterns and loading rates associated with traditional and minimalist running shoes. American Society of Biomechanics Annual Meeting. Gainesville, FL. August 2012.
21. Ridge S, Johnson A, Mitchell U, et al. Foot bone marrow edema after 10-week transition to minimalist running shoes. *Med Sci Sports & Exerc,* 2013. Publishished Ahead of Print. DOI: 10.1249/MSS.0b013e3182874769
22. Altman A, Davis D. Comparison of tibial strains and strain rates and barefoot and shod running. Presentation at American Society of Biomechanics August 18, 2012.

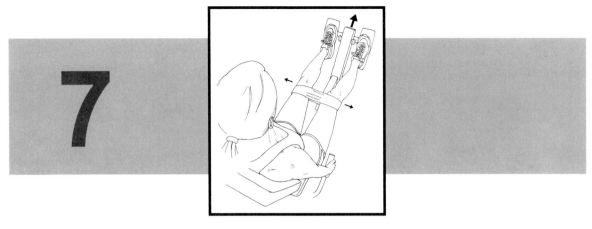

Chapter Seven

TREATMENT PROTOCOLS

In spite of the fact that our bodies are remarkably well designed to handle the forces associated with recreational running, nearly 50 percent of runners are injured each year. After reviewing the literature to determine factors responsible for running injuries, van Mechelen et al. (1) conclude that up to 75 percent of all running injuries are the result of overtraining. This finding is consistent with several studies showing the potential for injury dramatically increases when you run more than 35-40 miles per week (2,3). This number makes perfect sense considering our ancient ancestors had foraging distances of only 4-10 miles per day, and most of that distance was covered while walking.

Because we were not designed for running long distances, the best way to prevent injury is to run less than 35-40 miles per week. Of course, this is not always possible because in order to run faster, many recreational athletes run more

than 60 miles per week and it is common for professional runners to run between 100 and 130 miles per week. Unfortunately, regularly running high mileage can have a detrimental effect on our musculoskeletal system, as an MRI study of runners' knees performed before and after a marathon revealed significant cartilage breakdown (4). The authors note that because the changes in the knee cartilage were present even after three months of reduced activity, the runners were at higher risk for arthritis. This may explain research confirming that although moderate exercise is not associated with the development of knee arthritis, elite athletes are more likely to develop arthritis as they get older (5).

Because running long distances is hard on our bodies, experts at Furman University (6) have developed a training approach that allows you to train for full and/or half marathons without having to run too many miles. By utilizing cross training techniques such as swimming and biking, these authors have developed specific training schedules based on your running goals and overall fitness. When you consider that near- ly 90% of first-time marathon runners become injured (3), a training routine that minimizes weekly mileage is the best way to get you to the starting line of a marathon. Obviously, faster runners have no choice but to train by running long distances and to avoid potential injuries, they have to stay strong and coordinated. High mileage runners also have to develop a running form that allows them to efficiently absorb high impact forces without overly stressing their joints.

Regardless of your weekly mileage, if you have the misfortune of becoming injured, it is important to identify and fix the specific prob- lems with strength, flexibility, coordination, and/ or bony alignment that might be responsible for producing the injury. Identifying the cause is essential, since once injured, reinjury rates among runners can be as high as 70% (1). This is consistent with research confirming the best predictor of future injury is prior injury (2,7). To help you recover and get you back to running, the following section reviews home treatment protocols for some of the more common run- ning-related injuries. Just to be safe, prior to ini- tiating any home program, consider setting up an appointment with a sports specialist familiar with treating running injuries to make sure you have the correct diagnosis. You should also consider scheduling a few sessions with an experienced trainer to have your form evaluated while you're performing your stretches and/or exercises.

Achilles Tendinitis

Despite its broad width and significant length, runners injure their Achilles tendons with surprising regularity. In a recent study of 69 military cadets participating in a six-week basic training program (which included distance running), 10 of the 69 trainees suffered an Achil- les tendon overuse injury (8). The prevalence of this injury is easy to understand when you consider the tremendous strain runners place on this tendon; e.g., during the push off phase of running, the Achilles tendon is exposed to a force of seven times body weight. This is close to the maximum strain the tendon can tolerate without rupturing. Also, when you couple the high strain forces with the fact that the Achilles tendon significantly weakens as we get older, it is easy to see why this tendon is injured so frequently.

Anatomically, the Achilles tendon represents the conjoined tendons of the gastrocnemius and soleus muscles. Approximately 5 inches above the Achilles attachment to the back of the heel, the tendons from gastrocnemius and soleus unite to form a single thick Achilles tendon (Fig. 7.1). These conjoined tendons are wrapped by a single layer of cells called the paratenon. This sheath- like envelope is rich in blood vessels necessary to nourish the tendon. The tendon itself is made primarily from two types of connective tissue known as type 1 and type 3 collagen. In a healthy Achilles tendon, 95 percent of the collagen is made from type 1 collagen, which is stronger and more flexible than type 3. It is the strong cross-links and parallel arrangement of the type 1 collagen fibers that gives the Achilles tendon its strength.

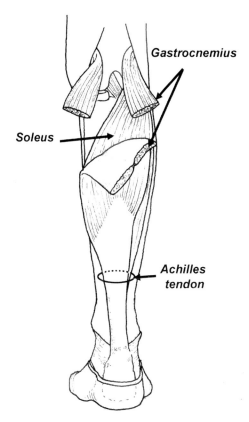

Gastrocnemius

Soleus

Achilles
tendon

7.1. The Achilles tendon represents the combined tendons from the gastrocnemius and soleus muscles.

Unlike the vast majority of tendons in the body, the Achilles tendon is unique in that at about the point where the gastrocnemius and soleus muscles unite, the tendon suddenly begins to twist, rotating a full 90 degrees before it attaches to the back of the heel. As mentioned in Chapter 3, this extreme twisting significantly improves efficiency while running because it allows the tendon to function like a spring, absorbing energy during the early phases of the gait cycle and returning it in the form of elastic recoil during the propulsive period.

Despite its clever design and significant strength, the extreme forces it is exposed to cause the Achilles tendon to break down all too frequently. Depending on the location of the damage, Achilles tendon overuse injuries are divided into several categories: insertional tendinitis, paratenonitis, and non-insertional tendinosis.

As the name implies, insertional tendinitis refers to inflammation at the attachment point of the Achilles on the heel. This type of Achilles injury typically occurs in high arched, inflexible individuals, particularly if they possess what is known as a Haglund's deformity, a bony prominence near the Achilles attachment on the heel. Because a bursa is present near the Achilles attachment (bursae are small sacs that contain lubricants that lessen shearing of the tendon against the bone), it is very common to have an insertional tendinitis with a bursitis (Fig. 7.2).

Until recently, the perceived mechanism for the development of insertional tendinitis was pretty straightforward: excessive running causes the Achilles tendon to break down on the back portion of the Achilles attachment, where pulling forces are the greatest. While this makes perfect sense, recent research has shown that just the opposite is true: the Achilles tendon almost always breaks down in the forward section of the tendon, where pulling forces are the lowest (9) (Fig. 7.3). By placing strain gauges inside different sections of the Achilles tendons and then loading the tendons with the ankle positioned in a variety of angles, researchers from the University of North Carolina discovered that the back portion of the Achilles tendon is exposed to far greater amounts of strain (particularly when the ankle was moved upward) while the forward section of the tendon, which is the section most frequently damaged with insertional tendinitis, was exposed to very low loads. The authors suggest that the lack of stress on the forward aspect of the Achilles tendon (which they referred to as a tension shielding effect) may cause that section to weaken and eventually fail. As a result, the treatment of an Achilles insertional tendinitis should be to strengthen the forward-most aspect of the tendon. This can be accomplished by performing a series of eccentric load exercises through a partial range of motion (Fig. 7.4). It is particularly important to exercise the Achilles tendon with the ankle maximally plantarflexed (i.e., standing way up on tiptoes), because this position places greater amounts of strain on the more frequently damaged forward portion of the tendon.

Runners with high arches are especially prone to insertional Achilles injuries and they often respond very well to lateral heel wedges.

These wedges, which are pasted to the outer portion of an insole, are used to distribute pressure away from the outer aspect of the tendon. Conventional heel lifts are always a consideration, but be careful, they may feel good at first but the calf muscles quickly adapt to their shortened positions and the beneficial effect of the heel lift is lost. Heel lifts also increase stress on the sesamoid bones and the plantar fascia, and should therefore be used for no more than a few weeks.

Rather than accommodating tight calves with heel lifts, a better approach is to lengthen the calves with gentle stretches. This can be accomplished with both straight and bent knee stretches to stretch the gastrocnemius and soleus muscles, respectively. Because aggressive stretching can damage the insertion, the stretches should be performed with mild tension only and held for less than 20 seconds. Performing 10 stretches throughout the day is usually enough to improve ankle flexibility. If calf inflexibility

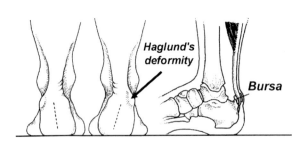

7.2. Insertional Achilles tendinitis injuries are frequently associated with a bony prominence called a Haglund's deformity. Because of chronic stress at the Achilles attachment point, an inflamed bursa often forms between the Achilles tendon and the heel.

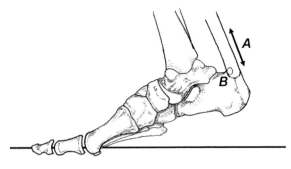

7.3. Location of Achilles insertional injuries. Tension in the Achilles tendon during pushoff places greater strain on the back of the Achilles tendon (**A**). Paradoxically, almost all insertional Achilles tendon injuries occur in the forward section of the Achilles tendon (**B**).

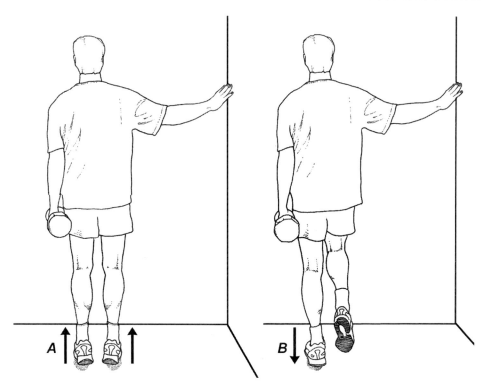

7.4. Insertional Achilles tendinitis exercise. Standing on a level surface while holding a weight with one hand and balancing against the wall with the other, raise both heels as high as you can (**A**) and then slowly lower yourself on just the injured leg (**B**). Three sets of 15 repetitions are performed daily on both the injured and uninjured side. Use enough weight to produce fatigue.

is extreme and does not respond to stretching, a night brace should be considered (Fig. 7.5). These braces, which are typically used to treat plantar fasciitis, are a very effective way to lengthen the gastrocnemius and soleus muscles.

The next type of Achilles tendon overuse injury is paratenonitis. This injury, which is very common in runners, represents an inflammatory reaction in the outer sheath of cells surrounding the tendon. Over-pronators are particularly prone to this injury because rapid pronation creates a whip-like action that can damage the tendon sheath (particularly the inner side). The first

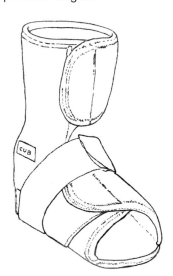

7.5. Night brace.

sign of the injury is a palpable lump that forms about two inches above the Achilles attachment. This mass represents localized thickening in response to microtrauma. If running is continued, the size of the lump increases and it eventually becomes so painful that running is no longer possible. Treatment for Achilles paratenonitis is to immediately reduce the swelling with frequent ice packs. If you're flat-footed, you might want to consider trying orthotics (start with over-the-counter models). Night braces are also effective with paratenonitis because tendons immobilized in a lengthened position heal more quickly.

If caught in time and the problem is corrected, Achilles paratenonitis is no big deal. However, if untreated, this injury can turn into a classic Achilles non-insertional tendinosis. This injury involves degeneration of the tendon approximately 1-2 inches above the attachment on the heel. Because this section of the tendon has such a poor blood supply, it is prone to injury and tends to heal very slowly.

Unlike insertional tendinitis and paratenonitis, non-insertional tendinosis represents a degenerative noninflammatory condition (i.e., the suffix *osis* refers to wear and tear, while *itis* refers to inflammation). In response to the repeated trauma associated with running through the injury, specialized repair cells called fibroblasts infiltrate the tendon, where, in an attempt to heal the injured regions, they begin to synthesize collagen. In the early stages of tendon healing, the fibroblasts manufacture almost exclusively type 3 collagen, which is relatively weak and inflexible compared to the type 1 collagen found in healthy tendons. If everything goes right, as

healing progresses, greater numbers of fibroblasts appear and collagen production shifts from type 3 to type 1. Unfortunately, many runners don't give the tendon adequate time to remodel (which can take up to 6 months) and a series of small partial ruptures begin to occur that can paradoxically act to lengthen the tendon, resulting in an increased range of upward motion at the ankle. At this point, pain is significant and the runner is usually forced to stop running altogether.

Various factors may predispose to the development of non-insertional tendinosis. In the previously mentioned study of military recruits, the recruits developing Achilles injuries were overly flexible and had weak calves (8). It is likely that these two factors create a whipping action that strains the Achilles tendons.

The good news about non-insertional tendinosis is that there is an exercise intervention that has excellent success, even with some of the worst injuries. Referred to as heavy load eccentric exercises, this treatment protocol involves wearing a weighted backpack while standing on the edge of a stair with your heels hanging off the stair (Fig. 7.6). Using both legs, you raise your heels as high as possible and then remove the uninjured leg from the stair. The injured leg is then gradually lowered through a full range of motion. The uninjured leg is then placed back on the stairway and both legs are again used to raise the heels as high as possible. Three sets of 15 repetitions are performed twice a day with the knees both straight and bent. In a 12-week study of 15 recreational runners with chronic Achilles non-insertional tendinosis, Swedish researchers had a 100 percent success rate at treating this difficult injury (10). The 100 percent success rate was impressive given the fact that these were older athletes (average age 45) that had symptoms for almost two years and had failed with every prior treatment protocol (e.g., nonsteroidal anti-inflammatory drugs, orthotics, physical therapy).

Non-insertional Achilles injuries also respond very well to the tibialis posterior strengthening exercise illustrated in figure 7.7. In a recent study comparing three-dimensional motion between runners with and without Achilles tendinopathy, researchers from East Carolina University determined that compared to controls, runners with Achilles tendinopathy failed to rotate their legs outward during the pushoff phase (11). The authors theorized that tibialis posterior weakness forced the leg to twist in excessively, which in turn increased strain on the Achilles tendon. After reading this article, I began adding tibialis

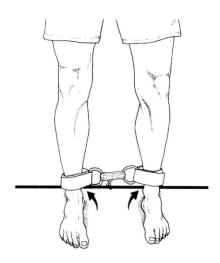

7.7. Closed-chain tibialis posterior exercise. By wrapping a TheraBand between two ankle straps (which can be purchased at www.perform-better.com), this exercise is performed by alternately raising and lowering your arches against resistance provided by the TheraBand. Three sets of 25 repetitions performed daily is usually enough to strengthen tibialis posterior.

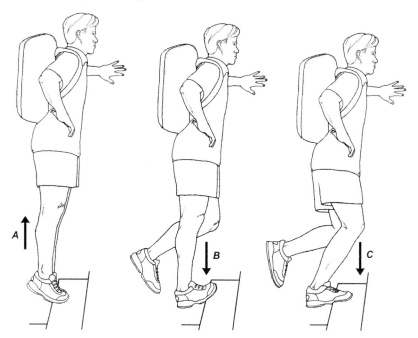

7.6. Heavy load eccentric Achilles exercise. Redrawn from Alfredson (10).

posterior exercises to the standard protocols for managing Achilles tendinitis and noticed reduced recovery times and better long-term outcomes.

In addition to strengthening exercises, an alternate method for improving Achilles function is deep tissue massage. The theory is that aggressive massage breaks down the weaker type 3 collagen fibers and increases circulation so healing can occur. To test this theory, researchers from the Biomechanics Lab at Ball State University (12) surgically damaged the Achilles tendons in a group of rats. In one group, an aggressive deep tissue massage was performed for three minutes on the 21st, 25th, 29th and 33rd day post injury. Another group served as a control. One week later, both groups of rats had their tendons evaluated with electron microscopy. Not surprisingly, the tendons receiving deep tissue massage showed increased fibroblast proliferation, which would create an environment favoring tendon repair.

A more high-tech method of breaking down scar tissue involves extracorporeal shock wave therapy. This technique involves use of costly machinery that blasts the Achilles with high frequency sonic vibrations. Recent research has shown comparable outcomes between shock wave therapy and heavy load eccentric exercises in the treatment of non-insertional Achilles tendinosis (13). As a result, shock wave therapy is typically used only after conventional methods have failed.

Regardless of whether the Achilles injury is insertional or non-insertional, a great method for lessening stress on the Achilles tendon is with flexor digitorum longus exercises. This muscle, which originates along the back of the leg and attaches to the tips of the toes, lies deep to the

Achilles and works synergistically with the soleus muscle to decelerate the forward motion of the leg before the heel leaves the ground during propulsion. Contraction of the flexor digitorum longus muscle while running significantly lessens strain on the Achilles tendon because it decelerates elongation of the tendon. The exercises to strengthen this muscle are simple to perform and require use of a small piece of TheraBand (Fig. 7.8). I recommend three sets of 40 repetitions performed daily.

It is also important that the runner forcefully curl the toes downward into the insole during

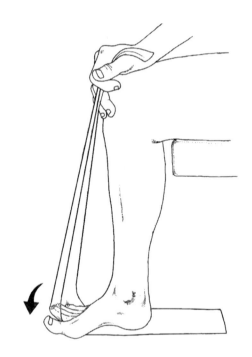

7.8. Flexor digitorum longus home exercise. Place a flat piece of TheraBand on the floor beneath your foot. Stabilize it with the heel and forefoot and pull the opposite end of the TheraBand to your knee, thereby lifting your toes. While maintaining tension on the TheraBand, force the toes downward (**arrow**).

the push off phase of the running cycle. This naturally strengthens the flexor digitorum longus muscle and reduces strain on the Achilles tendon. It's easy to see if you have weakness in this muscle by looking at the insole of your running shoe. Normally, when the flexor digitorum muscle is strong you will see well-defined indents beneath the tips of the second through fifth toes, whereas a weak flexor digitorum produces no marks beneath the toes and shows signs of excessive wear in the center of the forefoot only.

It's important to emphasize that runners with Achilles injuries should almost always avoid cortisone injections because they weaken the tendon by shifting the production of collagen from type 1 to type 3. In a study published in *The Journal of Bone and Joint Surgery* (14), cortisone was shown to lower the stress necessary to rupture the Achilles tendon and was particularly dangerous when done on both sides, because it produced a systemic effect that further weakened the tendon.

An overview of the management of Achilles tendon disorders can be summarized as follows: warm up slowly by running at least one minute per mile slower than your usual pace for the first mile and try to remain on flat surfaces. If you are a mid or a forefoot striker, consider switching to a rearfoot strike since this reduces strain in the Achilles tendon during initial contact. Because they increase strain in the Achilles by effectively lengthening the foot, runners with Achilles injuries should avoid wearing heavy motion control running shoes. In my experience, runners with Achilles injuries prefer neutral stability running shoes with duo-density midsoles, negative lateral midsole flares, and toe springs (refer back to

figure 6.4). Because they encourage a forward contact point, minimalist shoes and racing flats should be avoided. Lastly, if you have a tendency to be stiff, spend extra time stretching and if you're overly flexible, you should consider performing eccentric load exercises preventively. To evaluate strength, try doing 25 heel raises on each leg to see if you fatigue quicker on one side. If one leg is weaker, fix the strength asymmetry with the exercise illustrated in figure 7.6.

Sesamoiditis

The sesamoids are the two sesame seed-shaped bones located beneath the first metatarsal head. Situated inside the tendons of the flexor hallucis brevis muscle, the sesamoids are extremely important while running because they increase the mechanical advantage afforded to the flexor hallucis brevis muscle, greatly improving this muscle's ability to generate force. Because generating force beneath the big toe has been proven to lessen pressure beneath the central forefoot by as much as 30%, properly functioning sesamoids are necessary to prevent a wide range of forefoot injuries, including metatarsal stress fractures and interdigital neuromas.

Runners frequently injure their sesamoid bones because the sesamoids are located in a primary weight-bearing area and are subjected to tremendous forces during the pushoff phase while running. Runners with high arches are especially prone to sesamoiditis, because high arches cause an excessive amount of force to be centered beneath their inner forefeet (Fig. 7.9). The initial symptom associated with sesamoiditis is a "throbbing pain" located directly beneath the ball of the foot. Treatment for sesamoid injuries is to reduce pressure by incorporating a sub-one balance beneath the first metatarsal head (Fig. 7.10). This balance can be made at home by cutting a 1/8" thick piece of felt into a J-shaped balance and attaching it directly beneath the insole of the running shoe. If you don't feel like making one, pre-made sub-one balances can be purchased online and they are frequently referred to as dancer's pads.

Less often, runners with low arches injure their sesamoids. The most common mechanism for injury is that excessive pronation drives the inner forefoot into the ground with greater force, contusing the inner sesamoid (Fig. 7.11). Custom or over-the-counter orthotics are often effective when treating sesamoid injuries in low-arched runners because they distribute pressure

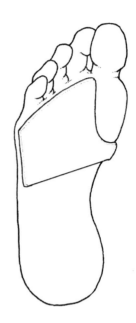

7.10. The sub-one balance.

A   B

7.9. Center of pressure distribution in runners with low arches (A), and high arches (B).

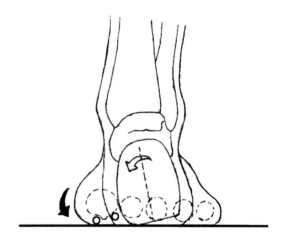

7.11. Excessive pronation (white arrow), drives the inner sesamoid into the ground (black arrow).

away from the sesamoid onto the medial arch.

Regardless of the cause, the flexor hallucis brevis muscle almost always responds to chronic sesamoid injury by reflexively tightening. Increased tension in flexor hallucis brevis (FHB) often worsens the sesamoid injury because it pulls the sesamoid into the bony groove located beneath the first metatarsal head when the big toe moves upward during push-off. A similar injury occurs in the knee, when chronic injury to the patella causes the quadriceps to tighten, which in turn causes the patella to jam against its bony groove. Tightness in the quadriceps is a proven perpetuator of chronic patellar injury and every sports medicine specialist knows the importance of stretching the quads when treating kneecap injuries. In contrast, the same sports experts rarely recommend lengthening the flexor hallucis brevis muscle to treat sesamoiditis. This is too bad because lengthening the FHB is a simple and effective way to treat sesamoiditis.

To determine if you have contracture in the FHB, gently bend your big toes back and compare the range between both feet. If the side with the painful sesamoid has a reduced range, you need to lengthen the FHB. To do this, start by massaging the muscle for a minute or so, and then gently pull the big toe back until you feel mild resistance (Fig. 7.12). At that point, hold the stretch for 35 seconds while simultaneously massaging the flexor hallucis brevis muscle. This stretch should always be comfortable and if it produces anything more than mild discomfort, you'll need an x-ray or an MRI to rule out stress fracture/tendon injury. On occasion, a severely injured sesamoid needs to be immobilized with a walking boot.

Metatarsalgia and Metatarsal Stress Fractures

Not surprisingly, given the central forefoot supports up to seven times body weight during pushoff, metatarsal injuries are extremely common in the running community. Metatarsalgia refers to a bruising of one of the metatarsals, while metatarsal stress fractures occur when the metatarsals can no longer tolerate the strain and begin to break. The second and third metatarsal heads are the most likely to produce metatarsalgia, while the third and fourth metatarsal shafts are the most likely to fracture. Metatarsalgia can

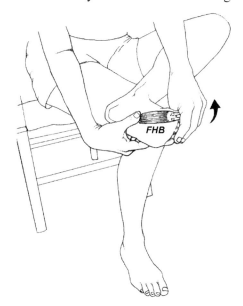

7.12. Flexor hallucis brevis mobilization.
Lightly massage the flexor hallucis brevis muscle (**FHB**) and follow with a gentle stretch by lightly pulling the big toe back (**arrow**). You can find the flexor hallucis brevis muscle by starting at the base of the big toe and angling down and back, making sure to massage the entire muscle. With practice, you can find tight points in the muscle.

easily be diagnosed by pressing firmly on the suspected metatarsal head. Conversely, metatarsal stress fractures can be diagnosed by feeling for a localized region of swelling along the shaft of the suspected metatarsal. Because x-rays miss about 40% of metatarsal stress fractures in the early stages, they are relatively useless for identifying stress fractures within the first few days following injury. After about a week, you can see the repair line forming in the fractured bone.

A frequently overlooked cause for metatarsalgia and metatarsal stress fractures is tightness in the gastrocnemius muscle. A tight gastrocnemius is dangerous while running because it forces the heel to leave the ground prematurely, driving the forefoot into the ground with excessive force. In a study evaluating the prevalence of tight ankles and metatarsal injuries, it was determined that individuals with tight calves were 4.6 times more likely to fracture their metatarsals than a more flexible control group (15). As a result, it is essential that runners keep their gastrocnemius muscles flexible with the straight knee stretch illustrated in figure 5.16, A. On occasion, runners with chronically tight calves should consider sleeping with night braces and/or perform prolonged stretches on slant boards.

The metatarsals are also prone to injury if the muscles to the toes are weak. As mentioned, strong toe muscles distribute pressure away from the metatarsal heads to the tips of the toes, while also lessening bending strains in the metatarsal shafts (see Fig. 3.31). These muscles can be strengthened with the exercises illustrated in figure 7.8. To evaluate if toe weakness is perpetuating a metatarsal injury, pull the insole out of your running shoe and look at the wear pattern: there should be clear indents beneath the toes. If you have more wear and tear beneath the center of the forefoot with little to no evidence of indentations beneath the toes, you need to perform toe strengthening exercises.

In addition to distributing pressure by strengthening the toes, another effective method for treating metatarsalgia is to try wearing metatarsal pads and/or toe crests (Fig. 7.13). In chronic cases of metatarsalgia, you can attach a Morton's platform beneath the first metatarsal head (Fig. 7.14). Because the first metatarsal is twice as wide and four times as strong as the neighboring metatarsals, it is better able to tolerate the redistribution of pressure away from the painful neighboring metatarsal heads. This addition is especially helpful when pain is centered directly beneath the second metatarsal head.

Regardless of the cause, all metatarsal injuries should be treated by reducing your stride length and avoiding forefoot contact points. Runners with a history of metatarsal injury should also avoid minimalist shoes, since they may cause a switch to a forefoot strike pattern, greatly increasing the weight borne by the metatarsals. Minimalist shoes are especially troublesome in runners with narrow forefeet and tight calves. As with all stress fractures, runners should avoid taking anti-inflammatory medications because they can interfere with bone healing. To improve bone health, runners should pay close attention to their diet, particularly their intake of vitamin D3, protein, and trace minerals.

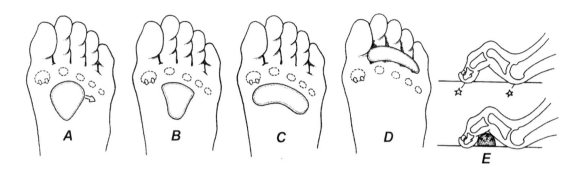

7.13. (A) Heart-, (B) stomach-, and (C) kidney-shaped metatarsal pads distribute pressure away from the metatarsal heads. These pads should be placed as close to the metatarsal heads as possible. Toe crests (**D**) are attached with an elastic strap that loops around the third toe. By distributing pressure over the entire toe (**E**), toe crests reduce pressure beneath the metatarsal heads in the tips of the toes (**stars**).

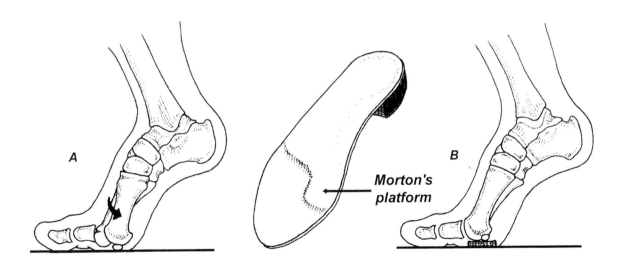

7.14. Morton's platform. Placing a 1/8 inch thick piece of felt beneath the first metatarsal head distributes pressure away from the neighboring second metatarsal. This can be added to an over-the-counter orthotic or placed beneath the bottom of your insole. A sports podiatrist can build a Morton's platform into a custom orthotic.

Interdigital Neuritis/Neuroma

This injury results from entrapment of one or more of the interdigital nerves located in the forefoot (Fig. 7.15). While this condition may occur at any of the interdigital nerves, the nerve located between the third and fourth toe is the most frequently injured. A common early symptom of this condition is a slight tingling between the toes. Affected runners often complain that their socks are "bunched" in the forefoot, and the discomfort is reduced when they take off their shoes. Initially, the nerve injury is mild and is referred to as an interdigital neuritis, because the nerve is inflamed but not seriously damaged. Over time, repeated irritation of the nerve results in the formation of a thickened ball of scar tissue inside the nerve called a Morton's neuroma. The formation of a Morton's neuroma is troublesome because it increases the likelihood of chronicity since the thickened nerve is more readily pinched. Clinically, it is often possible to identify a neuroma by squeezing the forefoot and feeling for the presence of a Mulder's click: a clunk-like sound that occurs when a swollen bursa located between the metatarsal heads is displaced.

Until recently, the most popular theory regarding the origin of interdigital neuritis was that upward motion of the toes during propulsion tethered the interdigital nerves against the transverse ligament (Fig. 7.16). This theory was recently disproved when researchers from Korea performed detailed dissections of 17 interdigital neuromas in order to identify the exact location of nerve entrapment (16). To everyone's surprise, in each case, the nerve was shown to be compressed

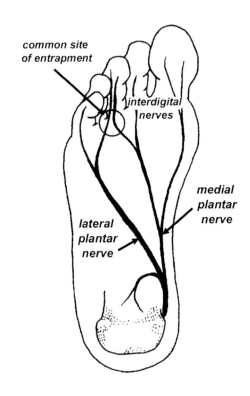

7.15. The interdigital nerves are branches of the medial and lateral plantar nerves.

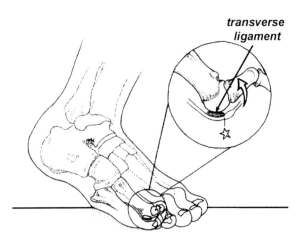

7.16. Until recently, it was believed that the interdigital nerve was tethered when it pulled against the transverse ligament.

beneath the tip of the metatarsal head and the base of the toe, not beneath the transverse ligament.

After reading this paper, I changed the way I treated interdigital nerve injuries. Prior to this study, like most sports doctors, I treated interdigital neuritis/neuroma by placing metatarsal pads behind the involved metatarsal heads in order to lift the transverse ligament off the inflamed interdigital nerve. After discovering the nerve is actually pinched downstream from this location, I began treating interdigital neuritis by placing a U-shaped felt support beneath the forefoot (Fig. 7.17). This treatment protocol turned out to be more effective than conventional metatarsal pads, because these pads do not support the metatarsal heads during the propulsive period (they are positioned too far back). In contrast, the U-shaped pad placed beneath the forefoot distributes pressure away from the involved metatarsals during the propulsive period, when the interdigital nerves are being compressed. The thickness of the pad is dependent upon the severity of the symptoms. I like to initially start with a 1/8 inch thick piece of felt with the U-shaped cutout placed directly beneath the third and fourth metatarsal heads. If symptoms persist, consider adding another 1/16 inch of felt to distribute a greater amount of pressure towards the neighboring metatarsals. Rarely, the nerve injury is so severe that the thickened neuroma needs to be surgically removed.

As with metatarsalgia, an often overlooked perpetuating factor for interdigital neuritis is tightness in the gastrocnemius muscle. As previously mentioned, tightness in the gastrocnemius muscle results in a premature lifting of the heel that can amplify forces centered beneath the

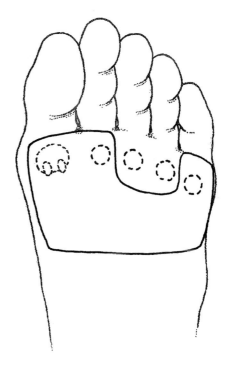

7.17. A U-shaped felt balance distributes pressure away from the third and fourth metatarsal heads during pushoff.

metatarsal heads during propulsion. Additionally, because the big toe can distribute pressure away from the central metatarsal heads, runners suffering with interdigital neuritis should perform the exercise illustrated in figure 7.8, with the band placed under the big toe. I tend to avoid strengthening the little toes because movement of the toes while performing the exercise sometimes irritates the interdigital nerve. Three sets of 40 repetitions are usually sufficient to strengthen the toe muscle.

Finally, to reduce pressure centered beneath the metatarsal heads during daily activities, women should avoid wearing high heels and runners with mid and forefoot strike patterns should consider switching to a rearfoot strike pattern. To lessen pressure on the nerve during propulsion, you should develop a shorter stride length with an increased cadence. Once the nerve injury resolves, you can begin running with your more natural stride but make sure you keep your calves flexible by performing straight leg stretches routinely. Interdigital neuromas can be frustrating to treat because once the nerve thickens, it never reduces in size and you will be prone to this injury in the future. As a result, it is important to treat interdigital neuritis very aggressively in the early stages of the injury.

Bunions

The medical term for a bunion is hallux abductovalgus, from hallux for *big toe* and abductovalgus for *pulled out and rotated* (Fig. 7.18). While no one is sure exactly why bunions form, an inherited tendency for loose ligaments seems to be a factor. In a series of interesting papers evaluating potential factors associated with the development of bunions, researchers found that laxity of the thumb (a marker for whole body laxity) was one of the best predictors of bunion formation (17) (refer back to Fig. 5.15). In fact, thumb laxity turned out to be a better predictor for the development of future bunions than x-ray measurements.

Runners with painful bunions are often difficult to treat because the inward angled big toe is ineffective at generating force. As a result, the pressure normally centered beneath the big toe is transferred to the central forefoot. Over time, a painful callus develops beneath the central forefoot that increases the potential for developing metatarsal stress fractures. Though rarely rec-

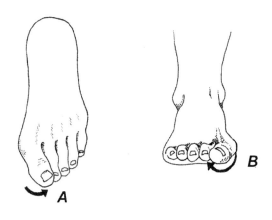

7.18. Hallux abductovalgus. The big toe is abducted (**A**) and in valgus (**B**).

ommended, an effective exercise for managing bunions in runners is to strengthen the peroneus longus muscle. With its strong attachment to the base of the first metatarsal, peroneus longus can help stabilize the inner forefoot by pulling the first metatarsal downward with enough force to unload the central forefoot (Fig. 7.19).

Despite a lack of clinical evidence supporting their use, the most common treatment for bunions is custom and prefabricated orthotics. Although there's no research suggesting they alter the long-term development of bunions, runners with painful bunions often respond very well to orthotics, possibly because they effectively distribute pressure over a broader area (18) and/or increase peroneus longus activity when worn by flatfooted individuals (19). These combined factors may help distribute pressure away from the overloaded central forefoot and improve stability of the first metatarsal. In my experience, runners tend to prefer graphite or thin

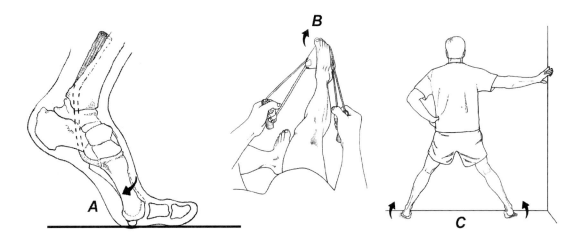

7.19. Peroneus longus exercises. Because of its ability to pull the first metatarsal head down (**A**), peroneus longus is an important stabilizer of the first metatarsal and can protect the central forefoot when a bunion is present. A simple peroneus longus exercise is to wrap a TheraBand or resistance tubing around the forefoot and press down with the first metatarsal head (**B**). Three sets of 25 repetitions performed daily is usually sufficient to strengthen the peroneus longus muscle. A more advanced peroneus longus exercise is performed by standing with your hips abducted and knees flexed (**C**). Peroneus longus is strengthened in this position by raising your heels while pronating your feet in so you are supported by the inner forefeet (**arrows**). As strength increases, this exercise can be performed with a weighted backpack.

plastic orthotics because these orthotics are less bulky and do not elevate the heel (even a slight heel lift increases pressure centered beneath the first metatarsal head). When large bunions are present, toe separators are often necessary to stop the toes from butting against one another.

As with all forefoot injuries, maintaining a flexible gastrocnemius muscle is important to reduce pressure on the forefoot during propulsion. Shoe gear must accommodate the widened forefoot and minimalist shoes should be avoided because they may switch initial ground contact from the heel to the forefoot. To reduce pressure on the forefoot, runners with bunions should consider reducing their stride length and increasing their cadence.

Hallux Limitus and Rigidus

From the Latin for *limited big toe motion,* hallux limitus is a degenerative condition in which the big toe becomes progressively stiffer and more painful. Hallux rigidus is an extreme version of this condition in which the big toe joint is completely fused and rigid. While hallux rigidus is relatively rare, hallux limitus is surprisingly common in the running community because even a slight reduction in the range of motion in the big toe joint can cause trouble while running. Occasionally the result of trauma, hallux limitus is more likely to develop in runners with Egyptian toes because a long big toe is exposed to greater force during propulsion (Fig. 7.20).

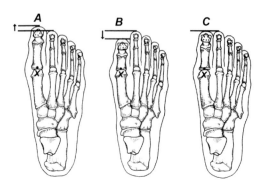

7.20. Variation in toe length. An Egyptian toe is present when the big toe is longer than the second toe (**A**). Conversely, Greek toes occur when the big toe is significantly shorter than the second toe (**B**). Square toes are present when the first and second toes are of equal length (**C**). The next time you go to the Museum of Natural History, take a look at the Greek and Egyptian statues: Egyptian sculptures almost always have long big toes, while Greek statues possess short big toes.

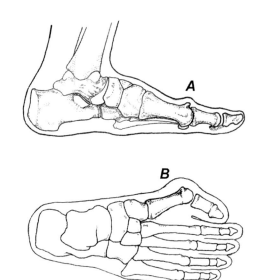

7.21. Bone spur formation in hallux limitus (A) and bunions (B).

Despite its prevalence, many doctors are unaware of this condition and frequently misdiagnose hallux limitus as a bunion. This is unfortunate since these two conditions are treated differently.

The easiest way to diagnose hallux limitus is by evaluating range of motion in the big toe joints. When hallux limitus is present, there is asymmetric motion between the right and left big toe joints. Another way to differentiate hallux limitus from a bunion is by noting the location of the bone spur on the metatarsal head. When a bunion is present, the spur forms on the side of the metatarsal head. In contrast, when hallux limitus is present, the bone spur forms directly on top of the metatarsal head (Fig. 7.21).

The severity of hallux limitus is determined by measuring the range of motion in the big toe joint (Fig. 7.22). Because this joint normally moves about 45° during propulsion, hallux limitus tends to produce pain when the range of big toe motion drops below 40°. Runners with low arches are especially prone to developing a painful hallux limitus because they have more force centered beneath their big toes during propulsion and their big toe joints need to move through larger ranges of motion (20,21).

The goal when treating hallux limitus is to restore as much motion as possible. As long as the spur on the top of the metatarsal head is not too large, it is possible to restore as much as 30° of motion by performing the massage and stretch illustrated in figure 7.12. In addition to increasing the range of motion available to the big toe joint with home stretches, it is also important to increase the range of motion available in the ankle. In my experience, runners with even severe hallux limitus rarely complain of pain as long as their ankles are flexible. In many cases, it is necessary to perform slant board exercises for up to five minutes per day in order to obtain ankle motion necessary to prevent hallux limitus from becoming painful.

Another popular treatment for hallux limitus is to prescribe custom or over-the-counter orthotics. While it was originally believed that orthotics allowed the big toe to move through a larger range of motion during propulsion, three-dimensional research has proven that this is not the case. Almost a decade ago, Dr. Deb Nowaczenski and I performed a pilot study in which we measured three-dimensional motion in the big toe joint while subjects wore different types of orthotics (22) (Fig. 7.23). While preliminary results suggested it was possible to improve motion, follow-up studies showed

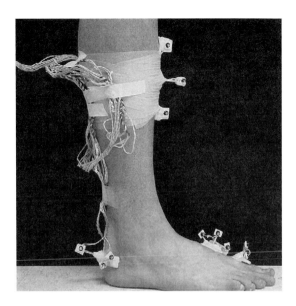

7.23. Measuring three-dimensional motion in the first metatarsal.

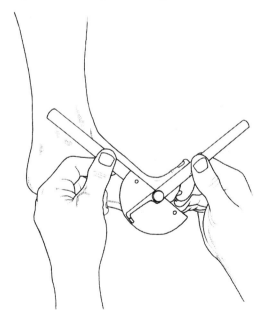

7.22. Measuring range of motion in the big toe joint. This measuring device can be purchased at any hardware store.

that no matter what type of orthotic the subjects wore, their big toe joints continued to move through the same range of motion. Nonetheless, orthotics have been proven to lessen pain in subjects with hallux limitus and should therefore be considered as a viable treatment option (23).

In situations where it is not possible to restore motion (e.g., a large dorsal spur has already formed) the goal of treatment is to accommodate the stiffened joint. The easiest way to do this is to wear running shoes with stiff midsoles and large toe springs that prevent the big toe joints from bending. In difficult cases, it is possible to accommodate hallux limitus by having a cobbler install a rocker bottom into the midsole of the running shoe (Fig. 7.24). Another option is to consider wearing an orthotic with a Morton's extension in the shell (Fig. 7.25). Despite slightly increasing strain on the Achilles tendon,

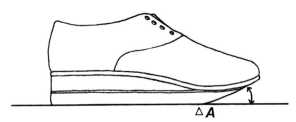

7.24. Rocker bottom. By tapering just past the metatarsals (**A**), a rocker bottom provides a pivot point that allows you to shift into your propulsive period with limited motion of the big toe.

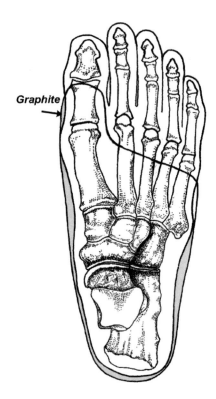

Graphite

7.25. A "Morton's extension in the shell" is usually made from a graphite material that is extended beneath the big toe. The graphite extension reduces movement of the big toe during pushoff.

this treatment approach is surprisingly well tolerated by most runners. If these treatment protocols fail, a surgical intervention known as a cheilectomy may be necessary (Fig. 7.26). While long-term outcomes for this approach are pretty good, surgery should always be a last option.

Plantar Fasciitis

By far, the most common cause for heel pain in runners is plantar fasciitis. The word fascia is Latin for *band,* and the inner portion of the plantar fascia, which runs from the heel to the base of the big toe, represents the strongest and most frequently injured section of the band. Until recently, it was assumed that excessive lowering of the medial arch in flat-footed individuals increased tension in the plantar fascia and overloaded the insertion of the plantar fascia on the heel bone. In fact, the increased tension on the heel was believed to be so great that it was thought to eventually result in the formation of a heel spur.

Although the connection between increased plantar fascial tension and the development of

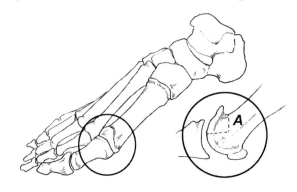

7.26. A cheilectomy is a surgical procedure in which the spur on the top of the first metatarsal is removed (A).

heel spurs is generally accepted in the medical community, recent research proves that it is not the plantar fascia that causes the spur to form. A detailed study of 22 heel bones with spurs revealed that bone spurs form at the origin of flexor digitorum brevis muscle, not the plantar fascia (24) (refer back to figure 3.26). This research emphasizes the important interactions occurring between the plantar fascia and the intrinsic muscles of the arch: the plantar fascia functions passively to store and return energy, while the arch muscles play a more dynamic role in "variable load sharing." Apparently, the intrinsic muscles work with the plantar fascia to prevent lowering of the arch during early stance, while also assisting with arch elevation during propulsion. This explains why the development of plantar fasciitis is not correlated with arch height and the best predictor of the development of plantar fasciitis is the speed in which the toes move upward during the propulsive period (25).

When flexor digitorum brevis is strong, it effectively decelerates upward movement of the toes during propulsion while equally distributing pressure between the tips of the toes and the metatarsal heads. Weakness of this small but important muscle allows the digits to move rapidly through larger ranges of motion, pulling on the plantar fascia with more force. As a result, successful treatment requires decelerating the speed in which the toes move up by strengthening the arch muscles (see figure 5.21, C). The speed in which the toes move may also be lessened by wearing a running shoe with a stiff midsole.

In addition to strengthening the toe muscles, chronic plantar fasciitis often responds well to low-dye taping and to custom and prefabricated orthotics, which are equally effective for the short-term treatment of plantar fasciitis (26). As demonstrated by researchers from the Orthopedic Bioengineering Research Lab in Illinois (27,28), buttressing the arch and/or placing a varus wedge beneath the rearfoot significantly reduces plantar fascial strain. Additional treatments include stretching of the calf and the use of night braces. Because the plantar fascia attaches to the base of the big toe, a group of researchers from Ithaca College of Physical Therapy (29) came up with a clever treatment for plantar fasciitis in which the big toe is stretched for 10 seconds, 30 times per day (Fig. 7.27). Compared to conventional treatments for plantar fasciitis, this stretch routine produced significantly better outcomes.

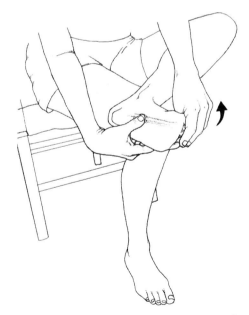

7.27. The plantar fascia home stretch. The stretch is held for 10 seconds and repeated 30 times per day. The plantar fascia should be lightly massaged while performing this stretch.

Whenever possible, runners with plantar fasciitis should avoid making initial ground contact with their mid or forefoot, since these strike patterns significantly increase tension in the plantar fascia. Because surgery often results in a gradual destruction of the medial arch (the plantar fascia is an important stabilizer of the arch and when it is surgically cut, the arch eventually collapses), surgical intervention should always be a last resort. An effective alternative to surgery is shock wave therapy, which is theorized to stimulate repair and accelerate healing. Many sports podiatrists perform this procedure in their office.

Heel Spurs and Calcaneal Stress Fractures

The second most common cause of heel pain is the calcaneal spur syndrome. These bony spurs are more likely to be a problem in slightly overweight older runners. The easiest way to differentiate heel spur pain from plantar fasciitis is to take a few steps while walking on your heels and while walking on your tiptoes. Because the plantar fascia is injured during pushoff and heel spurs hurt when your foot hits the ground, runners with plantar fasciitis complain of discomfort while walking on their toes, while runners with heel spur syndrome find it painful to walk on their heels. In fact, heel spur patients often make initial ground contact with the outer forefoot in an attempt to lessen pressure beneath the heel during the contact period.

It is important to diagnose these two conditions correctly because the treatment protocols for plantar fasciitis and heel spur syndrome are different: plantar fasciitis is treated with orthotics, stretches, and exercises, while heel spur syndrome is treated with heel cups and well-fitting heel counters. For both of these conditions, cortisone injections should be a last resort, especially in individuals with heel spur syndrome, because it may result in further degeneration of the calcaneal fat pad. In every situation, runners with heel spur syndrome should avoid minimalist shoes and should consider wearing running shoes with extra midsole material placed beneath the heel.

It is also possible that chronic heel pain is the result of an undiagnosed calcaneal stress fracture. A simple test to rule out calcaneal fracture is the squeeze test. Because the outer layer of bone in the heel is so thin, compressing the sides the calcaneus between the thumb and index finger produces significant discomfort when a stress fracture is present. This test should be performed on both sides. If you feel more pain on one side while applying the same pressure, set up a time to get an X-ray or MRI to make sure the bone isn't fractured. If a calcaneal stress fracture is present, it is important to identify what caused the stress fracture, such as underlying osteoporosis and/or vitamin D deficiency.

Baxter's Neuropathy

Baxter's neuropathy occurs when the nerve that supplies the little toe (also known as Baxter's nerve) becomes trapped beneath the plantar fascia. Although rare, high mileage runners occasionally get this injury. Because most sports docs aren't familiar with Baxter's neuropathy, the proper diagnosis is delayed and the injured runner spends a lot of time and effort receiving ineffective treatments.

To see if you might have Baxter's neuropathy, actively separate your toes: when a Baxter's neuropathy is present, you are unable to separate the fourth and fifth toes on the involved side (Fig. 7.28). If Baxter's neuropathy is present, custom and prefabricated orthotics are often helpful since they may lessen the "scissoring" of the nerve against the plantar fascia. I tend to prescribe soft over-the-counter orthotics because rigid custom orthotics occasionally dig into Baxter's nerve where it passes beneath the arch.

An alternate method for treating Baxter's neuropathy is to perform the nerve glides illustrated in figure 7.29. This technique has been proven to mobilize nerves in the arms and hands (30), and is believed to loosen adhesions

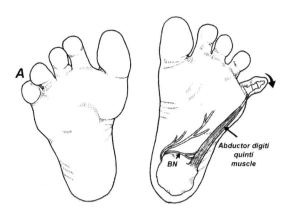

7.28. Baxter's neuropathy test. When the nerve to abductor digiti quinti is compressed, you are unable to abduct the fifth toe (**A**). **BN**=Baxter's nerve.

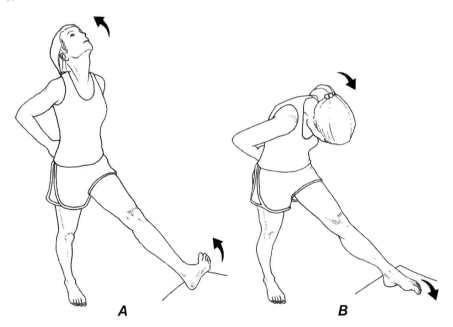

7.29. Nerve glide technique. To mobilize Baxter's nerve, place your heel on an elevated platform and then alternately tilt your neck back while moving your ankle and toes in the same direction (**A**). This position is held for five seconds and followed by bending your head and torso forward while pointing your ankle and toes (**B**).

responsible for maintaining the nerve in a fixed position. If conservative management of Baxter's neuropathy does not produce a rapid reduction in symptoms, consider setting up an appointment with a foot surgeon experienced in treating this condition. Surgical release of the scar tissue responsible for pinching Baxter's nerve has pretty good outcomes. Unfortunately, the longer you delay treatment, the less favorably this condition responds to surgical intervention.

Tibialis Posterior Tendinitis

Tibialis posterior is the deepest and most central muscle of the leg. The tendon of tibialis posterior forms in the lower third of the leg and angles sharply forward as it passes behind the inner ankle bone (Fig. 7.30). This tendon is similar to the Achilles tendon in that it rotates before it attaches, allowing it to store and return energy like a spring. This powerful muscle possesses extensive attachments throughout the midfoot mak-

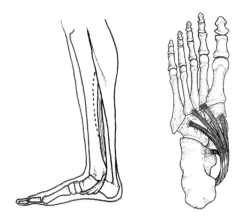

7.30. The tibialis posterior tendon. Notice the multiple attachment points to the bottom of the foot.

ing it the most important stabilizer of the arch.

When your foot hits the ground while running, tibialis posterior stores energy as the arch begins to flatten and returns this energy to elevate the arch during propulsion. In my experience, high mileage runners with low arches are especially prone to tibialis posterior tendinitis, especially if they are weak and/or hypermobile (check your thumb laxity with the test on page 92). The excessive force associated with repeatedly lowering the arch eventually overloads the tendon. Early symptoms associated with tibialis posterior tendinitis include pain beneath the inner ankle bone, especially while running on uneven surfaces.

Clinically, an early sign of tibialis posterior tendinitis is the inability to perform an equal number of heel raises on both sides. In the beginning stages of tibialis posterior tendon injuries, the tendon is inflamed but not lengthened and the arches are the same height. As the tendon injury progresses, the arch on the side of the damaged tendon begins to collapse and the runner is unable to lift his or her heel without significant discomfort.

Treatment for early-stage tibialis posterior tendon injuries consists of either over-the-counter or custom-made orthotics possessing large varus posts. Almost always, soft orthotics are preferred over hard orthotics.

In addition to orthotics, runners with mild tibialis posterior tendon injuries usually respond favorably to strengthening exercises. The exercise illustrated in figure 7.7 is especially helpful. Because aggressive exercises can injure the tendon, you should consult a sports specialist familiar with treating tibialis posterior injuries prior to performing stengthening exercises. Although mild to moderate tibialis posterior tendon injuries typically respond well to orthotics and exercises, severe tibialis posterior tendon injuries can be dangerous and early diagnosis is the key to keeping you running. Because of their potential to progress, it is very important to diagnose tibialis posterior tendon injuries early, and while I'm not an advocate of expensive tests, runners with chronic tibialis posterior tendon injuries should consider getting an MRI to evaluate the degree of tendon damage.

Ankle Sprains

In the United States alone, 23,000 people sprain their ankle each day (Fig. 7.31) resulting in 1.6 million doctor office visits yearly (31). The direct and indirect costs (e.g., lost days from work) associated with treating ankle sprains exceeds $1.1 billion annually (65). To make matters worse, these numbers do not take into account the long-term disability often associated with ankle sprains. In a 10-year follow-up of patients suffering ankle sprains, 72% showed signs of arthritis in the ankle joint (32).

Given the serious long-term consequences associated with ankle sprains, it is important to identify which runners are prone to spraining their ankles. Although numerous factors have been proven to correlate with the development of ankle sprains (such as high arches, impaired balance, tight calves, and decreased cardiovascular fitness), by far, the best predictors of future ankle sprain are prior ankle sprain and being overweight. In fact, overweight athletes with a prior history of ankle sprain are 19 times more likely to suffer another ankle sprain (33). Because

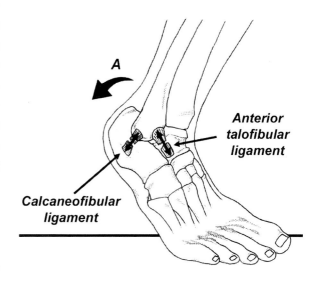

7.31. Inversion ankle sprain. Although an ankle can be sprained in any direction, the most common ankle sprain occurs when the rearfoot inverts (arrow **A**). The sudden movement can damage the anterior talofibular ligament and/or the calcaneofibular ligament.

force centered on the ankle can exceed seven times body weight while running, even a few extra pounds will greatly increase your potential for ankle sprain. Conversely, a previous ankle sprain can result in impaired coordination and calf tightness that can increase your potential for reinjury. In a three-dimensional study of motion in the foot and ankle while walking, individuals with a prior history of ankle sprain had reduced ground clearance during swing phase and the foot was tilted in excessively when it hit the ground (34).

Despite the strong connection between prior sprain and future sprain, there is a counterintuitive inverse relationship between the severity of ligament damage and the potential for reinjury.

In a two-year follow-up of 202 elite runners presenting with inversion ankle sprains, researchers determined that runners with the worst ligament tears rarely suffered reinjury (reinjury rates in this group were between zero and five percent), while runners with less severe ankle sprains suffered significantly higher rates of re-sprain (18% of runners with moderate sprains were reinjured during this two-year period) (35). This explains previous research confirming that patients with completely torn ankle ligaments treated with surgical reconstruction had worse short and long-term outcomes than individuals who refused surgical intervention (36). Clearly, runners with severe ankle ligament injuries should try to avoid surgery.

Regardless of the degree of ligament damage, the goal of treating an ankle sprain is to restore strength, flexibility, balance, and endurance as quickly as possible during the first few days following injury. Adding an elastic bandage to a standard air cast has been proven to reduce the length of time to full recovery by 50% (37). Table 1 outlines a popular treatment protocol for managing ankle sprains and figure 7.32 illustrates an effective tubing exercise that can be performed once symptoms of the acute sprain are reduced.

Besides the standard exercise routines, it is also important that problems with balance be addressed. The simple addition of an inexpensive foam balance pad can significantly reduce the risk of injury. In one study, there was a 77% decrease in the rate of reinjury when overweight athletes with a prior history of ankle sprain performed balance training on a foam stability pad for five minutes on each leg for four weeks (38). Another study from the Netherlands (39) found that

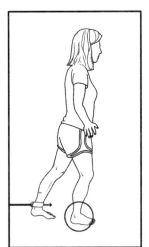  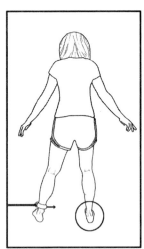 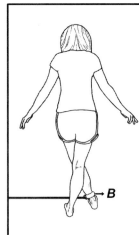

7.32. Ankle exercise. The sprained ankle (circled) is placed on the ground and a resistance band with an ankle cuff is wrapped around the opposite ankle. While maintaining balance on the injured ankle, the uninjured leg pulls the TheraBand forward (**A**), and to the side (**B**). You then rotate 180° and repeat the exercise by pulling the uninjured leg back and then out.

Phase 1. You are unable to bear weight.

A) Compressive wrap with U-shaped felt pad placed around fibula. Change every 4 hours.

B) Actively abduct/adduct toes for 5 seconds, repeat 10 times.

C) Write out alphabet with toes, 5 times per day.

D) Stationary bike, 15 minutes per day.

E) Ankle rock board performed while seated (off weight-bearing), 30 circles, performed clockwise and counter-clockwise 2 times per day. Perform on uninjured ankle while standing for 3 minutes (peforming the rock board on your uninjured ankle has been shown to increase stability in the injured limb).

Phase 2. You can walk with minimal discomfort and the sprained ankle has 90% full range of motion.

A) Stretch all stiff joints in the legs and hips.

B) Perform TheraBand exercises (Fig. 7.32) in all directions, 3 sets of 25 in each direction.

C) Double-leg and then single-leg heel raises on the involved side, 3 sets of 10 reps, performed 2 times per day.

D) Standing closed-eye balance, 30 seconds, 5 times per day.

E) Standing single-leg ankle rock board, performed for 1 minute, 5 times per day.

Phase 3. You can hop on involved ankle without pain.

A) Running at 80% full speed, avoid forefoot touch down.

B) Minitrampoline: 3 sets of 30 jumps forward, backward, and side-to-side. Begin on both legs, progress to single-limb.

C) Plyometrics performed on a 50 cm and a 25 cm box, positioned 1 meter apart. Jump from 1 box to the ground and then to the other box, landing as softly as possible. Perform 3 sets of 5 repetitions. This is an advanced drill and should be performed with care.

Table 1. Ankle Rehabilitation Program (35).

individuals treated with balance board exercises reduced their subsequent reinjury rates by 47%. Because foam pads and balance boards do not put your foot through a full range of motion, I prefer the *Two to One Ankle Rock Board* (available at www.humanlocomotion.org). Unlike conventional rockboards that move your foot equally in both directions, the *Two to One Ankle Rock Board* forces your foot to tilt in twice as much as it tilts out (which is how your ankle is designed to move). By standing with your hip and knee straight, you move your ankle so the periphery of the board touches the ground. The rock board places your foot in the position of a future sprain and then forces you to use your muscles to pull yourself out of the risky position. At first, you may need to do this exercise while seated, but after a few days, you can perform this exercise while standing.

Lastly, runners with sprained ankles occasionally develop a condition known as a lateral gutter syndrome. In this syndrome, scar tissue forms inside the ankle joint, which can get pinched when the ankle moves upward. Lateral gutter syndromes are particularly troublesome when running uphill. Even though this condition does not show up on x-ray or MRI, a simple test you can do to confirm this diagnosis is to stand with both feet straight and slowly squat down while keeping your heels on the ground. If a lateral gutter syndrome is present, you feel pinpoint pain localized slightly in front of the outer ankle. Unfortunately, lateral gutter syndromes do not respond well to conventional treatments and it is often necessary to have the scar tissue removed with arthroscopic surgery. The long-term outcomes for this procedure are excellent.

Compartment Syndromes

The muscles of the leg are located in five separate compartments, each of which is separated by specialized walls made of fascia (Fig. 7.33). Because exercise can increase muscular volume by as much as 20%, the fascial envelopes surrounding each compartment must be capable of stretching to accommodate the expanding muscle compartments. If the fascial envelopes are stiff and unable to expand sufficiently, pressure inside the affected compartment increases, causing the capillaries and veins to collapse. Without adequate venous drainage, the compartment's pressure continues to increase, eventually resulting in muscle and/or nerve damage.

Compartment syndromes are divided into two types: acute and chronic. Although rare, the acute form of compartment syndrome is a surgical emergency because pressure inside the muscle quickly becomes so high that the muscle may be badly damaged. Although sports specialists and runners need to be aware of the potential for acute compartment syndromes, this type of injury is uncommon. More often, runners develop chronic compartment syndromes in which the increased pressure causes discomfort but does not result in long-term muscle damage. Teenage runners are especially prone to compartment syndromes. The anterior and deep posterior compartments are most likely to be affected, and at first, the runner usually complains of a throbbing pain in the middle of the leg. If the condition worsens, runners with compartment syndromes may present with signs of nerve damage: tingling in the leg and/ or extreme muscle weakness. Approximately

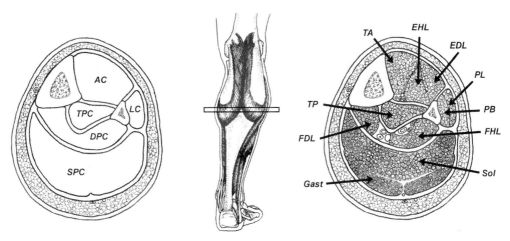

7.33. Cross-section through the middle of the leg revealing the 5 compartments. AC=anterior compartment; **TPC**= tibialis posterior compartment; **LC**=lateral compartment; **DPC**=deep posterior compartment; **SPC**= superficial posterior compartment. Muscle abbreviations: **TA**= tibialis anterior; **EHL**= extensor hallucis longus; **EDL**= extensor digitorum longus; **PL**= peroneus longus; **PB**= peroneus brevis; **FHL**= flexor hallucis longus; **Sol**= soleus; **Gast**= gastrocnemius; **FDL**= flexor digitorum longus; **TP**= tibialis posterior.

45% of individuals with chronic compartment syndrome also have fascial hernias, a condition in which a small portion of the muscle protrudes from its compartment. The herniated muscle looks like a small marble caught beneath the skin. Fortunately, muscle hernias are often asymptomatic and may even be protective, since they allow for reductions in internal muscle pressures.

The treatment of chronic compartment syndrome is dependent upon the specific compartment involved and the shape of the runner's foot: flat-footed runners presenting with a posterior compartment syndrome should be treated with over-the-counter or custom orthotics incorporating varus posts, while runners with high arches presenting with lateral compartment syndromes should be treated with valgus posts attached beneath the insoles.

Regardless of arch height, runners with an-terior compartment syndromes should be told to make initial ground contact with a midfoot strike pattern, while runners with superficial and deep posterior compartment syndromes should be encouraged to run with a heel-first strike pattern. In every situation, runners with chronic compartment syndrome should reduce their stride lengths and find a running shoe that works best for them. Because this injury tends to be chronic, it is often necessary to incorporate cross training techniques such as stationary bike riding and/or wet vest running in a pool. I tend to discourage runners with this injury from swimming because flutter kicks tighten the deep posterior compartment, which may prolong the length of time to full recovery.

To improve flexibility of the fascial envelopes, a home program of stretches and self-massage is invaluable (Fig. 7.34). Because these muscles are difficult to stretch, runners with compartment

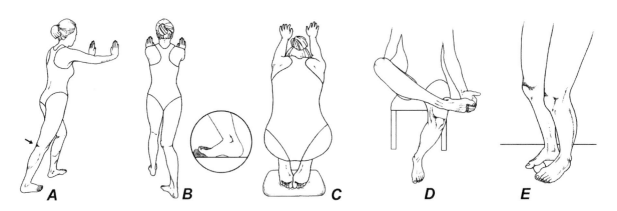

7.34. Compartment stretches. Gastrocnemius is stretched with the knee straight (arrow in **A**) while soleus and tibialis posterior are stretched with the knee bent and the foot pointing in (**B**). Flexor digitorum longus is isolated by placing a rolled-up towel beneath the toes while performing stretch B (inset). The anterior compartment is stretched by placing a towel beneath the toes and leaning back (**C**) or by sitting with your leg in a figure 4 position while pulling the toes back (**D**). Peroneus longus is stretched by placing a tennis ball beneath your forefeet while bending your knees (**E**).

syndromes should routinely incorporate massage sticks and/or foam rollers to more effectively lengthen the fascia. Heating the involved compartment prior to using massage sticks and/or rollers increases the speed in which the fascia is lengthened. Care must be taken when massaging the lateral compartment because the superficial peroneal nerve can easily be irritated (Fig. 7.35). If you feel tingling along the top of the foot or the outside of the leg while working on the lateral compartment, immediately stop massaging that area.

If compartment symptoms persist, surgeons often recommend a "fascial release" in which an incision is made along the length of one or more fascial envelopes. Although this type of surgery relieves pain in approximately 60% of cases (40), as many as 13% of patients may experience postoperative complications and for unknown reasons, women respond less favorably than men.

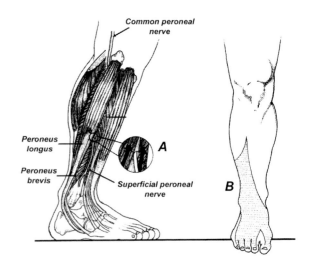

7.35. Location of the superficial peroneal nerve (A). When using massage sticks or foam rollers, avoid massaging the middle portion of the outside of the leg with too much force, since this may irritate the superficial peroneal nerve. You can tell if you're compressing the nerve because you'll feel a tingling along the outer leg and the top of the foot (**B**).

Medial Tibial Stress Syndrome

Medial tibial stress syndrome refers to a condition of localized pain along the inner aspect of the lower tibia. The classic sign of this injury is palpable tenderness over a 2 to 3 inch area just above the inner ankle bone. Originally believed to be caused by the soleus and/or flexor digitorum longus muscles pulling on the periosteum (a sensitive membrane surrounding the outer surface of bone), research confirms that medial tibial stress syndrome involves the bone itself. In a detailed study comparing bone geometry in injured and uninjured athletes, Franklin et al. (41) confirmed that runners with medial tibial stress syndrome have narrower tibias compared to an uninjured exercising control group, proving that medial tibial stress syndrome is also a bony injury, and not just a soft tissue injury. This is supported by other studies showing that the tibia in medial tibial stress syndrome subjects is more porous than in control subjects (42).

This injury is surprisingly common in the running community. In an online survey of 748 high school track and field athletes, 41% of females and 34% of males reported suffering a medial tibial stress injury. Injury to the medial tibia occurs 4 to 6 times more often than Achilles tendinitis and plantar fascial injuries, and the best predictor associated with the development of medial tibial stress injury is higher weekly mileage and faster running times. Although no single cause has been identified, numerous theories for the development of this injury have been suggested, including muscle weakness/tightness, decreased bone density, hormonal imbalances, and excessive pronation. Extrinsic factors such as running on asphalt and/or canted roads have also been implicated in the development of this condition.

To evaluate potential causes for the development of medial tibial pain, a prospective clinical study was performed in which 122 male and 36 female cadets were followed after measuring a variety of biomechanical risk factors, such as ankle flexibility, limb length discrepancy, and foot type (43). At the end of a 12-month training program, 23 cadets developed medial tibial pain and although no factors predicted injury in females, the injured males were more likely to present with greater ranges of hip rotation and smaller diameter calves. This research suggests that hip and calf strengthening exercises should be recommended for male runners presenting with this injury. In my experience, both male and female runners with medial tibial stress syndrome benefit from the flexor digitorum longus exercise illustrated in figure 5.21 (C) on page 103.

Although orthotics are almost always recommended in the treatment of medial tibial stress syndrome, research regarding their effectiveness has shown mixed results. Recently, a large, well-designed study confirmed that orthotics may prevent the development of medial tibial stress injury. In a randomized controlled trial of 400 military trainees performing a 7-week basic training program, researchers prescribed customized foam orthotics modified with posts, arch supports, and heel cups. These additions were added on a case-by-case basis depending upon the amount of pressure centered beneath each foot (44). A control group of military trainees was treated with standard insoles. After seven weeks of basic training, 22 cadets from the control group developed medial tibial stress syndrome, compared to only 2 in the orthotic group. Given the outcomes of this study alone, orthotics should be considered by all runners with a history of medial tibial stress syndrome.

The most popular home treatment for the management of medial tibial stress syndrome continues to be stretching. Despite its popularity, several studies have shown that stretching does not protect against the development of medial tibial injury (45). Nonetheless, once the injury has occurred, it is important to restore soleus and flexor digitorum longus to their degree of flexibility present prior to the injury. The stretches illustrated in figure 7.34, B (and inset), isolate these two muscles. Night braces are also helpful when treating this condition and a wedge can be placed beneath the toes to stretch the long toe muscles.

Because the development of medial tibial stress syndrome has been associated with high weekly mileage and faster running, runners with this injury should reduce their training volume and intensity until symptoms subside. Neoprene calf wraps are helpful when returning to sport and taping the inner side of the leg is also useful since it may enhance proprioception. To reduce strain on the medial compartment muscles, injured runners should run on soft trails. Because medial tibial stress syndrome is associated with reduced bone strength, it is important to evaluate dietary factors such as daily intake of vitamin D, calcium, magnesium, and daily protein intake (you need a minimum of 30 grams of protein each day). Finally, while anti-inflammatory medications are routinely prescribed for the management of this condition, an award-winning study by Cohen et al. (46) confirms that many nonsteroidal anti-in-

flammatory drugs can reduce tendon-to-bone healing in laboratory animals, and regular use of these drugs should therefore be discouraged.

Stress Fractures

In any given year, more than one in five runners will sustain a stress fracture (47). In the US alone, this translates into nearly 2 million stress fractures annually (48). In one of the largest studies to date, Matheson and colleagues (49) evaluated 320 athletes with stress fractures and noted that 4% of stress fractures occurred while playing basketball, 5% while playing tennis, 8% while in aerobics class, and a surprising 69% of these athletes developed stress fractures while running. Although it is generally believed that runners get stress fractures because the high impact forces associated with running cause the bones to break down, this is not always the case. In Matheson's classic study of 320 athletes with stress fractures, only 20% of the stress fractures could be related to an increase in running mileage and/or the transition to training on a hard surface (49).

In most situations, stress fractures are not the result of weak bones cracking when exposed to excessive stress, they are more likely to be the result of various biomechanical factors in which healthy bones break down when exposed to otherwise manageable impact forces. Though rarely considered, muscle strength plays an important role in the prevention of stress fractures. In an interesting study of muscle volume and the development of stress fractures, researchers from Australia (50) determined that a 10 millimeter reduction in calf circumference was associated with a fourfold increase in the incidence of tibial stress fracture. This is consistent with studies demonstrating certain muscles prevent tibial fractures by adjusting to bony vibrations by pretensing prior to heel strike (51,52).

In addition to dampening the potentially dangerous bony oscillations following heel strike, key muscles play an important role in creating compressive forces that allow various bones to resist bending strains present while running. For example, the piriformis muscle of the hip has been shown to reinforce the femoral neck, thereby preventing it from bending with the application of vertical forces (Fig. 7.36). Without adequate support from the piriformis and the neighboring hip abductor, the femoral neck might crack when exposed to the normal bending forces present during midstance while running. The best way to strengthen the muscles responsible for protecting the femoral neck are illustrated in figure 7.37.

While the piriformis has been proven to protect the femoral neck, the iliotibial band has recently been shown to create a stabilizing force that protects the shaft of the femur from stress fractures while running (Fig. 7.38). During the midstance phase, the tensor fasciae latae and gluteus maximus muscles create a compressive force in the iliotibial band that prevents the femur from bending. As a result, weakness of certain hip muscles may increase the likelihood of suffering a femoral shaft stress fracture. The exercises illustrated in figure 7.37 will help protect your femur from this injury.

As previously mentioned, the toe muscles play an important role in protecting the metatarsal shafts from stress fractures. Runners with a histo-

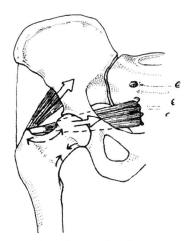

7.36. The piriformis and gluteus medius muscles (white arrows) create a compressive force that protects the femoral neck from stress fractures while running (black arrows).

ry of metatarsal stress fractures should do the toe exercises illustrated in figure 7.8 routinely. To determine if your toes are working properly, inspect the insoles of your running shoes. Ideally, you will notice indents beneath the tips of all of the toes.

Tightness in the gastrocnemius muscle is also an underappreciated cause of certain stress fractures. In addition to increasing the risk of metatarsal stress fracture by more than 400% (15), a tight calf also increases the potential of suffering a navicular stress fracture (53). Navicular stress fractures are extremely dangerous in runners since they tend to heal poorly because of the bone's naturally limited blood supply. In some cases, the navicular can only heal after surgeons reinforce the midportion of the bone with a metal screw. Because 45% of athletes suffering navicular stress fractures do not return to sport (54), tight runners should try to prevent this injury by routinely stretching their calves.

While strengthening exercises and stretches

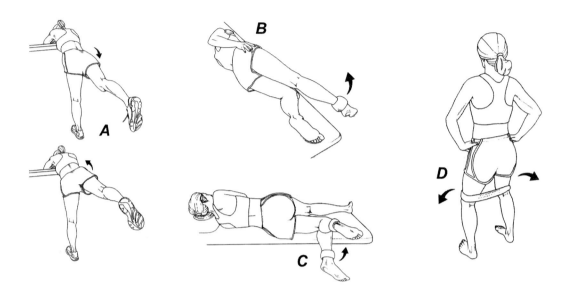

7.37. Piriformis and gluteus medius strengthening exercises. A) Standing piriformis exercise: while standing on the involved leg, raise and lower the opposite pelvis (**arrows**). **B**) Sidelying gluteus medius exercise: while lying on the edge of a bed or a bench, raise and lower the upper leg (**arrow**). To increase resistance, this exercise can be performed with an ankle weight. **C**) Piriformis exercise: this muscle can be exercised by lying on your side and raising and lowering the ankle with the knee flexed 90° (**arrow**). **D**) Standing piriformis exercise: with a TheraBand positioned above your knees, separate your knees against resistance provided by the band (**arrows**).

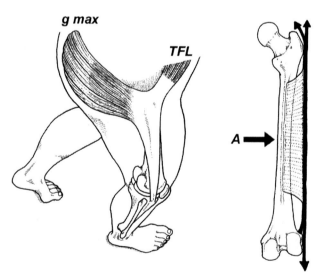

7.38. Because the iliotibial band has a fibrous slip that covers the back of the femur (A), glute max and the tensor fasciae latae create a compressive force that protects the femur from stress fractures while running.

are helpful when treating a variety of stress fractures, figuring out ways to prevent tibial fractures, especially in young women, has been difficult. This is unfortunate because tibial stress fractures are very common. In their 12-month study of 111 track and field athletes, researchers from The University of Melbourne (55) noted that almost 50% of all stress fractures occurred in the tibia.

To figure out why runners get so many tibial stress fractures, researchers from the University of Tennessee (56) performed three-dimensional motion analysis on female runners with and without a history of tibial stress fracture. To their surprise, runners with prior tibial stress fractures consistently attempted to absorb shock by excessively lowering their opposite hip rather than flexing their knee (refer back to figure 3.12). As a result, tibial stress fractures should be treated with gait modifications that specifically address the faulty movement pattern (see pages 111-118).

In order to allow runners to return to sport following a stress fracture, many practitioners continue to recommend the "10% rule," in which the injured runner is told to increase his/her running distance by 10% per week. Even though the 10% rule continues to be used by most sports experts, a study published in *the American Journal of Sports Medicine* in 2007 showed that this approach does not alter reinjury rates (57). Additionally, because runners heal at different rates, conventional formulas used to predict recovery time for specific stress fractures are extremely inaccurate. For example, some experts incorrectly claim that metatarsal stress fractures heal in 6 weeks while femoral stress fractures heal in 12 weeks. Rather than relying on inaccurate formulas, the most effective way

to return to sport following a stress fracture is to wait until the damaged bone is pain-free for two weeks with daily activity before attempting a trial run. If at any point during that two week period the bone begins to ache, you have to start all over again. To maintain fitness, runners with stress fractures can stationary bike ride and/or swim during the waiting period. Because swimming has a tendency to tighten the calf muscles, it is important to stretch after each pool workout, especially if you have a metatarsal stress fracture.

Depending upon the severity of the stress fracture, I recommend the injured athlete return to running with a walk/run combination. A typical first workout is to walk 1/4 mile, slowly jog 1/4 mile, and repeat this cycle for two miles. It is very important to run on alternate days and monitor symptoms: if the fracture site becomes uncomfortable, you'll have to take another two weeks off running and get back to cross training. As long as you remain symptom-free, you can increase the distance of your alternate day runs by one mile per week. At the end of the second week, you can transition to running only, but you've got to run at least two minutes per mile slower than your usual pace and keep your stride length short. Runners with stress fractures in the tibia or femur should be encouraged to switch to a midfoot strike pattern, while runners with midfoot or forefoot stress fractures should try landing on their heels. Because athletes recover at different rates, it is important to increase weekly mileage on a case-by-case basis with significant increases in weekly distance only after the first three weeks. If the stress fractures are recurrent and/or severe, you should consult with an experienced sports medicine specialist.

Patellofemoral Pain Syndrome

Also referred to as retropatellar pain, (or pain behind the kneecap), patellofemoral pain syndrome affects 25% of the running population. A classic sign that you have this injury is that your kneecap aches when you sit for long periods, and the pain goes away when you straighten your leg. Despite the fact that researchers have spent decades studying patellofemoral pain, identifying the cause for this condition has been difficult. Early research suggested the most likely cause for patellofemoral pain syndrome was a sideways shifting of the kneecap into the lower femur. The most frequently cited factors responsible for abnormal movement of the kneecap included an increased Q-angle and/or weakness of the inner quadriceps muscle (also know as the VMO) (Fig. 7.39).

To correct the abnormal sidewards movement of the patella, sports specialists prescribe a variety of VMO strengthening exercises, such as toe-out leg extensions and wall presses while squeezing a ball. Unfortunately, dozens of studies have shown that these exercises do not target the VMO. Rather, these exercises more effectively strengthen the outer quadriceps muscle, potentially worsening patellofemoral pain when the stronger outer quadriceps pulls the patella sidewards with more force. In spite of their proven ineffectiveness, VMO exercises continue to be a first-line intervention for the management of this common condition.

To get a better understanding of what really happens with patellofemoral injuries, a group of researchers placed people in specialized MRIs to evaluate patellofemoral movement while they flexed their knees (58). Surprisingly, the MRIs

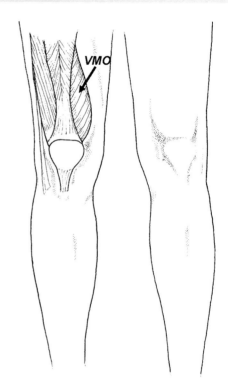

7.39. The vastus medialis obliquus (VMO).

revealed that the primary cause of patellofemoral problems was not a shifting of the patella into the stable femur, but a shifting of the outer aspect of the femur into the stable patella. Recent CT and functional MRI evaluations support this observation, confirming the most likely cause of patellofemoral pain while running is abnormal motion of the femur, not altered motion of the patella (59,60).

Hip weakness has been cited as the most likely cause for the exaggerated rotation of the femur. In a three-dimensional evaluation of runners with and without patellofemoral pain syndrome, researchers from Indiana University (61) proved that runners with weak hip abductors allow their femurs to turn in excessively, and the degree of rotation increases when fatigued.

As previously mentioned, in addition to the strengthening exercises listed in figure 5.21, runners with excessive inward rotation of the hips should perform gait retraining, in which they consciously focus on improving the faulty movement pattern (refer back to pages 73-74). The forward step-down test is a simple test that will help determine if hip weakness predisposes you to patellofemoral injury (see figure 5.26 on page 116). This test is also useful to monitor progress and you should consider cross training until you are able to perform the forward step-down test while keeping the hip and knee straight.

A frequently cited cause of retropatellar pain is low arches. The belief is that because runners with low arches pronate more, their lower legs are forced to twist in excessively, dragging the kneecap against the femur. While this seems logical, the connection between excessive and increased inward rotation of the leg is based on the mitered hinge analogy (refer back to Fig. 5.6), which has been proven to be incorrect. As discussed in chapter 5, recent three-dimensional research confirms that although runners with low arches do pronate more, their lower legs rotate the same amount as people with high arches (62). As a result, runners with low and high arches have the same potential for developing patellofemoral pain syndrome. The equal ranges of tibial rotation in runners with high and low arches explains why so many recent studies have shown a limited connection between pronation and patellofemoral pain.

Despite the limited connection between pronation and retropatellar pain, runners with painful kneecaps frequently report that orthotics lessen their discomfort. The easiest way to determine if an orthotic will lessen your patellofemoral pain is to do a simple trial in which you wear an over-the-counter orthotic while performing a few single-leg squats. According to researchers from Australia (63), if you feel more comfortable performing the squats while wearing the orthotics, the potential that orthotics will produce a marked reduction in knee pain increases from 25% to 45%.

The final factor to consider when treating chronic patellofemoral pain is flexibility of the quadriceps muscle. Researchers from Belgium (64) evaluated multiple factors associated with the development of patellofemoral pain and determined that tightness in the quadriceps muscle is a clear risk factor. In fact, quadriceps inflexibility was a better predictor of patellofemoral pain than an increased Q angle, which doctors often correct by surgically reconstructing the knee.

You can evaluate quadriceps flexibility by lying facedown and measuring the distance from the back of your heel to your hip (Fig. 7.40). The measurement should be repeated on both sides and in most situations, you should be able to get your heels within 4 inches of each hip. If either quadriceps is inflexible, roll the tight muscle with a foam roller or a massage stick and then perform the stretch illustrated in figure 7.41. The stretch should be held for 30 seconds and repeated five times per day. A common mistake is to only massage the lower portion of the quadriceps. Because the outer quadriceps runs up to the outside of the hip (Fig. 7.42), it is important to work the entire muscle, not just the lower portion.

To lessen patellofemoral pressure while running, consider shortening your stride and switching to a midfoot strike pattern. Increasing your

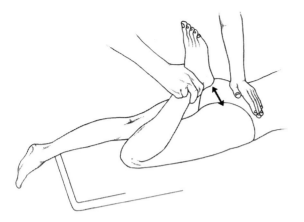

7.40. Measuring quadriceps flexibility.

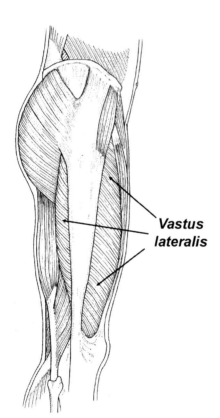

7.42. The vastus lateralis is a large muscle, running from the hip to the outer knee.

Vastus lateralis

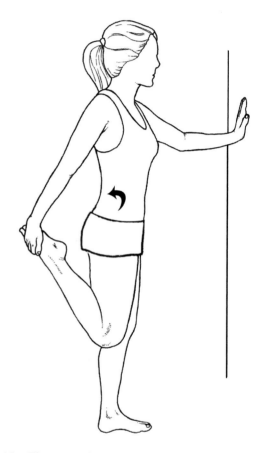

7.41. The quadriceps muscle is stretched while maintaining a pelvic tuck (arrow).

cadence by just 5% has been proven to reduce knee pressure (65). Finally, because running amplifies impact forces five-fold, overweight runners should consider losing a few pounds as even small reductions in body weight can significantly lessen pressure behind the kneecap. When returning to sport following a retropatellar injury, you may want to try wearing a neoprene knee brace or consider using Kinesiotape over the top of the patella. The Dual Action Cho-Pat Knee Strap is a common soft brace that is easy to use and helps stabilize the kneecap while you are recovering. As with almost all injuries, an active dynamic warm-up (Fig. 4.4) should be performed prior to running and you should make the first mile of your typical run at least one minute per mile slower than usual.

Patellar Tendinopathy

Patellar tendinopathy is a degenerative condition characterized by local tenderness of the patellar tendon at its attachment to the patella. Because stress in the tendon is greatest when the knee is flexed excessively, this injury is more prevalent in sprinters and high mileage endurance runners than in recreational runners. In an attempt to identify potential risk factors for the development of patellar tendinopathy, van der Worp (66) performed an extensive review of the literature and found some evidence suggesting that reducing body weight, increasing thigh flexibility, and using orthotics to control excessive pronation can be effective methods for reducing risk of injury. However, the evidence correlating a lessened potential for injury with a specific treatment intervention was weak. As with patellofemoral pain

syndrome, the ability of an orthotic to favorably modify symptoms associated with patellar tendinopathy is unpredictable. Because of these reasons, an orthotic device should only be prescribed if you respond favorably to specific functional tests while wearing an arch support; e.g., performing repeat step downs off a 4-inch high platform with and without over-the-counter orthotics.

Vigorous deep tissue massage followed by frequent stretching of the quadriceps is almost always helpful, since a flexible quadriceps absorbs force that would otherwise be absorbed by the patellar tendon. To understand why a more flexible quadriceps muscle is necessary to treat patellar tendinopathy, picture a metal chain that has been allowed to harden in a concrete block. If you were to repeatedly pull on this chain, the concrete at the base of the chain would rapidly break into small fragments. In contrast, if a rubber tube were allowed to harden in concrete and you were to pull on the tube with the same force, there would be less damage to the concrete at the attachment point because the rubber band would absorb the force that otherwise would be displaced into the concrete. The more flexible quadriceps is comparable to the rubber tube in that it absorbs force that would otherwise go into the tendon.

In addition to improving quadriceps flexibility, another way to reduce tendon strain while running is to wear a compressive strap around the knee (Fig. 7.43). Several studies have shown that compressive straps reduce tendon strain by distributing forces generated by muscle contraction over a broader area (67,68).

Of all the proposed treatment protocols, the most effective way to fix patellar tendinopathy is

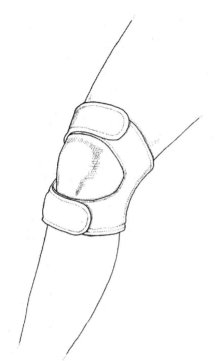

the exercise group developed an increase in the number of small tendon fibers, which improved the overall flexibility of the patellar tendon (Fig. 7.44). These changes made the patellar tendon significantly more resilient, allowing the athletes to exercise with considerable reductions in tendon pain and swelling. The authors speculate that overuse may cause small tears to form inside the patellar tendon resulting in reduced formation of new fibrils (hence the older, fatter, less populated fibril population). It is theorized that heavy slow resistance training results in increased tendon production, which in turn produces an increased

7.43. The Dual-Action Cho-Pat compressive knee brace.

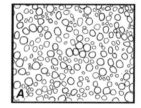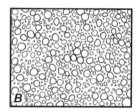

7.44. Electron microscopy of tendon biopsies taken before (A), and after (B), a 12-week strength training program. Note the significant increase in small-sized fibrils following strength training.

to increase strength in the quadriceps muscles. In an in-depth study of the effects of heavy weight training on patellar tendinopathy in athletes, researchers from Denmark (69) used electron microscopes to evaluate tendon fragments removed from individuals with and without patellar tendinopathy before and after completing a 12-week exercise protocol. The training sessions consisted of 3 weekly sessions of squats, leg presses, and hack squats. The subjects completed 4 sets of each exercise with a 2-3 minute rest between each set. Before and after completing this rigorous training program, biopsies of tendons in patients with patellar tendinopathy were compared to biopsies of tendons taken from a healthy control group. As demonstrated with electron microscopes,

number of tendon fibers with the formation of numerous small-sized fibrils. The changes in tendon fiber density occurred rapidly, and by week 12, there was no difference between the patellar tendinopathy and the control group. These researchers (69) related the reduced tendon stiffness to the increased production of new fibrils: because the smaller fibrils have fewer cross-links between them, the tendon itself becomes more resilient, since fewer cross-fibrils allow greater flexibility.

While heavy load resistance training increases tendon flexibility and decreases pain, the heavy weights used in this protocol could potentially cause injury when performed by recreational runners. An alternate protocol to strengthen the patellar tendon is to perform the long-step lunges without strides illustrated in figure 7.45. This exercise was proven to reduce strain on the patella and I recommend that runners with patellar tendinopathy perform this exercise 50 times per day with each repetition lasting 6 seconds (a 3-second eccentric phase followed by a 3-second concentric phase). In my experience, this exercise protocol is just as effective as the heavy resistance protocol described by the Danish researchers but because only light weights are incorporated, the risk of injuring the kneecap is greatly reduced.

As with patellofemoral pain, runners with patellar tendinopathy should consider switching to a midfoot strike pattern, reduce their stride lengths, and increase their self-selected cadence by 5%. Over-the-counter knee braces and/or placing Kinesiotape over the patellar tendon can make it a little less painful when returning to running.

Iliotibial Band Compression Syndrome

The iliotibial band is an interesting fibrous structure that originates from the gluteus maximus, medius, and tensor fasciae latae muscles and attaches to two separate points on the outside of the knee (Fig. 7.46). Runners with this injury often describe the pain as a burning sensation along the outside of the knee. While most sports textbooks will tell you that runners develop this injury when the band snaps back and forth over a small bony prominence located on the outside of the knee (traumatizing a bursa

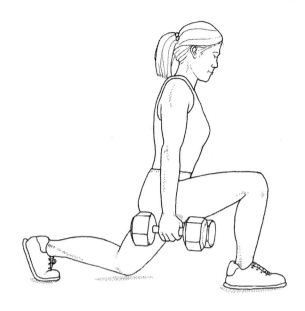

7.45. The long-step forward lunge. While maintaining your feet in a fixed position, raise and lower your body by straightening the legs. Redrawn from Escamilla (94).

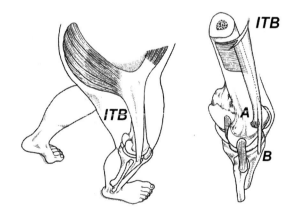

7.46. The iliotibial band (ITB) has two separate attachment points along the outer knee (A and B).

trapped beneath), more recent research confirms that the band does not snap back and forth and that a trapped bursa is not the cause of the pain.

In their thorough analysis of iliotibial band anatomy and function, researchers from the University of Wales (70) prove that what appears to be a forward/backward displacement of the band during knee flexion is actually an illusion created by alternating tensions generated by the tensor fasciae latae and gluteus maximus muscles (Fig. 7.47). Using MRI, the authors conclusively prove the band does not snap back and forth, but is compressed into the outer side of the femur when the knee is flexed, with peak compression occurring at 30° flexion.

To identify biomechanical factors potentially responsible for the development of this common injury, William Ferber and colleagues (71) performed 3-dimensional motion analysis of 35 runners with iliotibial band syndrome and compared rearfoot, knee, and hip movements to 35 age-matched controls. Compared to the control group, the iliotibial band syndrome group exhibited significantly greater collapse of the opposite hip with increased inward rotation of the involved knee. Importantly, there was no appre-

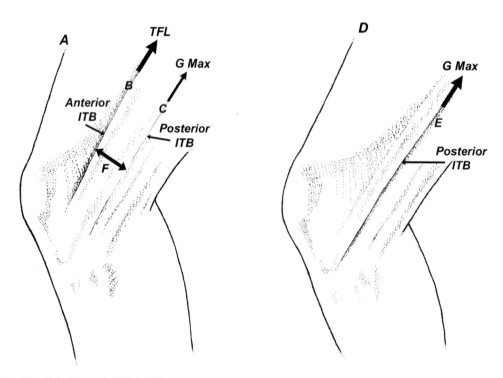

7.47. The iliotibial band (ITB). When the knee is slightly bent (**A**), the tensor fasciae latae muscle (**TFL**) pulls with more force than the gluteus maximus muscle (**G Max**) causing the front of the ITB to become more prominent (compare **B** and **C**). When the knee bends more (**D**), greater tension is created in the gluteus maximus muscle and the back of the iliotibial band becomes more prominent (**E**). The shifting of tension from the front to the back of the ITB (**F**) creates the illusion that the band is snapping forward and backward.

ciable difference in rearfoot pronation between the two groups. In fact, runners with iliotibial band syndrome had slightly reduced ranges of pronation compared to the control group, which is consistent with research suggesting this injury is more likely to happen in people with high arches (72). The authors state that the excessive dropping of the opposite hip and twisting of the involved knee causes an amplified compression of the band against the outer side of the knee. To treat this condition, runners with this injury should strengthen their hips and perform the gait retraining techniques described on page 118.

While strengthening exercises and gait retraining play an important role in the management of this condition, it is also important to evaluate hip abductor flexibility, since tightness in the tensor fasciae latae, gluteus medius, and gluteus maximus muscles can increase tensile strain on the band. In an extremely detailed study of the effect of stretching on the iliotibial band and proximal muscles, researchers surgically implanted strain gauges into the iliotibial bands of 20 cadavers and evaluated the effect of three different stretches on lengthening the band (73). These same researchers also evaluated elasticity of the iliotibial band in live athletes by using special ultrasound machines. Their detailed analysis confirmed that the iliotibial band itself is extremely rigid and resistant to stretch, since it lengthened less than 0.2% when pulled by the hip muscles with maximum force. Because of the extreme inflexibility of the iliotibial band, the authors stress that treatments aimed at reducing tension in the band are a waste of time, since massage will not loosen the band.

Other experts confirm that it is physically impossible to loosen the band itself because the connective tissue that makes up the band is as strong as Kevlar, the material used in bullet-proof vests (74). Rather than needlessly massaging the band, a more effective approach is to reduce tension in the muscular component of the band by massaging trigger points in the gluteus maximus, medius, and tensor fasciae latae muscles. After a few minutes of massage, these muscles should be lengthened with the stretches illustrated in figure 7.48.

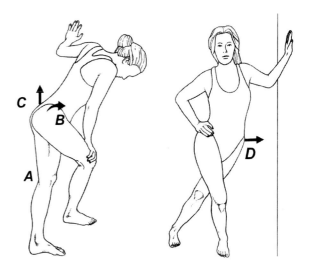

7.48. Iliotibial band stretches. The involved leg is kept in a straight position (**A**), while you bend forward at the hip (**B**). To stretch the back portion of the band, the involved hip is moved towards the wall (**C**). To stretch the TFL component of the band, move the involved hip towards the wall while keeping your spine upright (**D**).

Hamstring Strains

Of all the gait-related muscle injuries, hamstring strains have the highest rate of recurrence, with as many as one-third of injured runners suffering reinjury within the first few weeks following return to sport. With stride lengths exceeding 14 feet, sprinters are especially vulnerable to this injury and it can take up to 4 months of aggressive rehabilitative exercises before return to sport is possible.

Even though the hamstrings consist of four different muscles, runners almost exclusively injure the outer hamstring muscle, the long head of the biceps femoris. The reason for the higher injury rate in the outer hamstring was a mystery until recently, when researchers from the University of Wisconsin determined that because the biceps femoris muscle attaches lower down the leg, it is under greater strain when the swinging leg is moving forward (75) (Fig. 7.49). In a recent MRI study evaluating the location of hamstring strains in different athletes, the only runner to injure a hamstring other than the biceps femoris was an older man who severely strained his inner hamstring muscle while performing stretches prior to running, not while running (76). This is consistent with research showing that dancers almost always injure their inner hamstrings, which are very sensitive to stretch injuries.

Runners typically strain the biceps femoris muscle just before the lead foot hits the ground, when tension in the outer hamstring muscle is greatest. As with most injuries, the single best predictor of future injury is prior injury, possibly because the injured muscle heals with less flexibility and/or impaired coordination. Because of the extremely high recurrence rate associated with biceps femoris strains, rehabilitation of this injury must be comprehensive and address all possible factors associated with chronicity. While hamstring inflexibility is often cited as a potential cause, there is little evidence to support this theory. Recent research confirms that strength, not muscle stiffness, plays the most important role in preventing hamstring injury.

In an impressive study comparing the success of different treatment regimens used in the management of acute hamstring strains, Sherry and

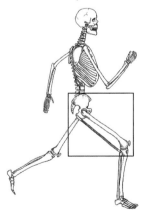
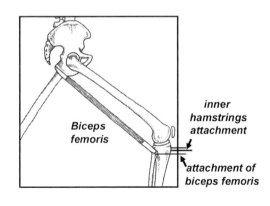

Biceps
femoris

inner
hamstrings
attachment

attachment of
biceps femoris

7.49. Because the biceps femoris attaches lower down the leg, runners tend to strain this hamstring muscle almost exclusively.

Best (77) prove that compared to a conventional protocol of static stretching and hamstring resistance exercises, an exercise regimen including agility and trunk stabilization exercises produces significantly better short and long-term outcomes (see Table 2 for a summary of these exercises). Compared to conventional rehabilitation, the agility and stabilization group returned to sport sooner (22 days versus 37 days), and suffered fewer reinjuries during the first two weeks after returning to sport (55% of the conventional rehab group were reinjured, compared to no reinjuries in the progressive agility and trunk stabilization group).

The beneficial effects of the agility and stabilization exercises were even present one year following return to sport, as 70% of the athletes treated with conventional stretches and exercises were reinjured, compared to only 7.7% of the athletes completing the progressive agility and trunk stabilization program. The alternate hamstring exercises illustrated in figure 7.50 are also helpful when treating hamstring injuries.

The fact that hamstring inflexibility does not cause hamstring strains does not suggest that an injured hamstring should never be stretched. On the contrary, since a flexible muscle is able to tolerate higher eccentric forces with less muscle damage (78), and individuals with flexible hamstrings are less prone to a variety of injuries (79), lengthening the hamstring muscles with gentle stretches is almost always appropriate. The stretch illustrated in figure 7.51 isolates the long head of the biceps femoris muscle. To reduce stiffness in the upper hamstring, this stretch should be performed with the knee flexed 45° and 90°.

Since fatigue increases the potential for hamstring injury, Verral et al. (80) recommend stretching the hamstrings for 15 seconds with the knee bent at different angles while exercising. Over a 2-year period, the authors demonstrated significantly reduced rates of hamstring injuries in Australian Rules football players when the stretches were performed during workouts and competition. As it applies to runners, the results of this study suggest that occasionally stopping to stretch the outer hamstring during your long runs may lessen the potential for reinjury.

In another study of Australian rules football players, Hoskins et al. (95) demonstrate that occasional chiropractic care can reduce the rate of hamstring injuries and reinjuries. In a one-year study of nearly 60 Australian rules football players, the authors demonstrate that players treated with occasional chiropractic care throughout the entire season developed significantly fewer hamstring injuries (1 vs. 5) and reinjuries (0 vs. 2) than an age-matched control.

While stretches and chiropractic care may be helpful in treating and preventing hamstring injuries, comprehensive strengthening exercises play the most important role in the management of hamstring strains. Because nonsteroidal anti-inflammatories may result in impaired tendon healing (46), the routine use of these drugs should be reconsidered. A safer alternative to improve healing is to perform deep tissue massage directly over the damaged tendon, since this may stimulate repair without adversely affecting tendon strength (81,82).

Phase 1.

1. Low- to moderate-intensity sidestepping, 3 x 1 minute.

2. Low- to moderate-intensity grapevine stepping (lateral stepping with the trail leg going over the lead leg and then under the lead leg), both directions, 3 x 1 minute.

3. Low- to moderate-intensity steps forward and backward over a tape line while moving sideways, 2 x 1 minute.

4. Single-leg stand, progressing from eyes open to eyes closed, 4 x 20 seconds.

5. Prone abdominal body bridge (performed by using abdominal and hip muscles to hold the body in a face-down straight-plank position with the elbows and feet as the only point of contact), 4 x 20 seconds.

6. Supine extension bridge (see figure 5.21, X). Repeat 4 times, holding 20 seconds.

7. Side plank (figure 5.21, W). Repeat 4 times, hold 20 seconds on each side.

8. Ice with hamstrings in a stretched position for 20 minutes.

Phase 2.

1. Moderate- to high-intensity sidestepping, 3 x 1 minute.

2. Moderate- to high-intensity grapevine stepping, 3 x 1 minute single-leg windmill touches (figure 7.50, B).

3. Push-up stabilization with trunk rotation (performed by starting at the top of a full push-up, then maintain this position with one hand while rotating the chest toward the side of the hand that is being lifted to point toward the ceiling, pause and return to the starting position), 2 x 15 reps on each side.

4. Fast feet in place (performed by jogging in place with increasing velocity, picking the foot only a few inches off the ground), 4 x 20 seconds.

5. Symptom-free practice without high-speed maneuvers.

6. Ice for 20 minutes if any symptoms of local fatigue or discomfort are present.

Key: Low intensity: a velocity of movement that is less than or near that of normal walking. Moderate intensity: a velocity of movement greater than normal walking but not as great as sport. High intensity: a velocity of movement similar to sport activity. Progression criteria: subjects progressed from exercises in phase 1 to exercises in phase 2 when they could walk with a normal gait pattern and do a high knee march-in-place without pain.

Table 2. Hamstring Exercise Protocol as described by Sherry and Best (77).

7.50. Hamstring exercises. **A**) Prone plank march: hold a plank position and alternately raise one leg at a time for 5 seconds. **B**) Single-leg windmill: while standing on the involved leg, pivot at the hips while maintaining alignment of opposite arm and leg. **C**) Upper hamstring exercise: stand on the involved leg with the opposite knee slightly bent. While maintaining an arch in your low back, pivot forward at the hips (**arrow**). The opposite leg should barely be contacting the ground during this exercise. **D**) Lower hamstring exercise: with arms supported on a stable surface, the involved knee flexes and extends while turning the leg in and out.

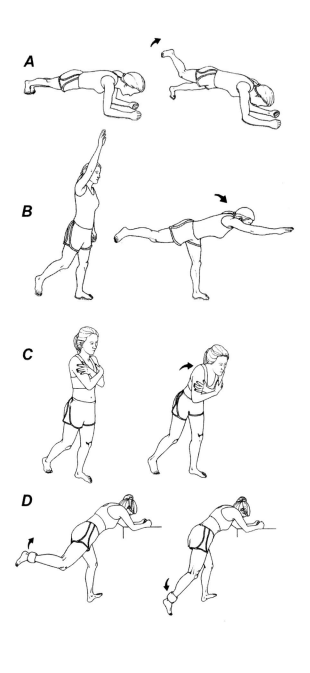

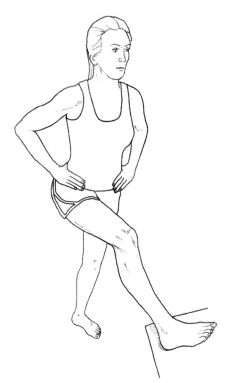

7.51. Stretch for the long head of the biceps femoris. While keeping your spine in a neutral position, lean forward by pivoting at the hip while the leg is turned in with the knee slightly bent.

Piriformis Syndrome

The word piriformis is Latin for *pear-shaped,* since the muscle's wide base and tapered attachment resembles a pear. This small but important muscle creates a compressive force that prevents the femoral neck from fracturing while running (refer back to figure 7.36). Despite the protection afforded the femoral neck, the piriformis muscle causes a lot of trouble in runners because it sits directly on top of the sciatic nerve (Fig. 7.52). In fact, in about 2% of the population, the sciatic nerve exits the pelvis directly through the middle of the piriformis muscle, greatly increasing the potential for developing sciatica. The increased activity present in this muscle while running can produce a chronic pinching of the sciatic nerve, which is the largest nerve in the body. Common symptoms associated with piriformis-related sciatica include a toothache type of pain along the outside of the leg and/or a tingling that can travel all the way to the foot.

To differentiate piriformis syndrome from other causes of sciatica (such as a herniated disc in the low back), a simple test you can do on yourself is to pull your knee towards your opposite shoulder while lying on your back. Hold the involved knee towards the opposite shoulder for about 30 seconds and if a piriformis syndrome is present, you'll feel a slight tingling along the outside of your leg. In my experience, piriformis syndrome is much more common than herniated discs in runners.

While most researchers refer to piriformis syndrome as an isolated entity in which the

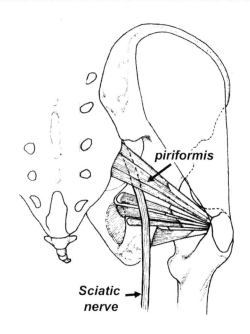

7.52. The sciatic nerve exits the pelvis directly beneath the piriformis muscle.

sciatic nerve is irritated only by the piriformis muscle, researchers from Austria determined that the piriformis muscle fuses with the neighboring obturator internus and/or gluteus medius muscle in more than 40% of the population (83) (Fig. 7.53). In addition to getting pinched beneath the piriformis, these researchers proved that the sciatic nerve can also be trapped against the obturator internus muscle.

Regardless of which muscles are involved, conventional treatments for piriformis syndrome emphasize stretching the hip rotators to lessen tension on the sciatic nerve. Because gluteus medius, piriformis, and obturator internus work together to cause this syndrome, it is important to stretch the hip abductors as well as the hip rotators. The most effective method to lengthen the hip external rotators is with the muscle en-

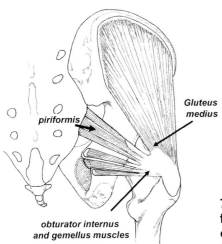

7.53. The tendon of the piriformis muscle frequently merges with the tendons of the obturator internus and gluteus medius muscles.

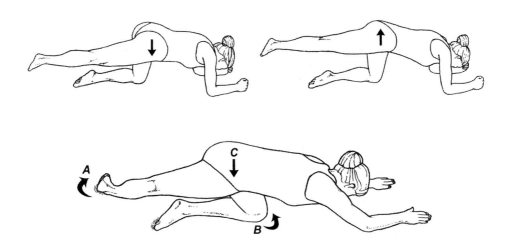

7.54. Hip rotator muscle energy stretch. This is an important stretch because it allows you to access specific fibers of each of the hip external rotators. To stretch the left hip external rotators, get on all fours with your weight supported by the left knee. At first, the right leg is held in a horizontal position. By using the left hip external rotator muscles, raise and lower the right hip up and down (**arrows**). Once the left hip fatigues slightly (after about a minute), touch the right leg to the ground by pulling it back and towards the left (**arrow A**). By varying the degree of hip flexion (**arrow B**) you can isolate specific muscle fibers responsible for limiting motion. The piriformis stretch illustrated in figure 5.16, Q, is also an effective way to lengthen the hip external rotators.

ergy stretch illustrated in figure 7.54. Prior to performing this stretch, I like to have runners use a softball to massage the piriformis and gluteus medius muscles. Because the piriformis muscle is thickest where it leaves the sacrum, it is important to loosen this specific area prior to stretching (Fig. 7.55). You should be careful while massaging the piriformis muscle to make sure you don't irritate the sciatic nerve by focusing the massage near the sacrum and along the outside of the hip. You can tell if you're accidentally hitting the sciatic nerve because your leg will go slightly numb. To avoid irritating the nerve, it is important to hold stretches for no more than 20 or 30 seconds, since a prolonged stretch can also pinch the nerve. As a rule, the stretches should be done frequently throughout the day for short durations only.

Even though sports doctors suggest that piri-

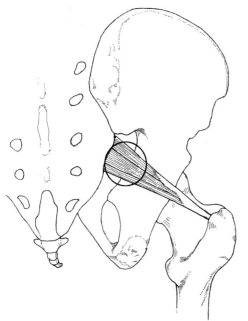

7.55. Prior to stretching, it is important to loosen the section of the piriformis muscle closest to the sacrum (circle).

formis syndrome can be corrected with stretches alone, it is almost always necessary to strengthen the hip musculature when treating this condition. Recent research shows that compared to conventional stretches alone, hip strengthening exercises hasten recovery and result in improved outcomes when treating piriformis syndrome (84,85). Figure 7.56 describes specific exercises that target the gluteus medius and maximus muscles.

To decrease the potential for reinjury, runners with piriformis syndrome often have to change the way they sit and sleep. Because rotating the hip up and out reduces tension in the piriformis muscle, runners with this injury tend to sit and sleep with their legs folded in a figure 4 position; i.e., with the foot of the involved side touching the opposite knee. Even though this position reduces tension on the sciatic nerve and feels comfortable, it is troublesome because it allows the piriformis muscle to tighten even more, potentially worsening the discomfort while running. Most runners are unaware they are rotating the injured side outward and it can take months to correct the faulty sitting and sleeping positions. To reduce the potential for chronicity, runners with piriformis syndromes should sleep on their side with a pillow folded between their knees, and sit with their knees straight. Because a piriformis syndrome tends to produce low grade discomfort that can go on for months, it is usually possible to continue running with this injury. To reduce strain on the piriformis muscle while running, consider shortening your stride by increasing your cadence 10% and try switching to a midfoot strike pattern.

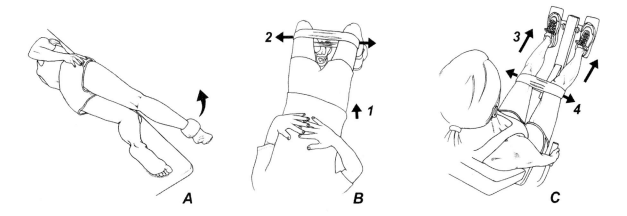

7.56. Gluteus maximus and medius strengthening exercises. A) While keeping the pelvis stationary with the upper leg hanging off the edge of a workout bench, raise and lower the upper leg through a 45 degree range of motion. **B**) With your shoulders resting flat on the floor, perform a plank by raising your pelvis (**1**) and then actively abduct your hips by pushing your knees outward against resistance provided by a TheraBand (**2**). **C**) This exercise requires a leg press, which is available at most gyms. The leg press is performed by moving your knees through the final 30° of extension (i.e., with the knees almost straight). While pushing the press (**3**), you simultaneously abduct your hips against resistance provided by a TheraBand (**4**).

Greater Trochanteric Pain Syndrome

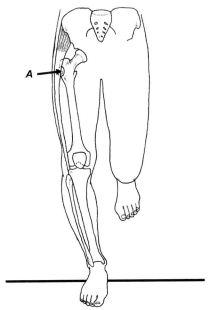

The greater trochanter is the large bone you feel on the outside of your hip, and greater trochanteric pain syndrome is a condition in which the soft tissues around this bony prominence become chronically painful. Next to arthritis, greater trochanteric pain syndrome is the most frequently encountered hip injury in older runners, especially women. Until recently, it was assumed that this injury resulted from a chronic pinching of the bursa located between the greater trochanter and the iliotibial band. This bursa was thought to be compressed when the upper portion of the band snaps over the greater trochanter while running (Fig. 7.57). The standard medical intervention has been

7.57. Until recently, greater trochanteric pain syndrome was thought to result from the iliotibial band compressing a bursa located on the outside of the hip (A).

to inject the inflamed bursa with corticosteroids.

Although effective in the short term, corticosteroid injections have been proven to have poor long-term outcomes. More recently, research has shown that it is not the bursa that causes the chronic pain associated with this syndrome, it is degeneration of the gluteus medius tendon insertion. By comparing MRI findings between the painful greater trochanter and the opposite symptom-free greater trochanter, researchers from New Zealand proved that inflammation of the bursa has nothing to do with this injury and in every situation, the pain could be related to degeneration of the gluteus medius tendon (86). As a result, treatment interventions to correct greater trochanteric pain syndromes should focus on improving tendon function, not reducing inflammation in the bursa.

The most effective way to treat this common condition is with the stretches and exercises described in Table 3. In a recent paper published in the *American Journal of Sports Medicine*, strengthening exercises were found to be more effective than corticosteroid injection for the long-term management of greater trochanteric pain syndrome (87). In addition to these exercises, deep tissue massage of the tendon attachment is an effective way to stimulate repair. My favorite way to access the gluteus medius tendon is to have a runner lie face up with the hip pulled slightly outward. I then use my thumb to get right on the attachment point of the gluteus medius tendon and perform cross friction massage. Although this can be a little painful, most runners are willing to tolerate the discomfort in order to get over this annoying condition.

Greater trochanteric pain syndrome is notorious for lasting more than six months and it is often necessary to cross-train on a bike or begin swimming while you gradually strengthen the tendon. To avoid reinjury, many runners with this condition report less discomfort upon switching to a midfoot strike pattern. Reducing your stride length and increasing your cadence by 10% may also be helpful to get over this injury. Greater trochanteric pain syndrome is a surprisingly difficult injury to treat and it is very important to remain patient while this injury gradually resolves.

Adductor Strains

The adductor muscle group is located in the upper thigh and consists of the adductor longus, brevis, and magnus muscles. Adductor strains are the most common cause of groin pain in runners. Fast runners with long strides are especially prone to developing this injury. Although any of the adductor muscles may be involved, the adductor longus muscle is by far the most frequently injured. While some experts suggest the adductor longus is injured because it has such a poor blood supply, the real reason adductor longus is so frequently injured is because its tendon is so small. In a detailed 3-dimensional study of the cross-sectional shape of the adductor longus tendon, researchers from NYU (88) observed that within an inch of its attachment to the pelvis, the tendon of adductor longus thinned rapidly and was less than 1/8 inch in diameter. The rapid narrowing of its upper tendon makes the adductor longus muscle susceptible to strains, particularly when the adductors are assisting with

Piriformis stretch. "Lie on your back with both knees bent and the foot of the uninjured leg flat on the floor. Rest the ankle of your injured leg over the knee of your uninjured leg. Grasp the thigh of the uninjured leg, and pull that knee toward your chest. You will feel a stretch along the buttocks and possibly along the outside of your thigh on the injured side. Hold this stretch for 30 to 60 seconds. Repeat 3 times."

Iliotibial band stretch standing. "Cross your uninjured leg in front of your injured leg, and bend down and touch your toes. You can move your hands across the floor toward the uninjured side, and you will feel more stretch on the outside of your thigh on the injured side. Hold this position for 30 seconds. Return to the starting position. Repeat 3 times."

Straight leg raise. "Lie on the floor on your back, and tighten up the top of the thigh muscles on your injured leg. Point your toes up toward the ceiling, and lift your leg up off the floor about 10 inches. Keep your knee straight. Slowly lower your leg back down to the floor. Repeat 10 times. Do 3 sets of 10."

Wall squat with ball. "Stand with your back, shoulders, and head against a wall, and look straight ahead. Keep your shoulders relaxed and your feet 1 foot away from the wall, shoulder-width apart. Place a rolled-up pillow or a ball between your thighs. Keeping your head against the wall, slowly squat while squeezing the pillow or ball at the same time. Squat down until your thighs are parallel to the floor. Hold this position for 10 seconds. Slowly stand back up. Make sure you are squeezing the pillow or ball throughout this exercise. Repeat 20 times."

Gluteal strengthening. "To strengthen your buttock muscles, lie on your stomach with your legs straight out behind you. Tighten your buttock muscles, and lift your injured leg off the floor 8 in, keeping your knee straight. Hold for 5 seconds, and then relax and return to the starting position. Repeat 10 times. Do 3 sets of 10."

All exercises are performed twice a day, 7 days a week, for 12 weeks.

Table 3. Home training program for greater trochanteric pain syndrome recommended by Rompe et al. (87). Written exactly as described by the authors.

flexing the hip at the initiation of swing phase.

While early research suggested that a lack of flexibility was likely to produce adductor strain, more recent research suggests that prior injury and/or adductor weakness is more likely to produce an adductor injury. In their evaluation of various risk factors responsible for the development of adductor injuries, Engebretsen et al. (89) found that previously injured individuals were more than twice as likely to sustain a new adductor injury, and individuals with weak adductors were four times more likely to be injured. This is consistent with research published in the *American Journal of Sports Medicine* in which athletes with adductor weakness were 17 times more likely to develop adductor muscle strain, and there was no correlation between adductor inflexibility and future injury (90).

The fact that adductor injuries are the result of adductor weakness, not tightness, is consistent with an evaluation of exercise protocols by Holmich et al. (91). By comparing a conventional treatment program of massage, stretching, and various physical therapy modalities to a 12-week strengthening program, the authors demonstrated that while the conventional treatments of massage and stretching were ineffective, 79% of the strengthened athletes were able to return to their prior level of sport within five months. Table 4 lists the exercises used in this study.

Perpetuating factors such as sleeping on your side with the injured hip adducted and/ or sitting in chairs with knees higher than hips should be avoided. Aggressive strengthening exercises should only be prescribed after a full range of hip abduction has been restored. While you're waiting for the adductor injury to heal, compressive thigh wraps made of neoprene reduce stress on the adductor tendon and can allow you to run short distances. Because the adductor tendon is strained at the initiation of swing phase, it is important to run with short strides. Once this condition has healed, you should consider routinely incorporating grapevine drills prior to running. Remember, once this tendon has been injured, it is prone to being chronically reinjured so you have to warm this tendon up carefully.

Osteitis Pubis

Also referred to as pubic symphysitis, osteitis pubis occurs when excessive movement of the pelvic bones produces pain in and around the pubic symphysis (Fig. 7.58). In the early stages of this condition, the runner complains of vague lower abdominal pain and/or adductor muscle discomfort. As symptoms progress, the pain becomes more localized to the pubic symphysis, and may be amplified by running on uneven surfaces such as trails. On occasion, the pubic symphysis may make a clicking sound when you stand from a seated position. Because the pubic symphysis is well designed to manage the forces associated with running, osteitis pubis tends to occur only in high mileage long distance runners. Elite females returning to sport after having a baby are especially susceptible to developing this injury.

The most common biomechanical causes for osteitis pubis are limb length discrepancy and muscle imbalances. Limb length discrepancies greatly stress the pubic symphysis because the pelvic bones rotate in opposite directions to

First 2 weeks

1) Place a soccer ball between your *ankles* while lying face up and squeeze for thirty seconds. Repeat 10 times.

2) Place a soccer ball between your *knees* while lying face up and squeeze for thirty seconds. Repeat 10 times.

3) Sit-ups, both in straightforward direction and in oblique direction; 5 sets of 10 reps.

4) Combined sit-up and hip flexion: lying on your back with a soccer ball placed between your knees, do a sit-up while flexing your hips and torso (folding knife exercise); 5 sets of 10 reps.

5) Balance training on wobble board for 5 minutes.

6) One-foot exercises on sliding board, with parallel feet; 5 sets of 1 minute continuous work with each leg in both positions. Because most runners don't have access to a sliding board I recommend doing the grapevine running drills illustrated in the bottom of figure 4.4.

Weeks 3 to 12.

(Two sets of each exercise, done twice at each training session.)

1) Continue step 2 from above.

2) Perform low back extension exercises while lying facedown over a workout bench or physioball; 5 sets of 10 reps. See figure 5.21 R, on page 107.

3) One leg weight-pulling abduction/adduction standing; 5 repetitions for each leg (see figure 5.21, L and N).

4) Abdominal sit-ups both in straightforward direction and in oblique direction; 5 sets of 10 reps.

5) One leg coordination exercise flexing and extending knee and swinging arms in same rhythm (cross-country skiing on one leg), 5 sets of 10 reps on each leg.

6) Training in sidewards motion on a "Fitter' (a rocking platform that rolls laterally on tracks positioned on top of curved base) for 5 minutes. If not available, perform the grapevine exercises illustrated at the bottom of figure 4.4 for 5 minutes.

7) Balance training on wobble board for 5 minutes.

8) Skating movements on sliding board; 5 times one minute continuous work.

Table 4. Adductor strengthening program, modified from Holmich et al. (91).

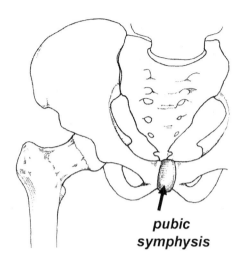

**pubic
symphysis**

**7.58. The pubic symphysis is a fibrocartilag-
inous disc located in the front of the pelvis.**

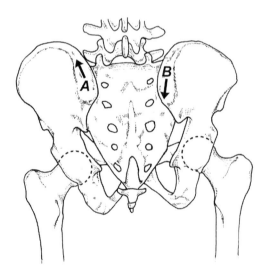

**7.59. To accommodate a limb length discrep-
ancy, the pelvis on the side of the short limb
tilts forward (A), while the pelvis on the side
of the long limb tilts back (B).**

accommodate the discrepancy (92) (Fig. 7.59). While these counter-rotations level the pelvis and lessen strain on the lumbar spine, they twist the pubic symphysis and increase the likelihood of developing this injury. As a result, limb lengths should be carefully evaluated, including the evaluation of asymmetrical pronation as a possible cause of limb length discrepancy. When necessary, asymmetrical pronation should be treated with the appropriate lift and/or orthotic.

The typical muscle imbalance responsible for the development of osteitis pubis is weakness of the core muscles coupled with excessive tightness in the hip flexors. This combination allows the pelvis to hyperextend during late midstance, which creates a shearing of the pubic symphysis (Fig. 7.60). Treatment in this situation is to improve hip flexibility and strenthen the core muscles. Unfortunately, even when treated properly, osteitis pubis can last 6 months or more and the best way to deal with this troublesome condition is to prevent it from occurring in the first place by keeping your hips flexible and your core strong.

Low Back Disorders

Over the past 7 million years, the low back has been gradually redesigned so it can easily manage the impact forces associated with walking and running. In fact, you're more likely to herniate a disc with prolonged sitting than with high mileage running. Nonetheless, running related back injuries do occur and they can usually be related to a variety of mechanical factors, such as muscle weakness/tightness and/ or compensation for limb length discrepancy.

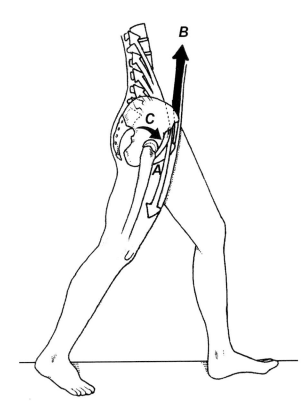

7.60. Tightness in the hip flexors (A) and weakness of the core (B), stresses the pubic symphysis because the pelvis on that side hyperextends during propulsion (C).

A common cause of low back pain in runners is weakness of the core muscles. When your foot hits the ground, weak core muscles allow your lowest lumbar vertebrae to shift forward, potentially damaging the joints of the low back. Weak core muscles are particularly likely to produce low back pain if your hip flexors are tight, because the lumbar spine is forced to hyperextend with each stride. A classic sign of core weakness is that your low back pain is worsened while running downhill and relieved while running uphill.

To test your core strength, try holding a side plank for 60 seconds on each side. If you're unable to maintain the plank for the full 60 seconds, start doing the exercises illustrated in figure 7.61. Begin by holding each position for 20 seconds and repeat 3 times daily. After a few weeks, you should be able to easily hold a side plank for 60 seconds.

Another cause for low back pain in runners is tightness of the spinal stabilizer muscles (Fig. 7.62). Because these muscles help absorb impact by decelerating forward motion of the spine, almost all high mileage runners have tight spinal stabilizers. Tightness in these muscles can produce delayed onset muscle soreness following long runs and can even hurt during the run, since excessive tightness in these muscles can compress the joints of the low back.

To test the flexibility of your spinal stabilizers, stand up and tilt sidewards while moving your hand towards the outside of your knee (Fig. 7.63). Repeat this motion on the opposite side and compare flexibility. If you can reach farther on one side than the other, perform the stretches illustrated in figure 7.64. Each stretch is typically held for about 20 seconds and repeated at least three times per day. It usually takes about a month of regular stretching to improve flexibility and after that, you will have to perform the stretches preventively to maintain flexibility.

Despite its strong ligaments, the sacroiliac joint is also an occasional source of pain in runners. Although difficult to diagnose, sacroiliac sprains usually produce a toothache type pain directly over the joint, and the ligaments covering the back of the joint are frequently painful to touch. The process of transitioning from a sitting to a standing position is surprisingly uncomfort-

7.61. Core exercises. With the front heel touching the toes of the back foot (**A**), maintain a sidelying plank for 20 seconds. By placing your arms parallel, rotate your torso 90° into a conventional plank (**B**). Try to hold this position for 20 seconds while raising one leg at a time for five seconds (**C**). You finish this exercise by again rotating 90° (**D**), holding the final side plank for 20 seconds. This cycle is usually repeated three times. Another excellent core exercise is to maintain a standard bridge position while raising a straightened lower leg (**E**). The leg is held in an elevated position for five seconds while maintaining the pelvis in a fixed position. Three sets of five repetitions while alternating legs is usually sufficient to strengthen the core.

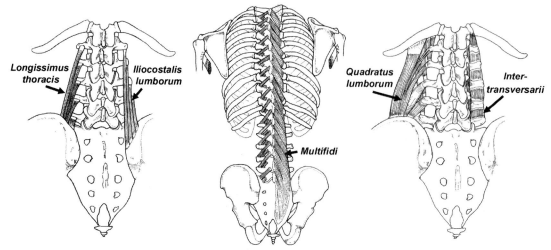

7.62. The spinal stabilizers.

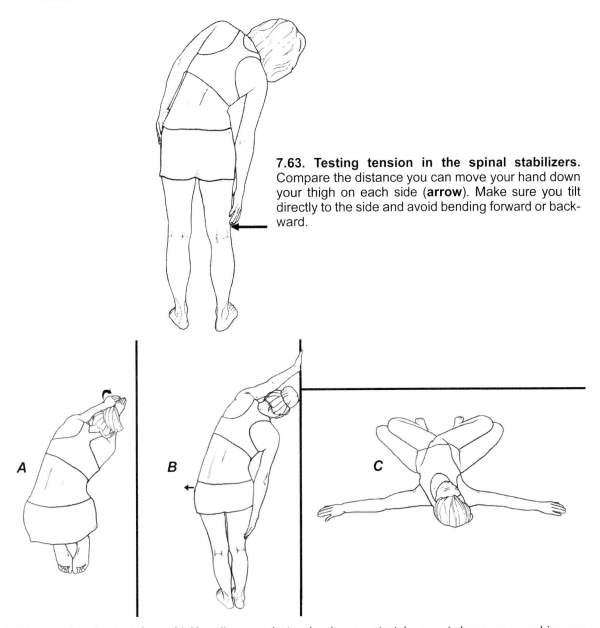

7.63. Testing tension in the spinal stabilizers. Compare the distance you can move your hand down your thigh on each side (**arrow**). Make sure you tilt directly to the side and avoid bending forward or backward.

A

B

C

7.64. Low back stretches. A) Kneeling quadratus lumborum stretch: squat down so your hips are directly over your heels and use your hands to pull your torso to the right (**arrow**). This stretches the left quadratus lumborum. **B**) Standing quadratus lumborum stretch: with your feet touching, grab the top of a door jam and shift your pelvis away from the door (**arrow**). By grabbing the door jam at different points and altering the degree of spinal flexion, different spinal stabilizers can be stretched. **C**) Lumbar rotational stretch: lie on your back and gently rock your flexed knees from side to side. This motion stretches the multifidi and if asymmetrical rotation is present, spend more time moving in the direction of the restriction.

able and the runner often limps to the opposite side to avoid compressing the inflamed sacroiliac joint. Rare in older runners because the joint is fused by the time you are in your 50s, sacroiliac pain is more likely to occur in young female long distance runners, especially following childbirth because the hormone relaxin loosens the joints of the pelvis to assist with delivery.

Treating sacroiliac sprains can be difficult because the sacroiliac joint is stabilized almost exclusively by ligaments. One of the only muscles that can provide protection if the sacroiliac joint is unstable is the transverse abdominus, which sends muscle fibers across the front of the sacrum. To test if you are weak in the transverse abdominus, perform the Vleeming's test illustrated in figure 5.18. If your pelvis lifts off the table more than a few degrees, perform the strengthening exercises illustrated in figure 7.61.

An important perpetuator of sacroiliac pain that needs to be corrected is tightness in the piriformis muscle. Because this muscle attaches to the front of the sacrum, a tight piriformis can pull the sacrum to one side, chronically stressing the sacroiliac joints. The muscle-energy stretch illustrated in the bottom of figure 7.54 is my favorite way to lengthen the piriformis.

To help in the diagnosis and possibly assist in the treatment, runners with painful sacroiliac joints should consider wearing a sacroiliac stabilizing belt. If you feel better while wearing this belt, you probably have a sacroiliac joint injury. Runners with sacroiliac sprains should wear the stabilizing belt until they correct any problem with core weakness and/or piriformis tightness. In theory, these belts apply a stabilizing com-

pressive force that protects an unstable sacroiliac joint from the excessive shear forces present while running. Even though I see mixed results with these belts, chronic sacroiliac sprains can be difficult to treat so they are always worth trying.

Although unlikely to produce low back pain in the general population, small limb length discrepancies can cause chronic low back pain in runners. By embedding metal beads in the sacrum and pelvis while subjects stood on different sized heel lifts, researchers determined that the pelvis shifts in very specific directions when limb length discrepancies are present (92) (Fig. 7.65). As a result, in addition to lifts, runners with limb length discrepancies should perform the stretches illustrated in figure 7.66. In some situations, chiropractic adjustments may be needed to restore motion and reduce tension in the surrounding muscles and ligaments.

Ironically, many runners injure their low backs while performing stretches and exercises designed to prevent low back pain. For example, many yoga instructors inappropriately recommend spinal unwinds in which individual vertebra are gradually flexed forward. As pointed out by the spinal researcher Stuart McGill (93), the discs of the lumbar spine were not designed to tolerate forward bending, so to remain injury-free, you should avoid flexing your spine excessively. The stretches most likely to injure your back are illustrated in figure 7.67.

Another common practice that may inadvertently result in low back injury is the recommendation that runners should run with their spines flat and their belly buttons tucked in. These concepts are taken from tai chi and Pilates in which

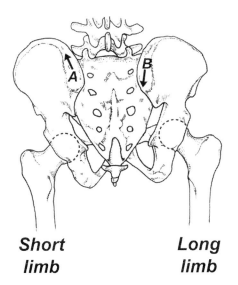

Short limb   **Long limb**

7.65. Pelvic movements to compensate for limb length discrepancy. The pelvis on the side of the short limb tilts forward (**A**), while the pelvis on the side of the long limb tilts back (**B**).

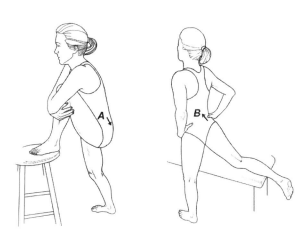

7.66. Home mobilizations for limb length discrepancy. On the side of the short limb, pull your knee towards your chest (**A**). This motion flexes the pelvis on that side. On the side of the long limb, place your knee on a chair or workout bench and extend the hip on that side (**B**). The stretches are typically held for 20 seconds and performed five times daily.

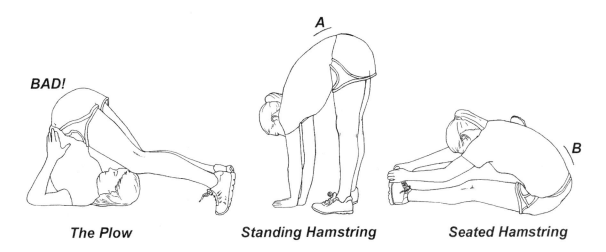

The Plow   **Standing Hamstring**   **Seated Hamstring**

7.67. Common stretches incorporating excessive forward flexion. While the plow stretch is always troublesome, the standing and seated hamstring stretches can be useful as long as you avoid flexing your lumbar spine excessively (**A** and **B**).

drawing in of the bellybutton is believed to recruit the transverse abdominus muscle and stabilize the low back. Unfortunately, this belief is unsubstantiated since the spine is most stable when held with a slight arch. A mild curve in the low back has been proven to distribute force more evenly between the discs and the joints while displacing the gel component of the disc forward (Fig. 7.68). Maintaining a slight curve while running effectively distributes pressure between the joints in the discs and allows the muscles of the low back to work in a more efficient manner (Fig. 7.69).

As with all running injuries, the best way to manage low back pain is to identify and correct all potential sources for injury. As pointed out throughout this book, the annual reinjury rates for runners should not be 70%. By quickly treating running injuries with proven treatment protocols, you can markedly reduce your potential for reinjury. Remember, recreational running is no more stressful on the body than fast walking and with a little effort, there's no reason you can't continue running into your 80s and 90s.

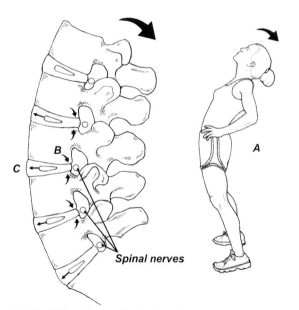

7.68. Side view of the lumbar spine. Arching your spine into extension (**A**), compresses the back portions of the lumbar discs (**B**), displacing the gel-like nucleus of the discs forward (**C**), away from the spinal nerves.

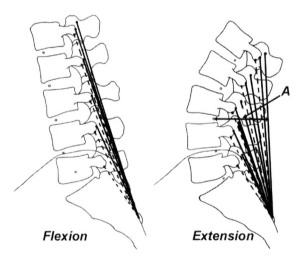

7.69. Extension of the lumbar spine improves muscle efficiency by increasing the length of the lever arm afforded the spinal stabilizers (A).

References

1. van Mechelen W. Running injuries: a review of the epidemiological literature. *Sports Med.* 1992;4:320.
2. van Gent R, Siem G, van Middelkoop M, et al. Incidence and determinants of lower extremity running injuries in long distance runners: a systematic review. *Br J Sports Med.* 2007;41:469-480.
3. Fredericson M, Anuruddh M. Epidemiology and etiology of marathon running injuries. *Sports Med.* 2007;37:437-439.
4. Luke A, Stehling C, Stahl R, et al. High-field magnetic resonance imaging assessment of articular cartilage before and after marathon running: does long-distance running lead to cartilage damage? *Am J Sports Med.* 2010;38:2273-2280.
5. Chakravarty E, Hubert H, Lingala V, et al. Long distance running and knee osteoarthritis: a prospective study. *Am J Prev Med.* 2008;35:133-138.
6. Pierce B, Murr S, Moss R. Run Less Run Faster. Rodale Publishing 2007.
7. Reinking M, Austin T, Hayes A. Exercise-related leg pain and collegiate cross-country athletes: extrinsic and intrinsic factors. *J Orthop Sports Phys Ther.* 2007;37:670-678.
8. Mahieu NN, Witvruow E, Stevens V, et al. Intrinsic risk factors for the development of Achilles tendon overuse injuries. *Am J Sp Med.* 2006;34(2):226-35.
9. Lyman J, Weinhold P, Almekinders LC. Strain behavior of the distal Achilles tendon. *Am J Sp Med.* 2004;32(2):457-61.
10. Alfredson H, Pietila T,Jonsson P et al. Heavy-load eccentric calf muscle training for the treatment of chronic Achilles tendinosis. *Am J Sp Med.*1998;26(3):360-6.
11. Williams D, Zambardino J, Banning V. Transverse-plane mechanics at the knee and tibia in runners with and without a history of Achilles tendinopathy. *J Orthop Sports Phys Ther.* 2008;38:761-767.
12. Davidson CJ, Ganion LR, Gehlsen GM, et al. Rat tendon morphological and functional changes resulting from soft tissue mobilization. *Med Sci Sp Exerc.* 1997;29(3):313-19.
13. Rompe J, Nafe B, Furia J. Eccentric loading, shock wave treatment or a wait-and-see policy for tendinopathy of the main body of tendo Achilles. *Am J Sp Med.* 2007;35(3):374-83.
14. Hugate R, Pennypacker J, Saunders M, Juliano P. The effects of intratendinous injections of corticosteroid on the biomechanical properties of rabbit Achilles tendons. *JBJS (American).* 2004;86:794-801.
15. Hughes L. Biomechanical analysis of the foot and ankle for predisposition to developing stress fractures. *J Orthop Sports Phys Ther.* 1985;3:96-101.
16. Kim J, Choi J, Park J, et al. An anatomical study of Morton's interdigital neuroma: the relationship between the occurring site and the transverse metatarsal ligament (DTML). *Foot Ankle Int.* 2007;28:1007-1010.
17. Carl A, Ross S, Evanski P, et al. Hypermobility in hallux valgus. *Foot Ankle.* 1988;8:264-270.
18. Redmond A, Lumb P, Landorf K. The effect of cast and noncast foot orthoses on plantar pressures and force during gait. *J Am Podiatr Med Assoc.* 2000;90:441-449.
19. Gray E, Basmajian J. Electromyography and cinematography of the leg and foot ("normal" and flat) during walking. *Anat Rec.* 1968;161:1-15.
20. Nawoczenski D, Houck J, Barnes E. Functional hallux limitus in the pronated foot: challenge to current theory. *J Orthop Sports Phys Ther.* 2003;33:A-12.
21. Ledoux W, Hillstrom H. Redistributed plantar vertical force of neutrally aligned and pes planus feet. *Gait Posture.* 2002;15:19.

22. Michaud TC, Nawoczenski DA. The influence of two different types of foot orthoses on first metatarsophalangeal joint kinematics during gait in a single subject. *J Manip Phys Ther.* 2006;29:60-65.

23. Welsh B, Redmond A, Chockalingam N, Keenan A. A case-series study to explore the efficacy of foot orthoses in treating first metatarsophalangeal joint pain. *J Foot Ankle Res.* 2010, Aug 27;3:17.

24. Abreu M, Chung C, Mendes L, et al. Plantar calcaneal enthesophytes: new observations regarding sites of origin based on radiographic, MR imaging, anatomic, and paleopathologic analysis. *Skeletal Radiol.* 2003;32:13-21.

25. Wearing S, Smeathers J, Yates B, et al. Sagittal movement of the medial longitudinal arch is unchanged in plantar fasciitis. *Med Sci Sports Exerc.* 2004;36:1761-1767.

26. Landorf K, Keenan AM, Herbert R. The effectiveness of foot orthoses to treat plantar fasciitis: a randomized trial. *Arch Intern Med.* 2006;166:1305-1310.

27. Kogler G, Solomonidis S, Paul J. Biomechanics of longitudinal arch support mechanisms in foot orthoses and their effect on plantar aponeurosis strain. *Clin Biomech.* 1996;11:243-252.

28. Kogler G, Veer F, Solomonidis S, Paul J. The influence of medial and lateral placement of orthotic wedges on loading of the plantar aponeurosis. *J Bone Joint Surg Am.* 1999;81:1403-13.

29. DiGiovanni B, Nawoczenski D, Lintal M, et al. Tissue-specific plantar fascia-stretching exercise enhances outcomes in patients with chronic heel pain. A prospective, randomized study. *J Bone Joint Surg.* 2003;85-A:1270–1277.

30. Coppieters M, Hough A, Dilley A. Different nerve-gliding exercises induce different magnitudes of median nerve longitudinal excursion: an *in vivo* study using dynamic ultrasound imaging. *J Orthop Sports Phys Ther.* 2009;39:164.

31. McKeon PC, Mattacola CG. Interventions for the prevention of first time and recurrent ankle sprains. *Clin Sports Med.* 2008;27:371-382.

32. Verhagen E, van Mechelen W, de Vente W. The effect of preventive measures on the incidence of ankle sprains. *Clin J Sport Med.* 2000;10:291-296.

33. Tyler TF, McHugh MP, Mirabella MR, Mullaney MJ, Nicholas SJ. Risk factors for noncontact ankle sprains in high school football players: the role of previous ankle sprains and body mass index. *Am J Sports Med.* 2006;34:471-475.

34. Delahunt E, Monaghan K, Caulfield B. Altered neuromuscular control and ankle joint kinematics during walking in subjects with functional instability of the ankle joint. *Am J Sports Med.* 2006;34:1970-1976.

35. Malliaropoulos N, Ntessalen M, Papacostsa E, et al. Reinjury after acute lateral ankle sprains in elite track and field athletes. *Am J Sports Med.* 2009;37:1755.

36. Kaikkonen A, Kannus P, Jarvinen M. Surgery versus functional treatment in ankle ligament tears: a prospective study. *Clin Orthop.* 1996;326:194-202.

37. Beynnon B, Renstrom P, Haugh L, et al. A prospective, randomized clinical investigation of the treatment of first-time ankle sprains. *Am J Sports Med.* 2006;34:1401.

38. McHugh M, Tyler T, Mirabella M, et al. The effectiveness of a balance training intervention in reducing the incidence of noncontact ankle sprains in high school football players. *Am J Sports Med.* 2007;35:1289.

39. Verhagen E, van der Beek A, Twisk J, et al. The effect of proprioceptive balance board training for the prevention of ankle sprains. *Am J Sports Med.* 2004;32:1385-1393.

40. Styf J. Chronic exercise-induced pain in the anterior aspect of the lower leg: an overview of diagnosis. *Sports Med.* 1989;7:331-339.

41. Franklyn M, Oakes B, Field B, et al. Section modulus is the optimum geometric predictor for stress fractures and medial tibial stress syndrome in both males and female athletes. *Am J Sports Med.* 2008;36:1179.

42. Magnusson H, Westlin N, Nyqvist F, et al. Abnormally decreased regional bone density in athletes with medial tibial stress syndrome. *Am J Sports Med.* 2001;29:712-715.

43. Burne S, Khan K, Boudville P, et al. Risk factors associated with exertional medial tibial pain: a 12-month prospective clinical study. *Br J Sports Med.* 2004;38:441-445.

44. Franklyn-Miller A, Wilson C, Bilzon J, McCrory P. Foot orthoses in the prevention of injury in initial military training : a randomized controlled trial. *Am J Sports Med.* 2011;39:30

45. Andrish JT, Bergfeld JA, Walheim J. A prospective study on the management of shin splints. *J Bone Joint Surg Am.* 1974;56:1697–700.

46. Cohen D, Kawamura S, Ehteshami J, Rodeo S. Indomethacin and Celecoxib impair rotator cuff tendon-to-bone healing. *Am J Sports Med.* 2006;34:362-369.

47. Bennell K, Malcolm S, Thomas S, et al. The incidence and distribution of stress fractures in competitive track and field athletes. A twelve-month prospective study. *Am J Sports Med.* 1996;24:211-217.

48. Crowell H, Milner C, Hamill J, Davis I. Reducing impact loading during running with the use of real-time visual feedback. *J Orthop Sports Phys Ther.* 2010;40:206.

49. Matheson GO, Clement DB, McKenzie DC. Stress fractures in athletes. A study of 320 cases. *Am J Sports Med.* 1987;15:46-58.

50. Burne S, Khan K, Boudville P, et al. Risk factors associated with exertional medial tibial pain: a 12-month prospective clinical study. *Br J Sports Med.* 2004;38:441-445.

51. Wakeling J, Nigg B. Modifications of soft tissue vibrations in the leg by muscular activity. *J Appl Physiol.* 2001;90:412-420.

52. Wakeling J, Liphardt A, Nigg B. Muscle activity reduces soft-tissue resonance at heel-strike during walking. *J Biomech.* 2003;36:1761-1769.

53. Agosta J, Morarty R. Biomechanical analysis of athletes with stress fracture of the tarsal navicular bone: a pilot study. *J Australasian Podiatr Med.* 1999.

54. Burne S, Mahoney C, Forster B, et al. Tarsal navicular stress injury: long-term outcome and clinical radiological correlation using both computed tomography and magnetic resonance imaging. *Am J Sports Med.* 2005;33;1875-1881.

55. Bennell K, Malcolm S, Thomas S, et al. The incidence and distribution of stress fractures in competitive track and field athletes: a 12-month prospective study. *Am J Sports Med.* 1996;24:211-217.

56. Milner C, Hamill J, Davis I. Distinct hip and rearfoot kinematics in female runners with a history of tibial stress fracture. *J Orthop Sports Phys Ther.* 2010;40:59-66.

57. Bulst I, Bredeweg S, van Mechelen W, et al. No effect of a graded training program on the number of running-related injuries in novice runners. A randomized controlled trial. *Am J Sports Med.* 2007;October 16:1-7.

58. Powers C, Ward S, Fredericson M, et al. Patellofemoral kinematics during weight-bearing and non-weight-bearing knee extension in persons with lateral subluxation of the patella: a preliminary study. *J Orthop Sports Phys Ther.* 2003;33:677-685.

59. Lin YF, Jan MH, Lin DH, Cheng CK. Different effects of femoral and tibial rotation

on the different measurements of patella tilting: An axial computed tomography study. *J Orthop Surg Res.* 2008;3:5.

60. Souza R, Draper C, Fredericson M, et al. Femur rotation and patellofemoral joint kinematics: a weight-bearing magnetic resonance imaging analysis. *J Orthop Sports Phys Ther.* 2010;40:277-285.

61. Dierks T, Manal K, Hamill J, Davis I. Proximal and distal influence on the hip and knee kinematics in runners with patellofemoral pain during a prolonged run. *J Orthop Sports Phys Ther.* 2008;38:448.

62. Williams D, McClay I, Hamill J, Buchanan T. Lower extremity kinematic and kinetic differences in runners with high and low arches. *J Applied Biomech.* 2001;17:153-163.

63. Collins N, Crossley K, Beller E, et al. Foot orthoses and physiotherapy in the treatment of patellofemoral pain syndrome: A randomised clinical trial. *Br Med J.* 2008;337:a1735.

64. Witvrouw E, Lysens R, Bellemans J, et al. Intrinsic risk factors for the development of anterior knee pain in an athletic population: a 2-year prospective study. *Am J Sports Med.* 2000;28:480.

65. Heiderscheit B, Chumanov E, Michalski M, et al. Effects of step rate manipulation on joint mechanics during running. *Med Sci Sports Exerc.* 2011;43:296-302.

66. van der Worp H, Ark M, Roerink S, et al. Risk factors for patellar tendinopathy: a systematic review of the literature. *Br J Sports Med.* 2011;March 2: Epub ahead of print.

67. Takasaki H, Aoki M, Oshiro S, et al. Strain reduction of the extensor carpi radialis brevis tendon proximal origin following the application of a forearm support end. *J Orthop Sports Phys Ther.* 2008;38:257.

68. Wadsworth C, Nielsen D, Burns L, et al.. Effect of the counterforce armband on wrist extension and grip strength and pain in subjects with tennis elbow. *J Orthop Sports Phys Ther.* 1989;5:192-197.

69. Kongsgard M, Qvortup K, Larsen J, et al. Fibril morphology and tendon mechanical properties in patellar tendinopathy. Effects of heavy slow resistance training. *Am J Sports Med.* 2010;38:749.

70. Fairclough J, Hayashi K, Toumi H, et al. The functional anatomy of the iliotibial band during flexion and extension of the knee: implications for understanding iliotibial band syndrome. *J Anat.* 2006;208:309-316.

71. Ferber R, Noehren B, Hamill J, et al. Competitive female runners with a history of iliotibial band syndrome demonstrate atypical hip and knee kinematics. *J Orthop Sports Phys Ther.* 2010;40:52.

72. Williams D, McClay I, Hamill J. Arch structure and injury patterns in runners. *Clin Biomech.* 2001;16: 341-347.

73. Falvey E, Clark R, Franklyn-Miller A, et al. Iliotibial band syndrome: an examination of the evidence behind a number of treatment options. *Scand J Med Sci Sports.* 2010;20:580-587.

74. Chaudhry H, Schleip R, Ji Z, et al. Three-dimensional mathematical model for deformation of human fasciae in manual therapy. *JAOA.* 2008;108:379-390.

75. Thelen D, Chumanov E, Best T, et al. Simulation of biceps femoris muscu-lotendon mechanics during the swing phase of sprinting. *Med Sci Sports Exerc.* 2005;37:1931-1938.

76. Askling C, Tengvar M, Saartok T, Thorstensson. Proximal hamstring strains of stretching type in different sports. Injury situations, clinical and magnetic resonance imaging characteristics, and return to sport. *Am J Sports Med.* 2008;36:1799.

77. Sherry M, Best T. A comparison of 2 rehabilitation programs in the treatment of acute hamstring strains. *J Orthop Sports Phys Ther.* 2004;34:116.

78. McHugh M, Connolly D, Eston R, et al. The role of passive muscle stiffness and symptoms of exercise-induced muscle damage. *Am J Sports Med.* 1999;27:594.

79. Hreljac A, Marshall RN, Hume PA. Evaluation of lower extremity overuse injury potential in runners. *Med Sci Sp Exerc.* 2000;32(9):1635-1641.

80. Verrall GM, Slavotinek JP, Barnes PG. The effect of sport specific training on reducing the incidence of hamstring injuries in professional Australian rules football players. *Br J Sports Med.* 2005;39:363-368.

81. Davidson C, Ganion L, Gehlson G, et al. Rat tendon morphologic and functional changes resulting from soft tissue mobilization. *Med Sci Sports Exerc.* 1997;2903:313.

82. Loghmani M, Warden S. Instrument-assisted cross-fiber massage accelerates knee ligament healing. *J Orthop Sports Phys Ther.* 2009;39:506-514.

83. Windisch G, Braun E, Anderhuber F. Piriformis muscle: clinical anatomy and consideration of the piriformis syndrome. *Surg Radiol Anat.* 2007;29:37-45.

84. Tonley J, Yun S, Kochevar R, et al. Treatment of an individual with piriformis syndrome focusing on hip muscle strengthening and movement reeducation: a case report. *J Orthop Sports Phys Ther.* 2010;40:103.

85. Hallin RP. Sciatic pain and the piriformis muscle. *Postgrad Med.* 1983;74:69-72.

86. Woodley S, Nicholson H, Livingstone V, et al. Lateral hip pain: findings from magnetic resonance imaging and clinical examination. *J Orthop Sports Phys Ther.* 2008;38:313.

87. Rompe J, Segal N, Cachio A, et al. Home training, local corticosteroid injection, or radio shock wave therapy for greater trochanteric pain syndrome. *Am J Sports Med.* 2009;37:1981.

88. Strauss E, Campbell K, Bosco J. Analysis of the cross-sectional area of the adductor longus tendon: a descriptive anatomic study. *Am J Sports Med.* 2007;35:996.

89. Engebretsen A, Myklebust G, Holme I, et al. Intrinsic risk factors for groin injuries among male soccer players: a prospective cohort study. *Am J Sports Med.* 2010;38:2051.

90. Tyler T, Nicholas S, Campbell R, McHugh M. The association of hip strength and flexibility with the incidence of adductor muscle strains in professional ice hockey players. *Am J Sports Med.* 2001;29:124.

91. Holmich P, Uhrskou P, Ulnits L, et al. Effectiveness of active physical training as treatment for long-standing adductor related groin pain in athletes: a randomized trial. *Lancet.* Feb 6,1999;353:439.

92. Cummings G, Scholz J, Barnes K. The effect of imposed leg length difference on pelvic bone symmetry. *Spine.* 1993;18:368-373.

93. McGill S. Low Back Disorders: Evidence-Based Prevention and Rehabilitation. Champaign, IL:Human Kinetics Publishing 2002.

94. Escamilla R, Zheng N, Macleod T, et al. Patellofemoral joint force and stress between a short and long-step forward lunge. *J Orthop Sports Phys Ther.* 2008;38:681-690.

95. Hoskins W, Pollard H, Orchard J. The effect of sports chiropractic on the prevention of hamstring injuries: a randomized controlled trial. *Med Sci Sports Exerc.* 2006;38:S27

Index

Bold italic numbers denote illustrations, tables and checklists.

About the Author

Since graduating from Western States Chiropractic College in 1982, Dr. Michaud has published numerous book chapters and dozens of journal articles on subjects ranging from the treatment of tibial stress fractures in runners, to the conservative management of shoulder injuries in baseball players.

In 1993, Williams and Wilkins published Dr. Michaud's first textbook, *Foot Orthoses and Other Forms of Conservative Foot Care*, which was eventually translated into four languages and continues to be used in physical therapy, chiropractic, pedorthic, and podiatry schools around the world. His latest textbook, *Human Locomotion: The Conservative Management of Gait-Related Disorders*, has over 1100 references and is one of the most detailed reviews of running biomechanics ever published.

In addition to lecturing on clinical biomechanics internationally, Dr. Michaud has served on the editorial review boards for *Chiropractic Sports Medicine* and *The Australasian Journal of Podiatric Medicine*. Over the past 30 years, Dr. Michaud has maintained a busy private practice in Newton, Massachusetts, where he has treated thousands of elite and recreational runners. You can find links to Dr. Michaud's articles and interviews, and order his textbooks online at www.humanlocomotion.org.